Secrets of Fat-Free Indian Cooking

SECRETS OF FAT-FREE INDIAN COOKING

Over 150 low-fat and fat-free traditional recipes – from samosas to mulligatawny soup to lamb curry

PRIYA KULKARNI
ANITA RANADE

Ave...

444 North Roxbury
Beverly Hills, California 90210

Cover Design: William Gonzalez
Cover Photograph: Victor Giordano
Text Illustrator: John Wincek
Interior Color Photographs: Victor Giordano
Photo Food Stylist: BC Giordano
Typesetter: Elaine V. McCaw
In-House Editor: Marie Caratozzolo
Printer: Paragon Press, Honesdale, PA

Avery Publishing Group
120 Old Broadway
Garden City Park, NY 11040
1-800-548-5757

Cataloging-in Publication Data

Kulkarni, Priya
    Secrets of fat-free Indian cooking : over 150 low-fat and fat-free traditional recipes from samosas to mulligatawny soup to lamb curry / Priya Kulkarni and Anita Ranade.
       p. cm.
    Includes index.
    ISBN 0–89529–805–8
    1. Low-fat diet—Recipes. 2. Indian cookery. I. Ranade, Anita. II. Title.
    RM237.7.K846 1998
    641.5'638—dc21   97–48422
                                                                      CIP

Printed in the United States of America

10   9   8   7   6   5   4   3   2   1

Contents

For
Sangeeta and Maya Ranade
and
Ela and Anjolie Kulkarni

our constant source of joy and inspiration.

Acknowledgements

We would like to thank various people who have helped and encouraged us in creating this cookbook.

Thanks to Rudy Shur and Avery Publishing Group for helping us make this book a reality. Special thanks to our editor, Marie Caratozzolo, for her tireless work and attention to detail that helped us transform our recipes and ideas into a finished work. She also displayed a keen understanding of our efforts to preserve our Indian culture and heritage throughout this book, for which we are grateful.

We wish to thank our mothers, Varsha Athawale and Sulabha Latey, who tolerated and encouraged our help in the kitchen ever since we were kids and sparked our interest in cooking. Their comments and suggestions throughout the development of this book were invaluable.

Last but not least, we wish to thank our husbands, Girish Ranade and Anirudh Kulkarni, who planted the seeds of the idea for this book in our minds, and for enduring, with smiles, all the taste tests we put them through.

Introduction

In recent years, Indian cuisine has gained wide popularity in the United States. The flavors, textures, smells, and cooking techniques have excited and intrigued the American palate. With Indian restaurants common in most cities and towns across the country, the exotic and authentic flavors found in curries and tandoori-cooked dishes are readily available.

Indian-style dishes are characteristically high in nutrient-rich ingredients like pulses, legumes, and fresh vegetables. However, the generous use of oils, butter, nuts, milk, and cream also make this cooking high in fat and cholesterol. The good news is that, with a few simple ingredient adjustments coupled with modified cooking methods, you can still enjoy authentic, taste-tempting low-fat and fat-free Indian foods.

While there are many Indian cookbooks on the market today, most include recipes that are fat- and cholesterol-filled. In addition, they often involve intricate cooking techniques and preparation methods. To the rescue comes *Secrets of Fat-Free Indian Cooking,* which pro-vides over 150 low-fat and fat-free Indian dishes that are nutritionally rich, flavorful, and satisfying. Helpful tips, techniques, and short-cuts are offered to easily guide you through the recipes, which are simple and easy to prepare. In addition, each recipe includes a nutritional breakdown, allowing you to see exactly what you are eating.

The book's first chapter helps familiarize you with India's traditional foods and its culinary heritage. It also presents a descriptive list of commonly used ingredients, including the many flavorful herbs and spices that are characteristic of Indian cooking. Also provided is a list of low-fat substitutions for high-fat ingredients to help you conform to a nutritious diet without compromising taste.

What follows are the recipe chapters, each of which is bursting with healthy versions of traditional Indian fare, as well as a number of original creations. Wonderful appetizers and snacks, including traditional Samosas (meat- or potato-stuffed pockets), grilled Barbecued Shrimp, and a smoky Eggplant Dip are just a sampling of the choices found in Chapter 2, "Snacks and Starters." Spicy Mulligatawny and tasty Tomato are just two of the soups found in Chapter 3 that are sure to tingle your palate and warm you up on a cold winter day. Combine any of the soups with one of the flatbreads or stuffed breads in Chapter 6 for a fat-free lazy weekend brunch.

Entrées include a wide variety of dishes, ranging from vegetarian Rice-Stuffed Green Peppers to Shrimp Pilaf, Royal Spiced Lamb with Rice, and Butterless Butter Chicken—all of which are satisfying, easy-to-prepare, and uniquely delicious. Looking for a break from the same old, humdrum salads? Why not enjoy the exotic Fenugreek with Split Mung Bean, Smoked Eggplant with Yogurt, or a Quick Garbanzo Bean Salad?

The beverage chapter is filled with traditional Indian drinks, such as the buttermilk-based *lassi,* as well as fruit drinks like Mango Milkshake and Fresh Lemonade. Our book wouldn't be complete without a wide assortment of delicious but low-fat Indian desserts such as Carrot Pudding, Creamy Saffron Yogurt, and Milk Delight.

Through the *Secrets of Fat-Free Indian Cooking,* we hope you will enjoy your experience with this exotic, flavorful cuisine. As you embark on this culinary journey, you will discover that cooking Indian food can be fun and easy. Above all, it will provide you with plenty of dishes that are not only low in fat but simple to prepare and delicious as well.

1.

Mastering Fat-Free Indian Cooking

In an effort to educate the American public about proper dietary nutrition, the United States Department of Agriculture (USDA) developed the Food Guide Pyramid. This graphic, presented on page 4, suggests a daily diet that includes a broad base of grains, adequate servings of fruits and vegetables, and moderate amounts of dairy products, meats, poultry, dry beans, and eggs. It also recommends a limited intake of sugar, salt, and alcohol, and advises Americans to cut back on products with high levels of cholesterol and fat (especially saturated fat).

Indian food, for the most part, naturally follows the dietary regimen suggested by the Food Guide Pyramid. Due to its large vegetarian population, India includes an abundance of vegetables, legumes, and whole grain dishes in its cuisine. Carbohydrates play an important and central role with meats and dairy products served in moderate amounts as side dishes. However, when prepared the traditional way, Indian dishes, which are commonly cooked in butter or oil and include ingredients such as coconut milk and cream, can be high in fat and cholesterol. In *Secrets of Fat-Free Indian Cooking,* you will learn how to cook a wide range of authentic Indian dishes that are low-fat or fat-free, yet easy to prepare and delicious, too.

In addition to presenting the various cooking techniques and ingredients used to cut the fat from Indian dishes, this chapter also includes detailed descriptions of commonly used herbs, spices, grains, and legumes in Indian cooking. It also details components of a harmoniously balanced Indian meal.

A WORD ABOUT FATS

A high-fat diet puts one at a greater risk for high blood pressure, diabetes, atherosclerotic heart disease, and many forms of cancer. Fat itself, however, is not bad; it is essential for proper body functioning. Some dietary fat is essential in maintaining cell walls, in storing and circulating fat-soluble vitamins, and in performing other functions to sustain a healthy

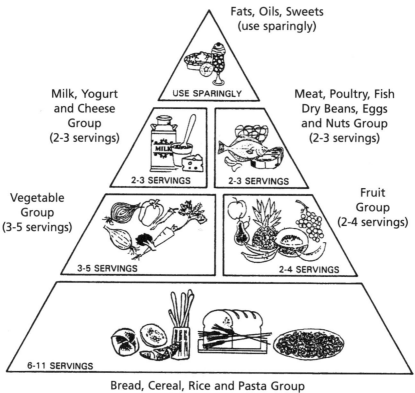

The Food Guide Pyramid

body. The problem comes from too much fat.

There are three main types of fat—saturated, polyunsaturated, and monounsaturated. *Saturated fat*, which is found primarily in animal products, dairy items, and some vegetable products, such as coconut oil and vegetable shortening, can cause a number of negative side effects when eaten in excess. Most seriously, it can significantly elevate blood cholesterol levels, increasing the risk of heart disease. *Polyunsaturated fat*, found in corn, sunflower, and safflower oils, and products made from these oils, contains *linoleic* acid, an essential omega-3 fat. Although an excess of polyunsaturated fat is believed to cause high blood pressure and blood clot development, a small daily amount of linoleic acid is necessary for good health. *Monounsaturated fat* is abundant in certain nuts like peanuts and almonds, and in oils such as olive, peanut, and canola. It contains *linolenic* acid—another essential omega-3 fat. Used in small amounts, monounsaturates may actually help decrease the risk of heart disease.

MAXIMUM DAILY FAT INTAKE

The average American consumes 40 percent of his or her calories from fat in a typical day. The American Dietetic Association and the American Heart Association suggest that no more than 30 percent of one's daily calories come from fat, and 20 to 25 percent would be even better. No more than 10 percent of these calories should come from saturated fats.

With the amount of daily fat you eat based on caloric intake, you must first establish how many calories you need in a day. Individual calorie needs differ depending on a person's weight, age, sex, rate of metabolism, and activity level. Generally, however, in order for most adults to maintain their weight, they must consume about 15 calories for each pound they weigh.

To establish your personal maximum daily calorie and fat intake, follow the steps presented here:

1. First, determine the number of calories your body needs in one day. This number will depend on your body weight. For example, let's say you weigh 130 pounds. To maintain this body weight, you would need to consume about 15 calories for every pound you weigh—approximately 1,950 calories:

$$
\begin{array}{rl}
130 & \text{pounds (total body weight)} \\
\times\ 15 & \text{calories (per pound)} \\
\hline
1,950 & \text{total daily calories (needed to} \\
& \text{maintain body weight)}
\end{array}
$$

2. Multiply the total daily calories by 0.25 (25 percent) to determine the maximum number of daily calories that should come from fat:

$$
\begin{array}{rl}
1,950 & \text{total daily calories} \\
\times\ 0.25 & \text{(25 percent)} \\
\hline
487 & \text{total calories from fat}
\end{array}
$$

3. As 1 gram of fat has 9 calories, divide the total daily calories by 9 to determine the total fat-gram allowance:

$$
\begin{array}{rl}
487 & \text{total calories from fat} \\
\div\ 9 & \text{calories per fat gram} \\
\hline
54 & \text{total daily fat grams}
\end{array}
$$

4. As no more than 10 percent of one's daily

calories should come from saturated fat, simply multiply the total daily calories by 0.1 (10 percent), then divide by 9:

$$
\begin{array}{rl}
1,950 & \text{total daily calories} \\
\times\ 0.1 & \text{(10 percent)} \\
\hline
195 & \text{total saturated fat calories} \\
\div\ 9 & \text{calories per fat gram} \\
\hline
21 & \text{total saturated fat grams}
\end{array}
$$

To summarize, a typical, moderately active 130-pound person should consume approximately 1,950 daily calories. No more than 487 of these calories should come from fat (54 grams) with less than 195 fat calories (21 grams) coming from saturated fat.

Table 1.1, presented below, shows the suggested maximum daily calories for a variety of different weights, along with a fat-gram budget based on 25 percent of these daily calories. If you are overweight, choose your goal weight, and follow the appropriate allowances. Keep in mind that these figures are approximate.

Table 1.1. Maximum Daily Fat Intake

Weight in pounds	Recommended Daily Calories (15 calories per pound)	Total Fat Grams (25% of total daily calories)	Total Saturated Fat Grams (10% of total daily calories)
100	1,500	42	16
110	1,650	46	18
120	1,800	50	20
130	1,950	54	22
140	2,100	58	23
150	2,250	62	25
160	2,400	67	27
170	2,550	71	28
180	2,700	75	30
190	2,850	79	32
200	3,000	83	33

SUBSTITUTING THOSE HIGH-FAT INGREDIENTS

In addition to cooking oil, there are a number of other high-fat ingredients that are commonly used in authentic Indian foods. Whenever possible, we have substituted high-fat ingredients with low-fat or fat-free products (see Table 1.2). These healthy ingredient choices are designed to trim the fat from Indian-style dishes without compromising taste.

TRADITIONAL INDIAN-STYLE MEALS

Americans, who are used to eating meals in which one course is followed by another, are usually puzzled when they first sit down to an authentic Indian meal. All courses are placed on one large plate. Even the soup is placed in a small bowl and served alongside the rest of the meal. Typically, bread and rice—great sources of carbohydrates—play a central role, with salads, vegetables, legumes, and meats acting as side dishes. Although there are regional variations, Indian flatbread is often served in the beginning of the meal along with the rest of the side dishes. Once the bread is eaten, it is replaced with rice.

A typical vegetarian Indian meal includes flatbread, rice, salad, a stir-fried vegetable, a vegetable curry, a legume curry, a chutney, and sometimes soup. On festive occasions, dessert is placed in a small bowl and included on the plate as well. In a non-vegetarian Indian meal, the legume dish is substituted with a meat or fish dish, and generally only one vegetable dish is served.

COOKING TECHNIQUES

There are four basic techniques used in Indian cooking—stir-frying (also called "searing and stirring"), deep-frying, steaming, and roasting. Presented below are modified versions of these techniques as they are used to prepare the low-fat and fat-free dishes in this book.

Stir-Frying

When preparing many Indian foods, the stir-frying cooking method is the one most commonly used. In this process, foods—and sometimes herbs and spices—are frequently stirred over medium-high heat in a nonstick wok or skillet until they reach a certain color and emit a distinctive aroma. Although traditionally this cooking method calls for lots of oil, we have found that only a very small amount of canola oil is necessary to provide equally tasty results.

Stir-frying is often used during more than one stage of the cooking process. For instance, many dishes begin with a little *tempered* oil—oil that has been flavored with whole spices. Traditionally, tempering begins with heated oil to which whole spices are added in quick succession. Once the oil is tempered (flavored), often herbs, such as onion, garlic, and/or ginger, are added to the oil and stir-fried. Depending on the recipe, other ingredients may be added, as well. (For

Table 1.2. Substitutions for High-Fat Ingredients

INGREDIENT	SUBSTITUTION
Coconut milk	Fat-free coconut milk (recipe on page 152).
Cream	Evaporated skim milk.
Eggs	Egg whites or egg substitute.
Oil and butter*	Vegetable cooking spray.
Paneer (fried whole-milk Indian cheese)	Tofu
Sour cream	Nonfat sour cream.
Yogurt	Nonfat yogurt.

* When cooking oil is necessary, use canola—an oil with monounsaturated fat that has no aroma or taste that might interfere with the subtle flavor of herbs and spices.

additional information on tempering oil, *see* inset below.) When cooking onions, be sure to cook them as instructed according to the individual recipe. Various degrees of a browned onion impart different flavors.

Pan-Browning

Pan-browning foods with cooking spray and a few drops of oil replaces the traditional high-fat deep-frying or pan-frying methods in which

Tempering Oil

The cooking process for many Indian dishes begins with a little tempered oil—oil that is heated and flavored with whole spices, often mustard or cumin seeds, and occasionally cardamom, cinnamon, bay leaves, and cloves. Turmeric, with its characteristic yellow color, is generally the only "ground" spice that is sometimes added to the whole spices when tempering oil.

Most often, tempering occurs at the onset of the cooking process. Tempered oil also can be used to garnish finished dishes such as dals. The oil is heated, then the whole spice is added but not stirred. When mustard seeds are added, they begin to pop. To prevent the seeds from popping out of the pan, we suggest using a splatter guard. Once the seeds have stopped popping (usually within 30 seconds), additional ingredients—generally other whole or ground spices and/or onion, garlic, and ginger—are added, combined with the tempered oil, and stir-fried a few seconds. When cumin seeds are used to temper oil, they start to sizzle (usually within 5 seconds) and often emit a wonderful aroma. This sign is an indication that the next ingredient should be added.

It is not necessary to stir the whole spices, like mustard and cumin seeds, during the tempering process. As soon as the mustard seeds stop popping or the cumin seeds sizzle a few seconds, quickly add the next ingredients as instructed in the individual recipe. (If a mild cumin flavor is desired, do not let the seeds sizzle before adding the next ingredients.) Keep in mind that it takes only a few seconds of overcooking to turn a flavorful aromatic herb into one that is bitter and acrid.

Traditionally, substantial amounts of oil are used in the tempering process. We have found that a very small amount of oil is all that is necessary to achieve equally flavorful results.

large amounts of oil are characteristically used. To properly pan-brown food, place it on a hot nonstick skillet that has been sprayed with vegetable cooking spray. Then, if needed, drizzle a few drops of canola oil around the food. The food should be allowed to cook until the bottom is brown, then it should be turned over to cook the other side.

Steaming

Once the oil has been tempered and the herbs and spices have been sufficiently cooked, generally vegetables, legumes, or meats are added. Often these ingredients are steamed. A bit of stock or water is added to the pot or skillet, the pot is covered, and the ingredients are left to cook in the steam.

An excellent cooking method, steaming results in tasty food without the use of oil. It improves the color of many ingredients, especially vegetables, enhancing the dish's eye appeal while maintaining its valuable nutrients. Steaming is the method of choice used in most curries. While ingredients are typically steamed after the oil has been tempered, they can also be steamed without tempered oil, such as the Whole Fish Stuffed with Mint Chutney (page 174).

Roasting (Tandoori Cooking)

Meats, chicken, and fish that are roasted in a tandoor—a huge bullet-shaped clay oven that is customarily set in the ground and heated with charcoal—are deliciously moist and tender. The meat is generally placed on skewers then set inside the intensely hot tandoor to cook. In addition to roasting meats, the tandoor, with its unique inner concave walls, can be used to cook a variety of flatbreads.

As most American homes do not have tandoors, an outdoor barbecue grill or a conventional oven set on 450°F can be used instead. The smoke and direct flame of an outdoor grill help flavor the meat, making it the recommended choice over a conventional oven. You can find small clay tandoors that fit inside conventional ovens in a number of cookware specialty shops.

SPICES

The heart and soul of Indian cooking lies in its unique spice combinations. These flavorful ingredients are blended and cooked to produce the taste that is characteristic of Indian cuisine.

In the past, affluent Indian households typically employed a cook with an assistant who did nothing but blend, pound, and grind various spices with a mortar and pestle as required by the chef. Today, the same job can be done quickly and efficiently with a coffee or spice grinder. In Indian cooking, whole, ground, and whole spices that have been dry-roasted and ground are used to flavor foods. Each of these spice forms is used during different parts of the cooking procedure.

Whole spices are used at the beginning of a dish's cooking process to flavor tempered oil (*see* Tempering Oil on page 7). They are not used at any other time. *Ground spices* like coriander, cumin, and paprika, are generally added during the middle of the cooking time; with the exception of ground turmeric, they are never used to temper oil. Ground spice blends, including masalas (*see* page 9) are added to a dish in the middle or near the end of its cooking time. Sometimes these blends, such as garam masala, are sprinkled on top of the food just before serving.

Dry roasting greatly enhances the intensity of a spice's flavor. These dry-roasted, ground spices are usually added to the wet masala or other herbs, then steamed with the other ingredients in a dish. They can also be sprinkled over a dish toward the end of the cooking process.

Masalas

Masalas can be either wet or dry herb and spice blends, or a mixture of dry ground spices. Generally, flavorful masalas are used in place of or along with the tempered herb spice blends. Wet masalas are always well-cooked along with other ingredients in a little water. When onion, ginger, and/or garlic are used in a masala, they must be properly cooked, or they can leave the food with an unpleasant aftertaste.

Dry spices like ground cumin seeds, ground coriander seeds, paprika, and garam masala are generally added to the food in the middle or at the very end of the cooking process. When added at the end, they maintain most of their aroma and flavor, so only small amounts are required. Turmeric, with its distinctive yellow color, is one of the few ground spices that is sometimes added to whole spices when tempering oil. Recipes for basic masalas called for in this book are provided in Making Your Own Masala, beginning on page 132.

About Dried Herbs

Although dried spices are important flavor enhancers in Indian cooking, dried herbs are not. Inferior in taste to fresh varieties, dried herbs should be used only when it's impossible to find fresh. Fresh ginger, onion, garlic, cilantro, and mint are all readily available in most grocery stores, so there is no need to use dried types.

COMMON INGREDIENTS IN INDIAN COOKING

The following is a description of ingredients commonly used in Indian cooking. While some of these ingredients, namely a few spices and grains, may require a trip to an Indian grocery store, most are easily found in major American supermarkets. If you are lucky enough to have access to an Indian grocery store, know that it will offer the best ingredient variety as well as the lowest prices.

Aniseed (*Sauf*). These small green seeds from the anise plant have a strong licorice flavor. They are widely used to flavor a number of meat dishes as well as pickles. A teaspoonful eaten at the end of a meal serves as a digestive aid.

Basmati rice (*Basmati chawal*). Basmati, which means "full of aroma," is a scented long-grain rice that is cultivated in the Himalayan foothills. Its distinctive nutty flavor and aroma make it an absolute must for Indian rice pilafs. Basmati grains nearly triple in size when cooked. For the best value, purchase basmati rice at an Indian grocery store. Texmati rice, which is available in most grocery stores, can be used as a substitute.

Bay leaves (*Tejpatta*). Aromatic whole bay leaves are commonly used to flavor curries and pilafs. Remember to remove and discard this inedible whole leaf from the dish before serving. The leaves are often included in a number of mixed spice blends.

Bishop's weed (*Ajwain*). These small light-brown seeds from the *Carum ajowan* plant closely resemble cumin and caraway seeds. Bishop's weed has a distinctive but slightly bitter flavor and is commonly used in root vegetable curry dishes, fried breads, and savory snacks. Also used as a digestive aid, bishop's weed is available in Indian grocery stores.

Black peppercorns (*Kali mirch*). These aromatic whole dried berries of the *Piper nigrum* pepper vine are hot and pungent. The ground peppercorns are an important ingredient in garam masala. Always use freshly ground pepper powder, within a week. After this period, the ground pepper loses its intensity.

Black-eyed peas (*Lobia*). These kidney-shaped light-brown beans from the *Vigna catjang* plant have a small black "eye." High in protein, flavor, and fiber, black-eyed peas are available in dried or canned form. They are a good nutritious choice for meatless dishes.

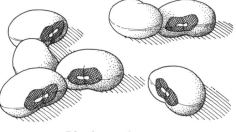

Black-eyed peas

Black garbanzo beans (*Kala chana*). These small dark-brown beans are smaller, darker, and stronger-flavored than regular garbanzo beans.

Black lentils (*Sabut urad* or *Urad dal*). These dried legumes with their black skin and white interior are available in whole, split, or husked form, and are a common delicacy in northern India. As black lentils are slightly difficult to digest, they should be eaten in small quantities. They are popularly used in the split form in such Indian delights as idlis (steamed fermented rice cakes) and dosas (pan-fried fermented rice and lentil pancakes).

Cardamom (*Elaychi*). From the pods of the *Elettaria cardamomum* plant come the aromatic cardamom seeds. Green and black varieties of cardamom grow abundantly in India and Sri Lanka. Green cardamom is commonly used to flavor sweet dishes, while the black pods are used in curries and pilafs. The whole black pods are sometimes used to temper the oil during a dish's early cooking stage, while the seeds of the green pods are ground and commonly added to curries during the final cooking stage. While ground cardamom is sold in most grocery stores, generally, the whole variety is available only in Indian and specialty food stores.

Chile peppers. *See* Green chile peppers; Red chile peppers.

Cilantro (*Hara dhania*). The fresh green leaves of the *Coriandrum sativum* plant, cilantro is generally chopped and used as a garnish. Cilantro, which is inexpensive, is easily found in most grocery stores and is also easy to grow at home. To store cilantro, first remove and discard the roots and any spoiled leaves, then let it air-dry for about an hour. *Do not wash.* Place the cilantro in a tightly sealed brown paper bag or plastic container lined with paper towels to absorb any excess moisture. Store in the refrigerator where it will keep for about one week. Wash the cilantro just before using.

Cinnamon (*Dalchini*). The dried inner bark of the *Cinnamomum cassia* tree, cinnamon is commonly used in curries and pilafs. It is also an important ingredient in garam masala.

Cloves (*Laung*). Cloves are the nail-shaped dried flower buds of the *Eugenia aromatica* tree. With a spicy, refreshing taste, whole cloves are used in curries, pilafs, and some desserts. Ground cloves are used in garam masala.

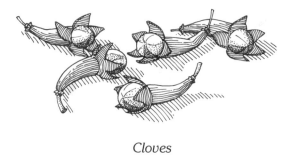

Cloves

Coconut essence. Blended with nonfat ricotta cheese to replace high-fat, high-cholesterol coconut milk, coconut essence comes in pure and imitation varieties. Pure coconut essence has a more authentic flavor than the imitation variety.

Coriander seeds (*Sukha dhania*). From the *Coriandrum sativum* plant, coriander seeds are occasionally tempered along with other spices for some northern Indian dishes. They impart a fresh, slightly citrus flavor to the oil. Ground coriander (*dhania)* is available in most grocery stores.

Coriander seeds

Cumin seeds (*Sabut jeera*). The light-brown seeds of the *Cuminum cyminum* plant, cumin closely resembles caraway seeds in appearance but not in taste. Cumin seeds are often used when tempering oil, adding a slightly spicy taste to the oil. Whole and ground cumin (*jeera*) is available in most grocery stores.

Cumin seeds

Curry leaves (*Kari patta*). These green leaves of the *Murraya keonigii* plant have a slightly

nutty, citrus flavor and are a common ingredient in western and southern Indian dishes. They are normally used as part of the oil tempering for curries and chutneys.

Curry powder. A purely British concoction, curry powder is actually a blend of a number of spices including turmeric, cumin, and cardamom. Available in most American grocery stores, it is one spice mixture that you cannot easily find in India.

Fenugreek (*Methi*). The green, slightly bitter leaves of the *Trigonella foenum graecum* plant, fresh fenugreek as well as dried (*kasoori methi*) is popularly used to flavor curries, potatoes, and certain vegetable dishes. Fresh fenugreek leaves are often combined with whole wheat flour to make flatbread. Dried fenugreek is an important ingredient in flavoring tandoori meat dishes. When purchasing fresh fenugreek, always choose leaves that are young and green (not discolored).

Fenugreek seeds are actually legumes that are generally used as a spice. They can be used whole or ground. When used in hot oil tempering, they impart a distinctive bitter taste to the dish. Because of this slightly bitter taste, fenugreek seeds should be used sparingly.

Garam masala. A classic blend of hot and aromatic spices, garam masala includes cumin seeds, cardamom, cinnamon, cloves, mace, and nutmeg. To preserve its flavor and aroma, garam masala is generally sprinkled over the food at the end of the cooking process. Although this spice blend is readily available in Indian grocery stores, you can easily make it yourself (*see* recipe on page 133).

Garbanzo beans (*Kabuli chana*). Also known as chick peas, garbanzo beans, from the *Cicer arietinum* plant, have a nutty, earthy flavor.

You can find canned garbanzo beans in most supermarkets. The dried variety, which is less expensive, is sold in Indian grocery stores.

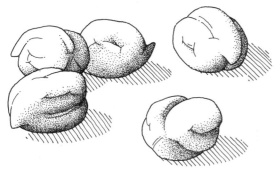

Garbanzo beans (chick peas)

Garlic (*Lasan*). White root bulbs of the *Allium sativum* plant, garlic is a popular herb used to flavor a wide variety of dishes. Fresh garlic is available year round. It also comes whole, minced, or crushed in jars, which must be refrigerated after opening. To freeze garlic, remove and discard the skin, then crush the bulbs. Transfer the crushed garlic to a resealable plastic bag and flatten it to an ⅛-inch thickness. Store the flattened paste in the freezer, breaking off pieces as needed. A ½-inch square is equal to 1 medium-sized clove.

Ginger (*Adrakh*). The underground root of the tropical *Zinziber officinale*, ginger is used for both its distinctive taste as well as its digestive properties. Fresh ginger is found in the produce sections of most grocery stores. It also comes minced or crushed in jars, which must be refrigerated after opening. To freeze, peel off the skin and finely grate the ginger. Transfer to a resealable plastic bag and flatten it to an ⅛-inch thickness. Store the flattened ginger in the freezer, breaking off pieces as needed. A 1-inch square of frozen ginger is equivalent to a ½-inch piece of fresh.

Green chile peppers (*Hari mirch*). Very hot and pungent, the long, narrow green chile peppers are available in Indian and southeastern Asian markets. Although not quite as hot, Mexican jalapeño peppers are adequate substitutes.

Kidney beans. *See* Red kidney beans.

Lentils (*Masoor*). These brown hulled seeds from the *Lens culinaris* plant are widely used in northern Indian cooking. Lentils are available in most grocery stores. *See also* Black lentils; Pigeon peas.

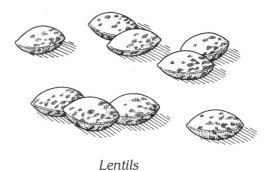

Lentils

Mango (*Aam*). In its unripe form, the mango is treated as a vegetable and is used to make relishes and chutneys. The ripe mango, called "king of fruits" in India, is used to flavor beverages and a variety of desserts. The best mango variety is the Alphanso, which is available in India, Canada, and England. Mangoes are available in the produce section of most grocery stores.

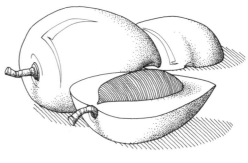

Mango

Mango powder (*Amchoor*). This tart greenish-brown powder that is made from sun-dried unripe mangoes is used like lemon juice. It is often added to legume curries, once the legumes are cooked.

Mace (*Javatri*). Made from the nutmeg's lacy outer shell, mace is generally ground and used in a number of masalas.

Masala. A dry or wet blend of ground spices or spice-herb combinations. *See* Garam masala; Sambar masala; Tandoori masala.

Mint leaves (*Podina*). Fresh green mint leaves are used extensively in drinks, vegetable dishes, legumes, and curries. They are most commonly used in mint chutneys. Avoid using dried mint, which is markedly inferior in taste to fresh.

Mint leaves

Mung beans (*Sabut mung or Mung dal*). Mung beans are green or yellow legumes from the *Phaseolus aureus roxb.* plant. Known as green grams in India, mung beans are used in their whole, sprouted, or split form. Whole mung beans, which are green in color, can be sprouted, greatly increasing their nutritional value. The yellow split mung beans are used in a variety of legume dishes, pilafs, and some desserts.

Mustard seeds (*Rai*). Whole black mustard seeds play an important role in Indian cuisine. They are commonly used when tempering oil,

Mung beans

during which their hot pungency is transformed into a mild nutty flavor. During the tempering process, these seeds pop, sputter, and change color. Yellow mustard seeds are available in most grocery stores and can be substituted for the black variety.

Nutmeg (*Jaiphal*). From the fruit of the *Myristica fragrans* tree comes the fragrant nutmeg kernel. Although mace and nutmeg come from the same fruit and have similar taste, mace is mainly used in garam masala, while nutmeg is used in desserts.

Paprika (*Kashmiri mirch*). This spice comes from the dried ripe pods of mild sweet red peppers. The seeds are normally discarded before the pepper is ground.

Peppercorns. *See* Black peppercorns.

Pigeon peas (*Toor dal*). This dry split lentil is from the *Cajanus cajan* plant. Similar in appearance to yellow split peas, pigeon peas are slightly smaller and possess a very different taste. Considered an everyday lentil, pigeon peas are used at least two or three times a week in most Indian homes. They are available plain or lightly coated in oil. This coating, which protects the peas from worms or insects, is a good choice if you plan to store the lentils for any length of time. We prefer the plain variety.

Plantain (*Kacha kela*). These green-skinned fruits from the *Musa sapientum* tree look a lot like large unripe bananas. They are used in a variety of curries and are traditionally combined with generous amounts of coconut milk or cream.

Poppy seeds (*Khus-khus*). These small white seeds of the *Papaner somniferum* plant are an important ingredient in many northern Indian dishes. With a flavor that is similar to but milder than sesame seeds, poppy seeds are used whole or ground in a variety of curries and flatbreads.

Red chile peppers (*Sukhi sabut lal mirch*). Whole, dried red chile peppers are sometimes used in curries, chutneys, and a number of southern Indian dishes. They are extremely hot, so use them sparingly.

Red kidney beans (*Rajma*). These kidney-shaped, red-skinned beans from the *Plaseolus vulgaris* plant are commonly used in a variety of Indian dishes. A rich source of protein and fiber, kidney beans are available canned or dried.

Red kidney beans

Rose water (*Gulab jal*). Made from highly scented rose petals, clear rose water is used to flavor a number of milk-based beverages and desserts. Bottled rose water is available in Indian grocery stores.

Saffron (*Kesar*). Deep reddish-brown saffron

threads are the stigmas of the *Crocus sativas* flower. Aromatic saffron imparts flavor and a pale yellow color to rice and curry dishes, as well as a number of desserts. Saffron is very expensive, but just a tiny pinch goes a long way.

Sambar masala. A unique dry blend of dals and spices, sambar masala is the main ingredient in south Indian curries. (*See* recipe on page 132.)

Split Peas. *See* Mung Beans; Yellow Split Peas.

Tamarind pulp (*Imli*). Obtained by soaking the dried, fleshy seed pod of the tamarind tree, tamarind pulp is very sour; it is used to flavor many curry dishes. Because it is so strong, just a little goes a long way. Bottled pulp is available in Indian and Asian grocery stores.

Tandoori masala. A blend of spices that is generally mixed with yogurt, ginger, and garlic, tandoori masala is used as a marinade for tandoor-cooked meat, poultry, or seafood. It is available in dry and wet (paste) forms. (*See* recipe on page 133.)

Turmeric (*Haldi*). Yellow powder obtained from the dried root of the *Curuma longa* plant, ground turmeric is an essential ingredient in Indian cuisine. Turmeric is one of the few ground spices that is sometimes added to whole spices when tempering oil. Fresh and ground turmeric is also used for its antiseptic and healing properties.

Vinegar (*Sirka*). Vinegar is rarely used in Indian cuisine, except in the coastal region of Goa, where it is used to flavor curries and pickles.

Whole wheat flour (*Atta*). A common everyday flour used to make Indian bread, whole wheat flour comes from ground whole-grain wheat kernels. In India, each family has its own blend of wheat kernels, which is taken regularly to a mill and ground into flour.

Yellow split peas (*Chana dal*). These round yellow split peas from the *Cicer arietinum* plant are also known as bengal grams in India.

Ordering Wisely in an Indian Restaurant

Most Indian restaurants provide plenty of choices for the low-fat diner. Healthful vegetables, legumes, chicken, fish, and steamed rice are offered throughout the menu. Unfortunately, there are also a large number of full-fat menu choices of which you should be aware.

The following guidelines will help you make wise food selections. As a general rule, avoid dishes that have the words "butter" or "coconut" in their titles. Steer clear of anything that is cooked in a "creamy" sauce or served with large amounts of nuts. Before ordering, always request that your food be prepared with as little butter or oil as possible, or ask that a particular dish be roasted or baked instead of fried in oil. Many restaurants will accommodate requests to bake such foods as stuffed Indian flatbreads and to dry-roast items such as papadums, both of which are traditionally deep-fried and oozing with oil.

FOODS TO CHOOSE

❑ Chana (garbanzo bean curry).

❑ Chicken or Shrimp Vindaloo.

❑ Chutney (spicy accompaniment).

❑ Dals (legume dishes—those without cream).

❑ Idlis (steamed rice cakes).

❑ Kachumbars (cut or shredded raw vegetable salads—those *without* tempered oil).

❑ Lamb or chicken kabobs.

❑ Mango or other fresh fruit.

❑ Naan (baked leavened flatbread).

❑ Raitas (yogurt-based salads).

❑ Roti or chapati (baked unleavened flatbread).

❑ Vegetable and dal (legume) soups.

❑ Vegetable, chicken, or seafood curry dishes (those *without* coconut, coconut milk, cream, or sour cream).

FOODS TO AVOID

❑ Bhatura (large, thick, deep-fried leavened bread made with white flour).

❑ Biryanis (vegetable, chicken, or seafood rice casseroles made with lots of oil).

❑ Butter Chicken.

❑ Coconut-based soups.

❑ Dosas (pan-fried, fermented rice and lentil pancakes).

❑ Gulab Jamun (sweet deep-fried whole milk balls).

❑ Kulfi (Indian ice cream).

❑ Malai Kofta (deep-fried vegetable dumplings served with cream sauce).

❑ Navrattan Korma (assorted vegetables cooked in cream sauce and topped with nuts).

❑ Pakora (vegetable fritters).

❑ Puri (small, thin deep-fried bread made with white and/or whole wheat flour).

❑ Papadums (fried lentil wafers).

❑ Samosas (fried turnovers).

❑ Shrimp in Coconut Curry.

This common everyday legume is popular throughout India and is easily found in most American grocery stores.

Yellow split pea flour (*Besan*). Pale yellow flour ground from roasted yellow split peas is also known as gram flour in India. Imparting a rather nutty taste, this flour is used as a binding agent in certain curries, flatbreads, and snack foods such as vegetable fritters.

A WORD ABOUT SALT

Salt provides our bodies with sodium, which is necessary for maintaining proper electrolyte balance. Most health experts recommend no more than 2,400 milligrams of sodium—about 1 teaspoon—per day. Sodium is present naturally in most fruits and vegetables.

Traditionally, salt is added to Indian foods, especially grains and legumes, to bring out their natural flavor. For the recipes in this book, the wise use of onions, tomatoes, lemon juice, and spices helps keep the salt to a minimum without compromising taste. Always add salt after the legumes are cooked, or the dry beans won't soften.

OILS AND COOKING SPRAYS

Even when cooking "low-fat," a little oil is sometimes necessary to enhance flavor, prevent sticking, or promote browning of food. In the case of Indian cooking, tempered oil is the basis for a number of traditional dishes. Typically, the various oils used in authentic Indian cuisine are canola, corn, cottonseed, safflower, sesame, and sunflower. Each has a distinctive flavor and aroma. Canola oil, which is rich in monounsaturated fat and has a neutral flavor, is an ideal choice to use in the preparation of Indian foods. A teaspoonful or two, used in combination with vegetable cooking spray, is usually adequate for tempering spices and for browning and stir-frying various ingredients.

Vegetable oil cooking sprays are useful when preparing low-fat and reduced-fat dishes. Although these sprays are pure fat, the amount that comes out in a spray is so small that the added fat is insignificant. Cooking sprays come in unflavored varieties, as well as a growing number of flavors. Be careful when buying generic brands as some have an unpleasant aftertaste. When using cooking spray to pan-fry or stir-fry foods, be sure to also use a nonstick pan. This will help minimize the need for additional oil.

ABOUT THE NUTRITIONAL ANALYSIS

The nutritional analysis for the recipes in this book was calculated using the information provided in *Nutrient Composition of Indian Foods* by B.S. Narasinga Rao, Y.G. Deosthale, and K. C. Pant, and *Food Values* by Jean Pennington. We have also relied on manufacturer product information when necessary.

Certain recipes in this book list optional ingredients. Generally, options are given for ingredients that are available only in Indian grocery stores, and are not essential to the successful preparation of the dish. Also, in some cases—especially desserts—nuts (which have a high fat content) have been listed as optional. Those on rigid low-fat diets may opt to omit the nuts, while others may prefer to include them. Of course, the nutritional facts have been calculated without the optional ingredients.

CONCLUSION

You are now ready to begin your journey into healthy Indian-style cooking. You will see how proper ingredients coupled with appropriate cooking methods can allow you to enjoy traditional Indian taste without the usual fat. Experience the pleasures.

2.

Snacks and Starters

Like most Americans, Indians love to snack. Whether eaten with afternoon tea, enjoyed at cocktail parties, or served as appetizers, snacks are very much a part of Indian cuisine.

In India, most snack foods are either made at home or purchased from street vendors. They include a vast array of offerings that range from dishes that are sweet and delicate to those that are hot and spicy. Frequently, traditional Indian snacks or appetizers are loaded with fat; often they are deep-fried in oil. We have adjusted both the ingredients and cooking methods in the following recipes to make them fat-free or very low in fat without compromising taste.

In this chapter, you will find a wide variety of appetizing delights. Be sure to try our low-fat versions of traditional Indian samosas—crisp flaky turnovers bursting with exotically seasoned meat or potato stuffing. Served with your favorite chutney or relish, they are sure to please even the most finicky guests. The flavorfully marinated Barbecued Shrimp, as well as the savory Stuffed Mushrooms and Potato Burger Bites are perfect cocktail or dinner party fare. And let us not forget the smoky Eggplant Dip—an ultimate topper for flatbread and pitas. Delicious!

We know you will enjoy making, serving, and eating these exotic, healthful, and delicious snacks and appetizers. They have been presented for your guilt-free enjoyment.

Angel Hair Stir-Fry

Sevaiya ka Upma

Yield: *6 servings*

12 ounces angel hair pasta

4 cups boiling water

1 teaspoon canola oil

½ teaspoon black or yellow mustard seeds

¼ teaspoon turmeric

1 medium green chile, finely chopped

4 curry leaves, washed and patted dry

1 medium onion, finely chopped

1 medium tomato, finely chopped

¼ teaspoon salt (or to taste)

1 tablespoon chopped fresh cilantro

This Western-influenced dish is one of our favorites. It is easy to prepare and calls for ingredients that are generally found in a well-stocked pantry. For variety, add ½ cup frozen thawed peas along with the tomatoes in Step 3.

1. Break the angel hair into 1-inch pieces and place in a medium bowl. Add the boiling water, stir a bit, then let the pasta sit for 30 minutes.

2. Generously spray a medium-sized nonstick skillet with vegetable cooking spray. Add the oil and place over medium heat. When the oil is hot, add the seeds. Cover the skillet with a splatter guard and allow the mustard seeds to pop. When the seeds have finished popping (within 30 seconds), add the turmeric, green chile, and curry leaves. Fry for a few seconds.

3. Add the onion and cook, while stirring, until golden brown. Stir in the tomato and continue to cook another 5 minutes.

4. Drain the angel hair and add to the skillet along with the salt. Mix well and cook about 5 minutes, stirring occasionally, until the ingredients are heated through.

5. Transfer to a medium sized serving bowl, garnish with the cilantro, and serve hot.

NUTRITIONAL FACTS (PER ¾-CUP SERVING)

Calories: 221   Carbohydrates: 43 g   Cholesterol: 0 mg
Fat: 1.9 g   Fiber: 1.2 g   Protein: 8.5 g   Sodium: 113 mg

SUGGESTED ACCOMPANIMENTS

Potato Samosas (page 33) and Mango Lassi (page 189).

HELPFUL HINT

- Reserve the pasta soaking water for another use, such as soup stock or for cooking rice.

Baked Eggplant Slices

Vaingya Che Kaap

Baked eggplant never tasted so good. Traditionally, this dish is pan-fried in lots of oil. For our healthier version, we bake the eggplant slices using vegetable cooking spray. This gives them a delicate crunch while preserving flavor and taste. Enjoy as an appetizer or side dish with any Indian meal.

Yield: *8 slices*

½ medium eggplant (about 8 ounces)

⅓ cup rice flour

1 tablespoon yellow split pea flour (optional)

¼ teaspoon salt (or to taste)

¼ teaspoon turmeric

¼ teaspoon paprika

¼ teaspoon ground cumin

1. Heat the oven to 350°F. Line a baking sheet with foil and lightly coat with vegetable cooking spray.

2. Cut the eggplant crosswise into ¼-inch-thick slices (about 8). Place in a pan and completely immerse in cold water to prevent the slices from turning brown.

3. In a shallow bowl or pie plate, combine the flours, salt, turmeric, paprika, and cumin. Remove each eggplant slice and drain the excess water, then dredge in the flour mixture, coating both sides. Dust off any excess flour and place the slices on the prepared baking sheet. Coat the tops lightly with vegetable cooking spray.

4. Cover with foil and bake for 45 minutes until tender, turning once halfway through the baking time. Serve hot.

NUTRITIONAL FACTS (PER SLICE)

Calories: 22   Carbohydrates: 5.1 g   Cholesterol: 0 mg
Fat: 0 g   Fiber: <1 g   Protein: 0.5 g   Sodium: 74 mg

SUGGESTED ACCOMPANIMENTS

Tamarind Chutney (page 183) and
Fresh Lemonade (page 189).

Barbecued Shrimp

Tandoori Jhinga

Yield: *24 medium shrimp*

8 ounces (about 24) medium shrimp

2 tablespoons nonfat yogurt

2 cloves garlic, crushed

½ teaspoon peeled and finely grated ginger

½ teaspoon homemade garam masala (page 133) or commercial variety

½ teaspoon cayenne pepper

½ teaspoon ground ajwain (bishop's weed), optional

1 tablespoon lemon juice

½ teaspoon salt (or to taste)

½ fresh lemon, sliced

Serve your guests these flavorful barbecued shrimp at your next cocktail party. The exotic marinade is also excellent for flavoring fish.

1. Peel, devein, and rinse the shrimp under cold water. Pat dry with paper towels and set aside.

2. In a medium-sized bowl, combine all of the remaining ingredients except the lemon slices.

3. Add the shrimp to the marinade and stir to evenly coat. Cover the bowl and refrigerate 2 hours.

4. Thread the marinated shrimp on skewers (if using the wooden type, be sure to soak them in water for at least 30 minutes before using).

5. Place the skewered shrimp on a heated barbecue grill and cook 3 to 4 minutes on each side, or until the shrimps are no longer translucent.

6. Line a platter with lemon slices. Remove the shrimp from the skewers and place on the platter. Serve hot.

NUTRITIONAL FACTS (PER SHRIMP)

Calories: 9   Carbohydrates: 0.2 g   Cholesterol: 11 mg
Fat: 0.1 g   Fiber: 0 g   Protein: 1.6 g   Sodium: 60 mg

SUGGESTED ACCOMPANIMENTS

Spicy Onion with Vinegar Relish (page 184) and Spicy Mint Drink (page 191).

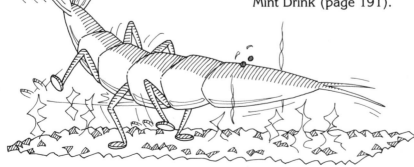

Cabbage Bake

Band Gobi Ke Tukde

Here is a quick and delicious snack that can also be served as a side dish. Be sure to finely shred the cabbage so that it bakes well and is easy to chew.

1. Preheat the oven to 375°F. Spray an 8-inch square baking pan with vegetable cooking spray and set aside.

2. Spray a medium-sized saucepan with vegetable cooking spray. Add the oil and place over medium heat. When the oil is hot, add the mustard seeds. Cover the pan with a splatter guard and allow the seeds to pop. When the seeds have finished popping (within 30 seconds), add the chile, turmeric, and onion. Cook covered while stirring often for about 2 minutes, or until the onions are beginning to brown.

3. Add the cabbage and stir in the water. Cover and cook another 5 minutes, or until the cabbage is tender. Remove from heat.

4. Stir the split pea flour, allspice, yogurt, cilantro, salt, and baking soda into the vegetable mixture. Spoon into the baking pan and spread evenly.

5. Cover with foil and bake for 20 minutes. Remove the foil and continue to bake another 5 minutes until the cabbage is slightly browned.

6. Cut into 2-inch squares and transfer to a medium-sized serving dish. Serve warm or at room temperature. Store any leftovers in an airtight container in the refrigerator for up to 5 days.

Yield: *16 squares*

1 teaspoon canola oil

1/4 teaspoon yellow mustard seeds

1 small green chile, finely chopped

1/2 teaspoon turmeric

1 medium yellow onion, finely chopped

4 cups very finely shredded green cabbage (packed)

2 tablespoons water

1 1/3 cups yellow split pea flour

1 1/2 teaspoons allspice

1 tablespoon plain nonfat yogurt

1 tablespoon finely chopped fresh cilantro

1/2 teaspoon salt (or to taste)

Pinch baking soda

NUTRITIONAL FACTS (PER SQUARE)
Calories: 48   Carbohydrates: 7.5 g   Cholesterol: 0 mg
Fat: 0.7 g   Fiber: 1 g   Protein: 2.7 g   Sodium: 78 mg

SUGGESTED ACCOMPANIMENTS

Cilantro Chutney (page 181) and Spicy Buttermilk Drink (page 193).

Tandoori Chicken Kabobs

Murg Tikka

Yield: *8 kabobs*

4 cloves garlic, crushed

½ teaspoon peeled and finely grated ginger

1½ tablespoons bottled tandoori marinade paste

2 tablespoons plain nonfat yogurt

1 pound skinless, boneless chicken breasts, cut into 1-inch chunks (about 32 pieces)

Although traditionally these kabobs are cooked in a tandoor, a barbecue grill will produce equally good results. (Using a conventional oven is not recommended but will do in a pinch. Just be careful not to overcook the chicken, as it dries out quickly).

1. In a medium-sized bowl, combine the garlic, ginger, tandoori paste, and yogurt. Mix well.

2. Add the chicken and mix well to coat. Cover and refrigerate for 1 hour.

3. Spray an outdoor barbecue grill with cooking spray and preheat for 10 minutes.

4. Thread 4 pieces of marinated chicken on each skewer (if using the wooden type, be sure to soak them in water for at least 30 minutes before using). Place on the heated barbecue grill and cook 5 to 6 minutes. Turn over and cook another 4 to 5 minutes until the chicken is no longer pink inside. If using a conventional oven, place the kabobs in a baking pan and cook in a preheated 450°F oven for 10 to 12 minutes.

5. Serve warm with your favorite chutney or relish.

NUTRITIONAL FACTS (PER KABOB)

Calories: 116   Carbohydrates: 0.3 g   Cholesterol: 48 mg
Fat: 2.4 g   Fiber: 0 g   Protein: 18 g   Sodium: 287 mg

SUGGESTED ACCOMPANIMENTS

Spicy Onion with Vinegar Relish (page 184) and Mango Lassi (page 189).

Eggplant Dip

Baingan Bharta

Versions of this smoky eggplant paté are common throughout India. Enjoy it warm as a side dish, or serve it at room temperature as a dip for pita bread, melba toast, or taco chips.

1. Preheat the oven to 400°F. Line a 9-x-13-inch baking pan with foil and lightly coat with vegetable cooking spray.

2. Spread the eggplant and onion in the pan. Cover with foil and bake for 30 minutes. Uncover and place under the broiler, stirring occasionally for 15 minutes, or until the onions are golden brown. Transfer the mixture to a bowl and mash well.

3. Coat a large nonstick skillet with cooking spray. Add the oil and place over medium heat. When the oil is hot, add the cumin seeds, garlic, and eggplant-onion mixture. Cook while stirring for 2 minutes.

4. Add the tomato paste, cilantro, ground cumin, ground coriander, and salt. Continue to cook for about 8 minutes, stirring often to prevent the mixture from sticking to the pan and burning.

5. Transfer to a serving bowl. Cool to room temperature, then use as a dip for chips or flatbread.

Yield: *1 cup*

1 medium eggplant (about 1 pound), peeled and cut into ½-inch cubes

1 medium onion, finely chopped

1 tablespoon canola oil

½ teaspoon cumin seeds

1 clove garlic, crushed

1 tablespoon tomato paste

1 tablespoon finely chopped fresh cilantro

½ teaspoon ground cumin

½ teaspoon ground coriander

1 teaspoon salt (or to taste)

NUTRITIONAL FACTS (PER 2 TABLESPOONS)
Calories: 27   Carbohydrates: 4.4 g   Cholesterol: 0 mg
Fat: 0.9 g   Fiber: 0.8 g   Protein: 0.8 g   Sodium: 146 mg

SUGGESTED ACCOMPANIMENTS
Raised Indian Flatbread (page 92) and Fresh Lemonade (page 189).

Eggplant Roll-Ups

Chatpata Baingan

Yield: *5 roll-ups*

1 small eggplant (about 8 ounces), peeled and cut lengthwise into five ½-inch slices

½ teaspoon canola oil

½ teaspoon cumin seeds

½ teaspoon aniseeds

3 scallions, cut into ¼-inch pieces

1 tablespoon bottled garlic and herb spaghetti sauce

2 teaspoons finely chopped fresh cilantro

⅛ teaspoon salt (or to taste)

⅛ teaspoon ground black pepper

¼ teaspoon chat masala (optional)

This elegant low-fat dish will make an attractive presentation at your next party.

1. Preheat the oven to 350°F. Lightly coat a nonstick cookie sheet with vegetable cooking spray.

2. Arrange the eggplant slices on the cookie sheet in a single layer. Spray with a little vegetable cooking spray and bake uncovered for 7 to 10 minutes. Turn the slices over and bake another 5 to 10 minutes until they are soft but not brown. Remove to a dish and allow to cool completely.

3. Coat a medium-sized nonstick skillet with vegetable cooking spray. Add the oil and place over medium heat. Add the cumin and aniseeds and cook, stirring constantly, until the seeds sizzle and emit a strong aroma. Add the scallions and continue to cook for 30 seconds.

4. Add the spaghetti sauce and cilantro. Mix well and cook, stirring constantly, for about 1 minute. The mixture should be somewhat dry. Remove from the heat and allow to cool completely.

5. Sprinkle the eggplant slices with salt and pepper. Spoon equal amounts of filling mixture on the bottom half of each slice. Beginning at the end with the filling, roll up each slice and place on the cookie sheet, seam side down.

6. Sprinkle the chat masala (if using) on the roll-ups and place under a broiler for 1 to 2 minutes, until the tops are golden brown.

7. Serve warm.

NUTRITIONAL FACTS (PER ROLL-UP)
Calories: 29   Carbohydrates: 3.8 g   Cholesterol: 0 mg
Fat: 0.6 g   Fiber: 2 g   Protein: 1.2 g   Sodium: 78 mg

SUGGESTED ACCOMPANIMENTS

Yellow Split Pea with Mango Relish (page 185) and Fresh Lemonade (page 189).

Ground Lamb Bites

Seekh Kebab

These exotic grilled lamb appetizers are perfect party fare. You can refrigerate any leftovers and simply heat them in a 350°F oven for 5 to 10 minutes, or until warm.

1. In a large bowl, mix together all of the ingredients except the salt. Cover and refrigerate about 10 minutes.

2. Remove the mixture from the refrigerator, add the salt, and divide into 16 equal portions. Mold the portions onto skewers and shape into 5-to 6-inch-long "sausages." Depending on the length of the skewers, you could mold one or two "sausages" on each.

3. Spray an outdoor barbecue grill with nonstick spray and preheat for 10 minutes.

4. Grill the meat about 2 to 3-inches from the heat, for about 5 to 8 minutes, turning until they are golden brown.

5. Slide the "sausages" from the skewer, cut in half, and serve.

Yield: *32 appetizers*

1 pound lean ground lamb

5 cloves garlic, crushed

1 small yellow onion, very finely chopped

1 jalapeño pepper, very finely chopped

2 tablespoons finely chopped cilantro

¾ teaspoon peeled, grated ginger

1 egg white

1 teaspoon lemon juice

1 teaspoon salt (or to taste)

NUTRITIONAL FACTS (PER APPETIZER)

Calories: 29   Carbohydrates: 0.4 g   Cholesterol: 12 mg
Fat: 1 g   Fiber: 0 g   Protein: 4.3 g   Sodium: 82 mg

SUGGESTED ACCOMPANIMENTS

Spicy Onion with Vinegar Relish (page 184) or Mint Chutney (page 182).

HELPFUL HINTS

- The onion and jalapeño pepper must be very finely chopped. Big pieces will cause the mixture to break apart as you try to mold it around the skewer.

- Adding salt to the mixture too early will cause the onion to produce water and spoil the consistency of the mixture. You will be unable to mold the mixture around the skewer.

- If using wooden skewers, be sure to soak them at least 30 minutes to keep them from burning on the grill.

Indian Chicken Salad Sandwiches

Murgi Salad ke Sandwiches

Yield: *6 servings*

6 ounces cooked chicken breast, cut into ½-inch cubes

½ medium ripe mango, peeled and cut into ¼-inch cubes

1 tablespoon nonfat sour cream

1 tablespoon nonfat mayonnaise

2 tablespoons plain nonfat yogurt

2 tablespoons finely chopped fresh cilantro

¼ teaspoon ground cumin

¼ teaspoon salt (or to taste)

3 large whole wheat pita bread pockets

This Indianized version of traditional American chicken salad uses lots of fresh green cilantro, a dash of ground cumin, and sweet flavorful mango. We serve it stuffed into whole wheat pita pockets, but feel free to enjoy it plain or with any bread of your choice.

1. Combine all of the ingredients except the pita pockets in a large bowl. Mix well, cover, and refrigerate for 1 hour.

2. Cut the pita pockets in half. Fill with equal amounts of the chilled salad and serve immediately.

NUTRITIONAL FACTS (PER SANDWICH)

Calories: 112   Carbohydrates: 17 g   Cholesterol: 12 mg
Fat: 0.6 g   Fiber: 1 g   Protein: 9.7 g   Sodium: 208 mg

SUGGESTED ACCOMPANIMENTS

Yellow Split Pea with Mango Relish (page 185) and Spicy Mint Drink (page 191).

Potato Burger Bites

Aloo Vada

This seasoned blend of mashed potatoes and yellow split pea flour is a fat free variation of Batata Vada, which is deep-fried in hot oil. Our tasty version is cooked in a nonstick skillet that is coated with cooking spray. To reheat any leftovers, simply pop them in a 300°F oven for 5 to 10 minutes.

Yield: *20 appetizers*

3 medium potatoes

2 scallions, finely chopped

1 green chile pepper, finely chopped

1 tablespoon finely chopped fresh cilantro

1 teaspoon finely chopped fresh mint

½ teaspoon chat masala (optional)

½ teaspoon cumin seeds

½ teaspoon salt (or to taste)

¼ cup fat-free egg substitute

½ cup split yellow pea flour

1 teaspoon canola oil

1. Peel the potatoes and cut into chunks. Place in a pot, add water to cover, and bring to a boil. Reduce the heat to medium and cook for about 3 to 5 minutes or until soft. Drain the potatoes and place in a large bowl.

2. Using a potato masher or the back of a large spoon, mash the potatoes until smooth. Add the scallions, chile, cilantro, mint, chat masala (if using), cumin seeds, and salt. Mix until well-combined.

3. Pour the egg substitute into a small bowl. Place the flour in a shallow plate or pie pan and set aside.

4. Coat a large nonstick skillet with cooking spray and preheat over medium heat.

5. Take level tablespoons of the potato mixture and form into small round burger shapes (approximately 20). Dredge each "burger" in the flour, coating both sides, then dip in the egg substitute and place in the pan. Drizzle the oil all around the pan, making sure each burger gets a bit.

6. Cook the "bites" over medium heat for 2 minutes, or until the bottoms are browned. Flip over and brown the other side. Sprinkle a few drops of water into the hot skillet and quickly cover for 1 minute. The steam created will cook any remaining uncooked coating on the potatoes.

7. Transfer the potatoes to a serving platter and enjoy warm with your favorite relish or chutney.

NUTRITIONAL FACTS (PER BURGER BITE)

Calories: 29   Carbohydrates: 5.7 g   Cholesterol: 0 mg
Fat: 0.3 g   Fiber: <1 g   Protein: 1.4 g   Sodium: 63 mg

SUGGESTED ACCOMPANIMENTS

Tamarind Chutney (page 183) or Sweet Buttermilk Drink (page 190).

Spicy Vegetable Platter

Masala Sabzi

Yield: *6 servings*

¼ cauliflower head

1 large carrot

1 medium cucumber

1 large tomato

½ teaspoon salt (or to taste)

1 teaspoon ground cumin

1 teaspoon pani-puri masala, or
 1 teaspoon lemon juice

This Indian-style raw vegetable platter is a great appetizer. Feel free to create your own version with your favorite vegetables.

1. Cut the cauliflower into medium-sized florets. Peel the carrot and cut it into ¼-inch circles. Place in a steamer and cook until tender-crisp. Remove from the steamer and cool.

2. Peel the cucumber and cut in half lengthwise. Cut each half into 6 spears.

3. Cut the tomato crosswise into 6 slices.

4. Arrange the vegetables on a platter. Sprinkle with salt, cumin, and pani-puri masala before serving.

NUTRITIONAL FACTS (PER SERVING)

Calories: 30   Carbohydrates: 6.4 g   Cholesterol: 0 mg
Fat: 0.2 g   Fiber: 1.4 g   Protein: 1.3 g   Sodium: 215 mg

SUGGESTED ACCOMPANIMENTS

Tuna Pita Pockets (page 36) and Mango Milkshake
(page 190).

Stuffed Mushrooms

Bhare Huai Khumb

The ever-popular stuffed mushroom appetizer takes on a delicious Indian twist in the following recipe.

1. Spray a medium-sized skillet with vegetable cooking spray. Add the oil and place over medium heat. When the oil is hot, add the cumin seeds, garlic, turmeric, and salt. Stir-fry for 30 seconds before adding the onion.

2. Continue to cook while stirring, until the onions are golden. Add a teaspoon of water as needed to prevent the onion from sticking to the skillet.

3. Add the tomato and stir-fry until the juices are absorbed. Stir in the cilantro, basil, and lemon juice. Cool completely.

4. Preheat the oven to 350°F. Spray a nonstick cookie sheet or baking pan with vegetable cooking spray.

5. Stuff about 1 teaspoon of filling mixture into each mushroom cap.

6. Place the stuffed caps in a single layer on the baking sheet and spray the tops with a little cooking spray. Bake for 15 minutes, or until the mushrooms are cooked and the tops are beginning to brown.

7. Transfer to a platter and serve warm.

Yield: *20 appetizers*

½ teaspoon canola oil

1 teaspoon cumin seeds

4 cloves garlic, crushed

½ teaspoon turmeric

¼ teaspoon salt (to taste)

½ medium yellow onion, thinly sliced

1 medium tomato, coarsely chopped

2 tablespoons finely chopped fresh cilantro

2 teaspoons finely chopped fresh basil

2 teaspoons lemon juice

20 medium white button or crimini mushrooms, stems removed

NUTRITIONAL FACTS (PER MUSHROOM)

Calories: 15   Carbohydrates: 1.7 g   Cholesterol: 0 mg
Fat: 0.2 g   Fiber: 0 g   Protein: 0.4 g   Sodium: 30 mg

SUGGESTED ACCOMPANIMENTS

Cilantro Chutney (page 181) and Spicy Buttermilk Drink (page 193).

Making Samosas

One of India's most popular foods is the samosa. These tasty turnovers consist of flaky homemade pastry that is stuffed with seasoned potatoes, vegetables, or ground meat. Traditionally, the pastry is made with lots of butter or shortening, and, once filled, is deep-fried in oil. For our low-fat samosas, we use flaky phyllo pastry to wrap around the filling, then pop them in the oven to bake. (And they are every bit as delicious as the traditional types.)

You can prepare samosas ahead of time, then store them in an airtight container in the freezer where they will keep up to two months. To cook the frozen samosas, simply place them seam side down on a baking sheet, spray the tops with cooking spray, and pop them into a preheated 425°F oven for 8 to 10 minutes until lightly browned.

To form samosas, you will need two sheets of phyllo dough.* Lay out one of the sheets on a clean dry surface. Lightly coat the sheet with vegetable cooking spray, then place the second sheet on top (Step 1). Cut the stacked sheets into 8 equal strips (Step 2). Place a heaping teaspoon of filling on the right side of one strip, about 1½ inches from the bottom. Fold the lower left corner up to enclose the filling in a triangular pocket (Step 3). Continue folding the pocket up the entire strip (Step 4). If you are left with any unfolded dough, simply tuck it under the pocket (Step 5).

* Sheets of frozen phyllo dough must be thoroughly defrosted before you start working with them. (Sheets that are even slightly frozen will tear and crack.) Because phyllo dries out very quickly, it is necessary to keep it covered with a clean damp cloth until ready to use. For this same reason, it is also important to work quickly when forming the samosas.

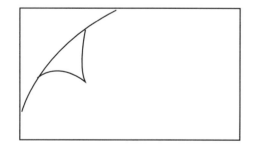

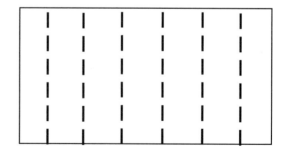

1. *Coat a sheet of phyllo with cooking spray and lay a second sheet on top.*

2. *Cut the stacked sheets into 8 equal strips.*

Forming Samosas

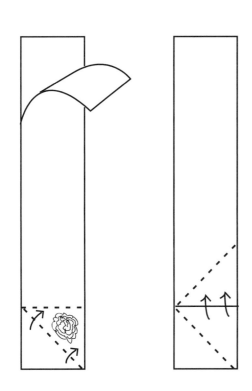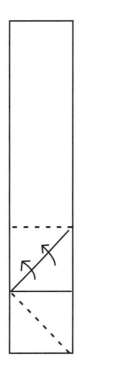

3. Place a heaping teaspoon of filling on the right side of the strip about 1½ inches from the bottom. Fold the lower left corner up to enclose the filling in a triangular pocket.

4. Continue folding the pocket.

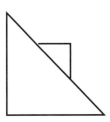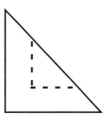

5. Tuck any unfolded dough into the pocket.

6. The completed samosa.

Turkey~Lamb Samosas

Meat Samosas

Yield: *32 appetizers*

5 ounces lean ground lamb

3 ounces lean ground turkey breast

1 medium yellow onion, finely chopped

2 teaspoons lemon juice

1 tablespoon finely chopped fresh cilantro

1 small green chile pepper, finely chopped

¼ teaspoon salt (or to taste)

8 sheets frozen phyllo dough, thawed and covered with a clean damp cloth

These savory stuffed turnovers will be a hit at your next party.

1. Coat a medium-sized nonstick skillet with cooking spray and place over medium heat. When hot, add the lamb and turkey and stir-fry until no longer pink.

2. Add the onion and sauté, stirring frequently, until golden brown.

3. Stir in the lemon juice, cilantro, chile, and salt. Mix well and continue to cook until the liquid has evaporated. Cool completely.

4. Preheat the oven to 425°F. Lightly coat 2 nonstick cookie sheets with cooking spray and set aside.

5. Place one sheet of phyllo dough on a clean dry surface. Lightly coat it with cooking spray and lay a second sheet on top. (Keep the remaining phyllo covered with a clean damp cloth to prevent it from drying out.) Cut the stacked sheets into 8 strips and form the samosas according to instructions beginning on page 30. Place the samosas seam side down under a damp towel and repeat with the remaining phyllo dough and filling. (This will yield 32 samosas.)

6. Place the samosas on the cookie sheets and lightly coat the tops with cooking spray. Bake about 10 to 15 minutes until light golden brown.

7. Serve warm with your favorite relish or chutney.

NUTRITIONAL FACTS (PER SAMOSA)

Calories: 37   Carbohydrates: 4.5 g   Cholesterol: 6 mg
Fat: 0.5 g   Fiber: 0 g   Protein: 2.7 g   Sodium: 60 mg

SUGGESTED ACCOMPANIMENTS

Mint Chutney (page 182) and Spicy Indian Tea (page 192).

Potato Samosas

Aloo Samosas

This nonfat vegetarian samosa is stuffed with a combination of seasoned potatoes, onions, and peas.

1. Coat a medium-sized nonstick skillet with cooking spray and place over medium heat. When hot, add the cumin seeds. Fry a few seconds, then add the onion and sauté, stirring frequently, until golden brown. (Add a teaspoon or two of water as needed to prevent the onion from sticking to the skillet.)

2. Stir in the potato, peas, and ginger. Mix well and continue cooking another 5 minutes.

3. Add the garam masala, ground coriander, cayenne pepper, and salt, and cook another minute. Remove from the heat, add the lemon juice and cilantro, and mix well. Allow the mixture to cool completely.

4. Preheat the oven to 425°F. Lightly coat 2 nonstick cookie sheets with cooking spray and set aside.

5. Place one sheet of phyllo dough on a clean dry surface. Lightly coat it with cooking spray and lay a second sheet on top. (Keep the remaining phyllo covered with a clean damp cloth to prevent it from drying out.) Cut the stacked sheets into 8 strips and form the samosas according to instructions beginning on page 30. Place the samosas seam side down under a damp towel and repeat with the remaining phyllo dough and filling. (This will yield 32 samosas.)

6. Place the samosas on the cookie sheets and lightly coat the tops with cooking spray. Bake about 6 to 8 minutes until light golden brown.

7. Serve warm with your favorite relish or chutney.

Yield: *32 appetizers*

½ teaspoon cumin seeds

½ small yellow onion, finely chopped

1 medium potato, boiled, peeled, and coarsely mashed

½ cup frozen peas, thawed

¼ teaspoon peeled and finely grated ginger

½ teaspoon homemade garam masala (page 133) or commercial variety

¼ teaspoon ground coriander

¼ teaspoon cayenne pepper

¼ teaspoon salt (or to taste)

2 teaspoons lemon juice

1 tablespoon finely chopped fresh cilantro

8 sheets frozen phyllo dough, thawed

NUTRITIONAL FACTS (PER SAMOSA)
Calories: 23   Carbohydrates: 4.6 g   Cholesterol: 0 mg
Fat: 0.1 g   Fiber: 0 g   Protein: 0.7 g   Sodium: 50 mg

SUGGESTED ACCOMPANIMENTS
Tamarind Chutney (page 183) and Spicy Indian Tea (page 192).

Mushroom-Onion Stuffed Sandwiches

Khumb aur Pyaz ke Sandwiches

Yield: *8 snack sandwiches*

¼ teaspoon canola oil

¼ teaspoon cumin seeds

1 clove garlic, crushed

1 small yellow onion, thinly sliced

½ cup thinly sliced mushrooms

1 medium tomato, coarsely chopped

¼ teaspoon salt (or to taste)

¼ teaspoon ground cumin

1 tablespoon finely chopped fresh cilantro

8 slices whole wheat bread

4 slices nonfat mozzarella cheese (optional)

Pile a savory mushroom-onion mixture between hearty slices of whole wheat bread in these tasty sandwich snacks. And don't feel restricted to this filling—you can use just about any leftover cooked vegetables you have on hand. Cabbage with Peas (page 96), Cauliflower with Tomato (page 98), and Yellow Mashed Potatoes (page 121) are all good choices. Enjoy with ketchup or your favorite chutney or dipping sauce.

1. Coat a medium-sized nonstick skillet or wok with vegetable cooking spray. Add the oil and place over medium heat. When the oil is hot, add the cumin seeds. Fry a few seconds until the seeds begin to sizzle, then add the garlic and onion. Cook while stirring, until the onions are pale and soft. (Add a tablespoon or two of water as needed to prevent the onion from sticking to the skillet.)

2. Add the mushrooms, cover, and steam for 30 seconds, then stir in the tomato. Increase the heat to high, and cook while stirring, until the juice from the tomato evaporates. If the tomato starts sticking to the pan, reduce the heat to medium-low.

3. Stir in the salt, ground cumin, and cilantro. Mix well and remove from the heat. Cool completely.

4. Lightly coat one side of each slice of bread with vegetable cooking spray. Turn four of the slices over and evenly spread 2 tablespoons of the mushroom mixture on top. Top each with a slice of mozzarella cheese (if using) and a remaining slice of bread (sprayed side up).

5. Place in a sandwich toaster* and cook a few minutes until golden brown. Remove the sandwiches, and serve.

* You can also grill the sandwiches in a nonstick skillet that has been coated with cooking spray. Cook each side 2 to 3 minutes over medium heat until brown.

NUTRITIONAL FACTS (PER APPETIZER)

Calories: 70   Carbohydrates: 13.5 g   Cholesterol: 0 mg
Fat: 1.3 g   Fiber: 2 g   Protein: 2.7 g   Sodium: 233 mg

SUGGESTED ACCOMPANIMENTS

Mint Chutney (page 182) and Sweet Buttermilk Drink (page 190).

Indian-Style Crisped Rice

Bhel

This crunchy fat-free treat from the western region of India is both sweet and tart. Its unusual ingredient combination results in a taste that will have you addicted. Because the crisped rice loses its crunch quickly, these treats should be eaten immediately after they are made.

Yield: *4 servings*

1. Combine the potato, tomato, onion, chile, mango, and cilantro in a large mixing bowl. Add the chutneys and mix thoroughly.

2. Just before serving, add the crisped rice and mix quickly.

3. Divide the mixture onto four serving plates and enjoy immediately.

1 medium potato, cooked, peeled, and cut into ¼-inch cubes

1 small tomato, finely chopped

1 small onion, finely chopped

1 small green chile pepper, finely chopped

2 tablespoons finely chopped raw, green mango

1 tablespoon finely chopped fresh cilantro

3 tablespoons Mint Chutney (page 182)

2 tablespoons Tamarind Chutney (page 183)

2 cups crisped rice cereal like Rice Krispies

NUTRITIONAL FACTS (PER SERVING)
Calories: 112   Carbohydrates: 23.4 g   Cholesterol: 0 mg
Fat: 0.3 g   Fiber: <1 g   Protein: 2.1 g   Sodium: 267 mg

SUGGESTED ACCOMPANIMENTS
Mango Milkshake (page 190) or Spicy Indian Tea (page 192).

Tuna Pita Pockets

Machchi Bhari Roti

Yield: *6 servings*

3 large whole wheat pita
breads

TUNA FILLING

1½ teaspoons canola oil

1 small yellow onion, finely
chopped

6-ounce can tuna packed in
water, drained

¼ teaspoon turmeric

1 teaspoon ground cumin

1 teaspoon ground coriander

½ teaspoon salt (or to taste)

⅛ teaspoon ground black
pepper

1 medium potato, boiled,
peeled, and mashed

1 tablespoon ketchup

GARNISH

1½ cups shredded lettuce

1 medium tomato, sliced

1 cup alfalfa sprouts

This low-fat tuna recipe is an Indianized version of an American favorite.

1. Coat a medium-sized nonstick skillet or wok with vegetable cooking spray. Add the oil and place over medium heat. When hot, add the onions and cook, stirring, until golden brown.

2. Add the tuna and cook for a minute, then add the turmeric, cumin, coriander, salt, and black pepper. Cook for 5 minutes, stirring occasionally.

3. Add the mashed potato and ketchup, and continue to cook, stirring occasionally, another 10 minutes. Remove from the heat and cool.

4. Cut each pita bread in half. Line each half with lettuce, tomato, and alfalfa sprouts. Spoon equal amounts of the tuna mixture into each half and serve.

NUTRITIONAL FACTS (PER PITA POCKET)

Calories: 130   Carbohydrates: 20.7 g   Cholesterol: 12 mg
Fat: 1.2 g   Fiber: 2 g   Protein: 9 g   Sodium: 412 mg

SUGGESTED ACCOMPANIMENTS

Spicy Mango Chutney (page 180) and Sweet Buttermilk Drink page 190).

3.

Soups for the Soul

There are very few traditional soups in India—the fiery Mulligatawny and the refreshing Tomato Saar being two of the most notable. There are, however, a number of legume- and tomato-based curries that are very thin and possess a soup-like quality. We have included a number of these "soups," such as the Easy Dal Soup and Mixed Legume Soup, in this chapter.

Having lived in the United States for a number of years, we have had the pleasure of enjoying many of the flavorful soups found here. To a number of these "American" soups, we have added a flavorful Indian touch. The Zesty Carrot and Spicy Corn are two delicious examples of western soups to which we have given a special Indian flair.

Enjoy this chapter's warm, comforting soups alone or alongside a bowl of steamed rice or some freshly made Indian flatbread (*see* bread recipes in Chapter 6). Some offerings, like the Dal Soup with Whole Wheat Dumplings and the Lentil and Vegetable Soup are nutritionally complete meals in themselves. But, no matter which soups you choose, you will find them all to be hearty, nutritious, and, best of all, delicious.

Buttermilk Soup

Kadhi

Yield: *4 servings*

2 cups buttermilk, at room temperature

2 cups water

¼ cup plus 1 teaspoon chick pea flour (besan)

1 teaspoon canola oil

½ teaspoon cumin seeds

¼ teaspoon fenugreek seeds

2 bay leaves

2 small whole dried red chile peppers

½ teaspoon turmeric

1 medium yellow onion, finely chopped

½ teaspoon ground cumin

½ teaspoon ground coriander

½ teaspoon paprika

½ teaspoon salt (or to taste)

2 teaspoons dried fenugreek leaves

¼ teaspoon homemade garam masala (page 133) or commerical variety (optional)

2 teaspoons finely chopped fresh cilantro

While buttermilk soup variations are enjoyed throughout India, this version from northern India is one of our favorites. It is thick, flavorful, and delicious.

1. Combine the buttermilk and water in a medium-sized bowl. Set aside.

2. Transfer ½ cup of the buttermilk mixture to a small bowl. Add the chick pea flour and stir to form a paste. Return this paste to the bowl of buttermilk and stir to dissolve. Set aside.

3. Place the oil in a medium-sized nonstick pan over medium heat. When the oil is hot, add the cumin seeds, fenugreek seeds, and bay leaf. When the seeds begin to sizzle and emit a strong aroma, add the chile peppers, turmeric, and onion. Stir-fry until the onion is pale and soft. (Add a tablespoon or two of water as needed to prevent the onion from sticking to the skillet.)

4. Add the ground cumin, ground coriander, and paprika. Stir for 15 seconds, then add the salt and buttermilk mixture. Quickly bring to a boil, then reduce the heat to low and simmer for 2 minutes.

5. Stir in the dried fenugreek leaves and garam masala (if using). Mix well and ladle the hot soup into individual serving bowls. Garnish with cilantro and serve.

NUTRITIONAL FACTS: (PER 1-CUP SERVING)

Calories: 91   Carbohydrates: 16.5 g   Cholesterol: 2 mg
Fat: 1.5 g   Fiber: 0.8 g   Protein: 6.2 g   Sodium: 404 mg

SUGGESTED ACCOMPANIMENTS

Quick Garbanzo Bean Salad (page 68) and Fenugreek Flatbread (page 84).

HELPFUL HINT

- It is important for the buttermilk to be at room temperature to prevent the soup from separating when heated.

Top: Eggplant Dip (page 23) and
Mint Chutney (page 182)
Left: Potato Burger Bites (page 27)
Right: Raised Indian Flatbread (page 92)
Bottom: Turkey-Lamb Samosas (page 32)

Top: **Spinach Buttermilk Soup** (page 45)
Right: **Mulligatawny Soup** (page 42)
Left: **Tomato Soup** (page 47)

Easy Dal Soup

Toor Dal ka Shorba

Dal refers to a wide variety of dried legumes including lentils and split peas. It also refers to curries made from legumes. Dal, in one form or another, is commonly consumed with every vegetarian meal.

1. Pick through the dried peas for any grit or debris, then place them in a strainer and rinse thoroughly. Transfer the peas to a medium-sized pot along with 3 cups of water. Soak for 2 hours.

2. Place the pot with the peas and their soaking water over high heat and bring to a boil. Reduce the heat to medium and cook, partially covered, for 35 minutes or until the peas are tender. As the peas cook, crush them against the sides of the pot with the back of a spoon.

3. Once the peas are cooked, stir in 2 cups of water. Remove from the heat and set aside. Blend, if necessary.

4. Spray a large nonstick skillet with vegetable cooking spray. Add the oil and place over medium heat. When the oil is hot, add the mustard seeds. Cover the skillet with a splatter guard and allow the seeds to pop. When the seeds have finished popping (within 30 seconds), add the cumin seeds and turmeric. Fry for a few seconds.

5. Add the onions and cook, while stirring, until light golden brown. (Add a tablespoon or two of water as needed to prevent the onion from sticking to the skillet.) Stir in the tomato and continue to cook another 5 minutes.

6. Add the cooked pigeon peas, ground coriander, ground cumin, and salt, and bring to a boil. Reduce the heat to medium-low and continue to cook another 5 minutes while stirring constantly. Ladle the hot soup into bowls, garnish with mint leaves, and serve.

Yield: *4 servings*

¾ cup split pigeon peas (toor dal), or yellow split peas

1 teaspoon canola oil

¼ teaspoon black or yellow mustard seeds

¼ teaspoon cumin seeds

¼ teaspoon turmeric

1 small yellow onion, finely chopped

1 small tomato, finely chopped

1 teaspoon ground coriander

½ teaspoon ground cumin

½ teaspoon salt (or to taste)

1 tablespoon coarsely chopped fresh mint

NUTRITIONAL FACTS: (PER 1-CUP SERVING)

Calories: 145   Carbohydrates: 23.7 g   Cholesterol: 0 mg
Fat: 1.8 g   Fiber: 1.1 g   Protein: 8.5 g   Sodium: 299 mg

SUGGESTED ACCOMPANIMENTS

Cucumber Tomato Salad (page 57), Spinach Flatbread (91), and plain boiled rice.

Lentil and Vegetable Soup

Masoor Sabzi ka Shorba

Yield: *5 servings*

1 cup dry lentils

1 small yellow onion, finely chopped

1 medium potato, peeled and cut into ¼-inch cubes

3 cloves garlic, crushed

½ teaspoon peeled and finely grated ginger

¾ cup canned crushed tomatoes

½ teaspoon salt (or to taste)

¼ teaspoon cayenne pepper

1 teaspoon finely chopped fresh cilantro

1 teaspoon finely chopped fresh mint

This hearty soup combines proteins from the lentils with vitamins and carbohydrates found in the vegetables. Perfect to serve on a cold winter day with fresh bread or crackers.

1. Pick through the lentils for any grit or debris, then place them in a strainer and rinse thoroughly. Transfer to a medium-sized pot along with 2 cups of water. Soak for 2 hours.

2. To the soaked lentils add 2 cups of water, the onion, potato, garlic, and ginger. Place over high heat and bring to a boil. Reduce the heat to low and cook, partially covered, for 15 minutes, stirring occasionally.

3. Stir in the crushed tomatoes, salt, and cayenne pepper, and cook another 5 minutes. Add the cilantro and mint. Remove the pot from the heat and allow the soup to cool slightly.

4. Transfer all but 1 cup of the soup to a blender. Add a cup of water and blend to a coarse purée. Return the soup to the pot, and reheat until the mixture is heated through.

5. Ladle the hot soup into individual bowls and serve.

NUTRITIONAL FACTS: (PER 1-CUP SERVING)

Calories: 172   Carbohydrates: 31.4 g   Cholesterol: 0 mg
Fat: 0.3 g   Fiber: <1 g   Protein: 10.8 g   Sodium: 312 mg

SUGGESTED ACCOMPANIMENTS

Cucumber Yogurt Salad (page 56) and Raised Indian Flatbread (page 92).

Mixed Legume Soup

Dal Aur Sabzi ka Shorba

This hearty soup, which calls for carrots, potato, and spinach, makes an exotic and colorful soup.

1. Pick through the dried peas for any grit or debris, then place them in a strainer and rinse thoroughly. Transfer to a medium-sized pot along with 2 cups of water. Soak for 2 hours.

2. Add 3 cups water to the soaking beans and bring to a boil over high heat. Reduce the heat to medium-low and continue cooking, partially covered, for 35 minutes, stirring occasionally.

3. Add the remaining ingredients to the pot along with 1 cup water. Continue cooking another 15 minutes. Remove the pot from the heat and allow the soup to cool slightly.

4. Transfer the soup to a blender and purée in batches. Return the soup to the pot and bring to a gentle boil over medium-high heat.

5. Ladle the hot soup into individual bowls and serve.

Yield: *5 servings*

¼ cups each dry yellow split peas, pigeon peas, and split mung beans

2 medium carrots, cut into ½-inch circles

1 medium potato, peeled and cut into ½-inch cubes

1 cup thoroughly washed, chopped fresh spinach leaves, packed

½ teaspoon peeled, grated ginger

¼ teaspoon turmeric

1 teaspoon ground cumin

½ teaspoon ground coriander

¼ teaspoon cayenne pepper

½ teaspoon salt (or to taste)

NUTRITIONAL FACTS: (PER 1-CUP SERVING)

Calories: 152   Carbohydrates: 26.4 g   Cholesterol: 0 mg
Fat: 1.8 g   Fiber: 3.4 g   Protein: 7.8   Sodium: 263 mg

SUGGESTED ACCOMPANIMENTS

Indian Potato Salad (page 58) and Honey Wheat Flatbread (page 86).

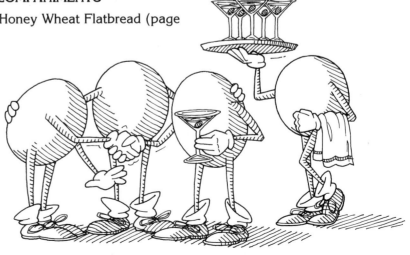

Mulligatawny Soup

Mullagatanni

Yield: 3 servings

2 tablespoons dry split pigeon peas

1 fresh red or green chile pepper, halved lengthwise

1/8 teaspoon turmeric

1 large tomato, coarsely chopped

1/2 teaspoon canola oil

1/4 teaspoon cumin seeds

1/4 teaspoon black or yellow mustard seeds

5 curry leaves

2 dried red chile peppers (or to taste)

3 cloves garlic, crushed

1/2 teaspoon salt (or to taste)

1 teaspoon freshly ground black pepper (or to taste)

3/4 teaspoon tamarind pulp dissolved in 1 tablespoon warm water*

2 teaspoons finely chopped fresh cilantro

*Can substitute 2 tablespoons lemon juice for the dissolved tamarind.

This fiery hot soup from southern India literally means "spice water." Its heat comes from fresh green chile peppers, as well as ground black pepper. Covered tightly and stored in the refrigerator, this soup will keep up to two days. Remember to add the cilantro just before serving.

1. Pick through the dried peas for any grit or debris, then place them in a strainer and rinse thoroughly. Transfer to a medium-sized pot along with 2 cups of water. Soak for 2 hours.

2. Place the pot with the peas and their soaking water over high heat. Add the fresh chile and turmeric and bring to a boil. Reduce the heat to medium-low and simmer partially covered for 30 minutes or until the peas are tender.

3. Strain the cooked peas through a strainer or sieve that has been set over another medium-sized pot. (The stock will drain into the pot.) Remove and discard the chile. Mash the peas through the strainer into the pot. Add a cup of water to the puréed mixture and set aside.

4. Place the tomato in a blender or food processor. Process it to a purée, remove to a small bowl, and set aside.

5. Coat a large nonstick pot with cooking spray. Add the canola oil and place over medium heat. When the oil is hot, add the cumin seeds and mustard seeds. Cover the pot with a splatter guard and allow the seeds to pop. When the seeds have finished popping (within 30 seconds), add the curry leaves, dried chile, and garlic. Reduce the heat to medium-low and stir once.

6. Stir in the tomato and salt, increase the heat to medium-high, and cook about 30 seconds. Add the pea mixture and increase the heat to high.

7. Add the black pepper and tamarind. Mix well, bring to a boil, and remove from the heat. Ladle the hot soup into bowls and garnish with cilantro.

NUTRITIONAL FACTS: (PER 1-CUP SERVING)

Calories: 49   Carbohydrates: 5.9 g   Cholesterol: 0 mg
Fat: 1.1 g   Fiber: <1 g   Protein: 2.5 g   Sodium: 392 mg

SUGGESTED ACCOMPANIMENTS

Banana Yogurt Salad (page 52) and Green Pea Flatbread (page 85).

Spicy Corn Soup

Makai ka Shorba

This easy-to-prepare soup is delicately flavored with fresh ginger, curry powder, and fresh cilantro. Adjust the cayenne pepper according to taste.

1. Combine the corn, onion, potato, ginger, turmeric, and water in a medium-sized stockpot and bring to a boil over a high heat. Reduce the heat to medium-low and simmer, partially covered, for 20 minutes, or until the vegetables are tender.

2. Transfer all but about 1 cup of the vegetables and broth to a blender. Add the salt, cayenne pepper, and curry powder, and blend to a coarse purée. Return the puréed soup to the pot.

3. Add the milk and cook over low heat for about 5 minutes, stirring until the soup is heated through.

4. Transfer to individual soup bowls, garnish with cilantro, and serve immediately.

Yield: *4 servings*

2 cups fresh or frozen corn kernels

1 small yellow onion, finely chopped

1 medium potato, peeled and cut into ¼-inch cubes

½ teaspoon peeled and finely grated ginger

⅛ teaspoon turmeric

2½ cups water

½ teaspoon salt (or to taste)

¼ teaspoon cayenne pepper

¼ teaspoon curry powder

½ cup evaporated skim milk

1 tablespoon finely chopped fresh cilantro

NUTRITIONAL FACTS: (PER 1-CUP SERVING)

Calories: 128   Carbohydrates: 28.6 g   Cholesterol: 0 mg
Fat: 0.3 g   Fiber: 2 g   Protein: 5.9 g   Sodium: 331 mg

SUGGESTED ACCOMPANIMENTS

Crunchy Cabbage Salad (page 63) and Green Pea Flatbread (page 85).

Mung Bean and Radish Soup

Mung Dal Aur Mooli ka Shorba

Yield: *4 servings*

¾ cup dry mung beans

¼ teaspoon turmeric

2 cloves garlic, crushed

6 small red radishes, peeled and grated

½ teaspoon salt (or to taste)

½ teaspoon curry powder

½ teaspoon ground cumin

½ teaspoon cayenne pepper (optional)

½ tablespoon lemon juice

1 tablespoon finely chopped fresh cilantro

This nourishing vegetable-bean soup is sure to warm you on a cold blustery day. You can also enjoy it as a curry dish served alongside plain boiled rice or naan.

1. Pick through the beans for any grit or debris, then place them in a strainer and rinse thoroughly. Transfer the beans to a medium-sized pot along with 3 cups water. Soak for 2 hours.

2. Place the pot with the beans and their soaking water over high heat. Add the turmeric and garlic and bring to a boil. Reduce the heat to medium-low and cook the beans, partially covered, for 30 minutes.

3. Add the radishes and 1 cup of water, and continue to cook another 15 minutes. Remove from heat and cool slightly.

4. Stir in the salt, curry powder, cumin, cayenne pepper (if using), and lemon juice. Mash the beans against the side of the pot with the back of a spoon until the mixture is smooth. Return the pot to the stove and place over medium heat until the soup is hot.

5. Spoon the soup into individual bowls, garnish with cilantro, and serve piping hot.

NUTRITIONAL FACTS: (PER 1-CUP SERVING)

Calories: 132   Carbohydrates: 22.8 g   Cholesterol: 0 mg
Fat: 0.5 g   Fiber: 0 g   Protein: 9.2 g   Sodium: 299 mg

SUGGESTED ACCOMPANIMENTS

Banana Yogurt Salad (page 52) and Fenugreek Flatbread (page 84).

Spinach Buttermilk Soup

Palak Bhaji

Nonfat buttermilk is the base for this nourishing soup.

Yield: *4 servings*

1. Place the fresh spinach in a medium-sized pot with 1 or 2 teaspoons of water, and steam until tender.

2. Transfer the cooked spinach to a blender, add the flour, ginger, salt, buttermilk, and water. Blend until well-combined.

3. Transfer the spinach mixture to a large pot and place over low heat until the mixture comes to a gentle boil.

4. Heat the oil in a small pan. Add the cumin, turmeric, green chile, and curry leaves (if using), and fry for a few seconds. Add to the spinach mixture.

5. Continue cooking the soup another 10 minutes. Ladle into individual serving bowls and enjoy hot.

8 ounces thoroughly washed fresh spinach, or 1 cup cooked

¼ cup yellow split pea flour

1 teaspoon peeled, grated ginger

½ teaspoon salt (or to taste)

2 cups nonfat buttermilk, at room temperature

1½ cups water

1 teaspoon canola oil

¼ teaspoon ground cumin

¼ teaspoon turmeric

1 small green chile

6 curry leaves (optional)

NUTRITIONAL FACTS: (PER 1-CUP SERVING)

Calories: 83   Carbohydrates: 10.7 g   Cholesterol: 0 mg
Fat: 1.4 g   Fiber: 1 g   Protein: 6.2 g   Sodium: 431 mg

SUGGESTED ACCOMPANIMENTS

Carrot Salad (page 65) and Honey Wheat Flatbread (page 86).

Spinach Dal Soup

Palak ka Shorba

Yield: *3 servings*

1 tablespoon dry split, skinned mung beans

1 cup chicken stock

½ cup water

1 cup thoroughly washed, chopped fresh spinach

½ cup thinly sliced mushrooms

1 cup skim milk

1 tablespoon cornstarch

An unusual combination of split mung beans and spinach enhanced with fresh mushrooms makes this soup unique. Tightly covered and refrigerated, it will keep up to twenty-four hours. Simply reheat and serve.

1. Pick through the beans for any grit or debris, then place them in a strainer and rinse thoroughly. Place them in a small bowl with ¼ cup water. Soak for 2 hours.

2. Bring the stock and water to a boil in a large saucepan. Add the mung beans and their soaking water, along with the spinach and mushrooms. Reduce the heat to low and simmer, loosely covered, about 35 minutes or until the beans are tender.

3. Strain the cooked beans through a strainer or sieve that has been set over a medium-sized bowl (The stock will drain into the pot.) Transfer the bean mixture to a food processor and purée. Add the remaining stock and continue to process another few seconds.

4. Measure the puréed mixture in a large measuring cup. If necessary, add enough water to measure 2 cups.

5. Place the mixture in a large saucepan, add the milk, and bring to a boil. Reduce the heat to low, stir the soup, and simmer. Dissolve the cornstarch in 2 tablespoons of water then add it to the soup. Stirring constantly, simmer the soup for 5 minutes, or until the soup has thickened and is heated through.

6. Ladle the hot soup into individual bowls and serve hot.

HELPFUL HINT

•When using canned chicken stock that is not fat-free, place the can in the refrigerator for a few hours. This will cause the fat to rise to the top, making it easy for you to remove the fat and discard it.

NUTRITIONAL FACTS: (PER 1-CUP SERVING)

Calories: 60   Carbohydrates: 7.7 g   Cholesterol: 2 mg

Fat: 0.8 g   Fiber: <1 g   Proteins: 6.0 g   Sodium: 316 mg

SUGGESTED ACCOMPANIMENTS

Beet Yogurt Salad (page 53) and Herbed Onion Flatbread (page 88).

Tomato Soup

Tomato Saar

This version of western India's classic soup, is refreshing, flavorful, and fat-free.

1. Place all of the ingredients except the cilantro in a blender and process until well-blended.

2. Transfer the mixture to a medium-sized pot. Bring to a boil, then reduce the heat to low and simmer about 10 minutes, stirring occasionally.

3. Ladle into soup bowls, garnish with cilantro, and serve.

Yield: 4 servings

16-ounce can whole peeled tomatoes (no salt added)

1 tablespoon cornstarch

1 cup water

½ teaspoon peeled, grated ginger

1 clove garlic, crushed

½ teaspoon ground cumin

½ teaspoon salt (or to taste)

1 tablespoon brown sugar

Dash of Tabasco sauce

1 tablespoon finely chopped fresh cilantro

NUTRITIONAL FACTS (PER 1-CUP SERVING)

Calories: 39   Carbohydrates: 8.7 g   Cholesterol: 0 mg
Fat: 0 g   Fiber: 1 g   Protein: 2 g   Sodium: 307 mg

SUGGESTED ACCOMPANIMENTS

Rice with Split Mung Beans (page 78) and Herbed Onion Flatbread (page 88).

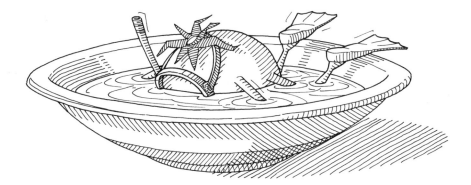

Dal Soup with Whole Wheat Dumplings

Dal Dhokli

Yield: *10 servings*

1 cup split pigeon peas (toor dal)

1 teaspoon canola oil

½ teaspoon black or yellow mustard seeds

½ teaspoon turmeric

1 medium green chile, halved

6 curry leaves

5 cups water

½ teaspoon ground cumin

½ teaspoon ground coriander

½ teaspoon peeled, grated ginger

2 teaspoons tamarind pulp dissolved in ¼ cup warm water*

¼ cup dark brown sugar, packed

1 teaspoon salt

DUMPLINGS

1 cup whole wheat flour

¾ cup unbleached flour

¾ cup yellow split pea flour

½ teaspoon turmeric

½ teaspoon salt

½ teaspoon ground ajwain (optional)

¾ cups water

*Can substitute 2 tablespoons lemon juice for the dissolved tamarind.

This hearty vegetarian soup makes the perfect weekend brunch, especially on cold days. The only accompaniment it requires is a hungry appetite. Traditionally garnished with loads of melted butter, we find that fat-free butter buds or a sprinkling of chopped fresh cilantro works just as well.

1. Pick through the dried peas for any grit or debris, then place them in a strainer and rinse thoroughly. Transfer to a medium-sized pot along with 3 cups of water. Soak for 2 hours.

2. Place the pot with the peas and their soaking water over medium heat. Cook, partially covered, for 35 minutes or until the peas are tender. Stir occasionally.

3. While the peas are cooking, prepare the dough for the dumplings. Place the flours, turmeric, salt, and ajwain (if using) in a mixing bowl. Add ¾ cup water, a tablespoon at a time, mixing with your hands to get a firm dough. You may need slightly more or less water. Knead for 2 minutes. Cover the dough with plastic wrap and set aside on the counter.

4. Place the oil in a large pot over medium heat. When the oil is hot, add the mustard seeds. Cover the pot with a splatter guard and allow the seeds to pop. When the seeds have finished popping (within 30 seconds), add the turmeric, chile, and curry leaves, followed by the cooked split pigeon peas. Stir in 5 cups of water, then add the cumin, coriander, ginger, tamarind, brown sugar, and salt. Bring the ingredients to a boil.

5. While the soup is coming to a boil, make the dumplings. Lightly dust a clean dry work surface with flour. Sprinkle the dough with some flour then roll it out into an 18-inch circle (Step 1). Cut the circle in half with a sharp knife (Step 2). Cut ¾-inch strips on one half of the dough (Step 3), then cut the strips into diamond shapes (Step 4). Repeat procedure with the other half of the dough (Step 5).

6. When the soup begins to boil, add the squares of dough to the pot. Stir once and reduce the heat to medium. Cover the pot and cook the dumplings, stirring occasionally, for 1 hour or until the dumplings are cooked.

7. Ladle the soup and dumplings into individual serving bowls and enjoy hot.

NUTRITIONAL FACTS: (PER 1-CUP SERVING)
Calories: 191   Carbohydrates: 30.6 g   Cholesterol: 0 mg
Fat: 1.5 g   Fiber: 1.1 g   Protein: 9.1 g   Sodium: 354 mg

SUGGESTED ACCOMPANIMENTS

Green Bean Salad (page 67) and Spicy Buttermilk Drink (page 193).

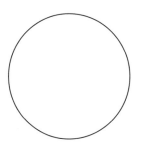

1. Roll the dough into an 18-inch circle.

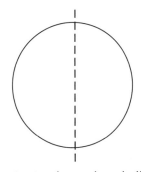

2. Cut the circle in half.

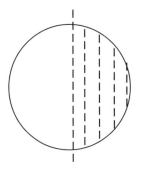

3. Cut one half into ¾-inch strips.

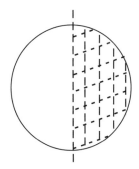

4. Cut the strips at an angle to form diamonds.

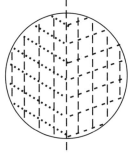

5. Repeat procedure with the remaining dough.

Forming Dumplings

Zesty Carrot Soup

Gajar ka Shorba

Yield: *6 Servings*

5 cups water

6 medium carrots, peeled and cut into circles

6 scallions, coarsely chopped

2 medium potatoes, peeled and cut into ¼-inch cubes

1 stalk celery, finely chopped

2 cloves garlic, crushed

½ teaspoon salt (or to taste)

½ teaspoon ground cumin

½ teaspoon ground coriander

½ teaspoon packaged curry powder

¼ teaspoon cayenne pepper

½ cup evaporated skim milk

1 tablespoon finely chopped fresh cilantro

Here's another western soup with a zesty Indian touch.

1. Place the water, carrots, scallions, potatoes, celery, and garlic in a medium-sized stockpot. Bring to a boil over high heat. Reduce the heat to medium and cook uncovered for 20 minutes, or until the vegetables are tender.

2. Add the salt, cumin, coriander, curry powder, and cayenne pepper, and cook for another 5 minutes. Remove from the heat and cool slightly.

3. Transfer the cooked vegetables and some of the broth to a blender and purée until smooth. Return to the pot, add the skim milk, and bring to a gentle boil over medium heat for 5 minutes.

4. Ladle the hot soup into individual soup bowls, garnish with cilantro, and serve hot.

NUTRITIONAL FACTS: (PER 1-CUP SERVING)

Calories: 92   Carbohydrates: 19.9 g   Cholesterol: 0 mg
Fat: 0.3 g   Fiber: 1 g   Protein: 3.7 g   Sodium: 251 mg

SUGGESTED ACCOMPANIMENTS

Quick Garbanzo Bean Salad (page 68), Pumpkin Flatbread (page 90), and Shrimp Pilaf (page 74).

4.

Exceptional Salad Creations

Salads, always eaten as side dishes, are an integral part of Indian meals. They help balance the variety of flavors presented by the different side dishes, while adding a cool, refreshing touch to hot and spicy curries and other foods. Although a salad does not compete with the main dish for attention, an Indian meal would be incomplete without it.

Indian salads fall into two categories—raitas and kachumbars. Raitas are yogurt-based salads of steamed or raw vegetables that are cubed, shredded, or mashed. Kachumbars consist of raw vegetables that are cut or shredded and flavored with a bit of tempered oil, a sprinkling of lemon juice, or an assortment of dry spices and sometimes crushed peanuts.

Be sure to season kachumbars just before serving. This is because salt, which is generally included in the seasoning, causes some vegetables like cucumbers and onions to release water, resulting in limp, mushy salads. Also, to ensure the crunch of fresh cilantro, always add it to any salad just before serving.

When preparing raitas without cucumbers, you can mix together all of the ingredients except the cilantro, then chill in the refrigerator before serving. (Chilling is a matter of personal preference and not a necessary step.) Just before serving, garnish with cilantro. For raitas that include cucumbers, do not add the salt or the cilantro until just before serving. The salt will cause the cucumbers to turn limp.

The salads in this book are quick and easy to make. They call for basic ingredients found in most refrigerators or pantries, and most are fat- and cholesterol-free. Whenever possible, nonfat versions of high-fat ingredients, such as yogurt and mayonnaise, are called for. Other full-fat ingredients, like flavorful oils and peanuts, are used in minimal amounts to provide uncompromising taste.

Banana Yogurt Salad

Kele ka Raita

Yield: *4 servings*

2 cups plain nonfat yogurt

2 teaspoons granulated white sugar

¼ teaspoon salt (or to taste)

½ teaspoon honey mustard

1 medium banana, peeled and cut into ¼-inch cubes

1 tablespoon finely chopped fresh cilantro

This delicious, fat-free salad complements spicy curry dishes very well. You can also enjoy it as an unusual pancake topping by simply eliminating the mustard and cilantro.

1. Whisk together the yogurt, sugar, salt, and mustard in a small mixing bowl until well-blended.

2. Add the bananas and mix well.

3. Garnish with cilantro and serve.

NUTRITIONAL FACTS: (PER ½-CUP SERVING)

Calories: 100   Carbohydrates: 17.4 g   Cholesterol: 2 mg
Fat: 0.4 g   Fiber: 0 g   Protein: 6.8 g   Sodium: 240 mg

SUGGESTED ACCOMPANIMENTS

Chicken Xacutti (page 150), Green Beans with Potatoes (page 103), and Raised Indian Flatbread (page 92).

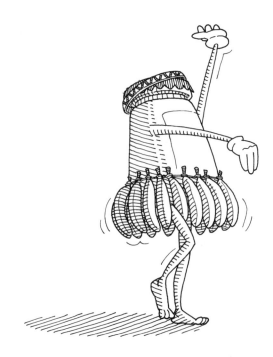

Beet Yogurt Salad

Chakundar ka Raita

This colorful fat-free salad is delicious and extremely easy to make. Enjoy it by itself or as a side dish with flatbread and a vegetable dish.

1. Steam the beets for about 15 minutes or until tender. Transfer to a medium mixing bowl and cool.

2. Combine the yogurt, sugar, and salt. Blend well and add to the beets. Mix well to coat.

3. Refrigerate about 2 hours. Garnish with cilantro and serve chilled.

Yield: *4 servings*

2 small beets, cut into ½-inch cubes (about 1 cup)

1 cup plain nonfat yogurt

½ teaspoon granulated white sugar

¼ teaspoon salt (or to taste)

1 teaspoon finely chopped fresh cilantro

NUTRITIONAL FACTS (PER ½-CUP SERVING)

Calories: 47   Carbohydrates: 7.7 g   Cholesterol: 1 mg
Fat: 0.1 g   Fiber: 0 g   Protein: 3.7 g   Sodium: 208 mg

SUGGESTED ACCOMPANIMENTS

Potato Curry with Aniseed and Fenugreek Seeds (page 105) and Spinach Flatbread (page 91).

Making Homemade Yogurt

In the cuisine of India, yogurt (dahi) is a staple ingredient. Customarily, fresh milk is purchased each day in India, and any leftover milk is used to make yogurt. Often enjoyed by itself, yogurt is sometimes flavored with salt and ground cumin or sugar. It is the base for raitas, and is served as part of a meal with flatbread and rice dishes.

Homemade yogurt is a lot tastier and much more economical than commercial brands. It is also very easy to make, as you can see from the following recipe. You will, however, need a small amount of store-bought yogurt with live, active cultures to use as a "starter," which is necessary to begin the fermentation process. The following recipe yields 4 cups of fresh yogurt. Although it can be prepared on the stovetop, we find using a microwave is quicker and less complicated (you can use the same pot to set the yogurt).

Homemade Yogurt

4 cups 1% milk

2 level tablespoons nonfat powdered milk

1 tablespoon plain nonfat yogurt (with live, active cultures), at room temperature

1. Heat the milk in a plastic or glass bowl in the microwave oven for 7 to 10 minutes on High power, or until it boils. Stir the milk a few times as it heats up.

2. Remove the milk from the oven and cool to lukewarm (105° to 110° F).

3. Combine the yogurt and milk powder in a small bowl to form a paste, then add to the lukewarm milk. Stir to mix.

4. Cover the bowl with a warm tea cozy and set in a warm place for 12 hours or overnight. Do not move or stir the mixture, or the yogurt will not set properly.

5. Once the yogurt is set, you can eat it immediately, or store it in a covered container in the refrigerator for up to 10 days.

NUTRITIONAL FACTS: (PER ½-CUP SERVING)

Calories: 58   Carbohydrates: 6.8g   Cholesterol: 5 mg
Fat: 1.3 g   Fiber: 0 g   Protein: 4.7 g   Sodium: 71 mg

Carrot Yogurt Salad

Gajar ka Raita

Serve this tasty salad as a side dish with any Indian meal. To make it completely fat-free, simply skip the tempered oil.

1. Steam the carrots for about 5 minutes or until tender. Transfer to a medium bowl and cool.

2. Combine the yogurt and salt. Blend well and add to the carrots. Mix and set aside.

3. Place the oil in a small skillet over medium-high heat. When the oil is hot, add the mustard seeds. Cover the skillet with a splatter guard and allow the seeds to pop. When the seeds have finished popping (within 30 seconds), add the turmeric and remove from the heat. Add this tempered oil to the carrot-yogurt mixture and stir well.

4. Garnish with cilantro and serve.

Yield: *4 servings*

1 cup grated carrot (about 2 medium)

1 cup plain nonfat yogurt

¼ teaspoon salt (or to taste)

1 teaspoon canola oil

¼ teaspoon black or yellow mustard seeds

¼ teaspoon turmeric

1 teaspoon coarsely chopped fresh cilantro

NUTRITIONAL FACTS (PER ½-CUP SERVING)

Calories: 58   Carbohydrates: 8 g   Cholesterol: 1 mg
Fat: 1.3 g   Fiber: 0 g   Protein: 3.6 g   Sodium: 200 mg

SUGGESTED ACCOMPANIMENTS

Green Pea Pilaf (page 70) and Mixed Legumes (page 129).

Cucumber Yogurt Salad

Kakdi ka Raita

Yield: *5 servings*

2 cups plain nonfat yogurt

½ teaspoon granulated white sugar

¼ teaspoon salt (or to taste)

2 teaspoons ground unsalted roasted peanuts (optional)

1 green chile, seeded and finely chopped (optional)

½ cup peeled and finely chopped cucumber

1 teaspoon finely chopped fresh cilantro

This refreshing salad is the perfect choice for accompanying spicy curry dishes and vegetable pilafs.

1. Whisk together the yogurt, sugar, and salt in a medium-sized mixing bowl until well-blended. Stir in the peanuts and chile (if using).

2. Add the cucumbers and mix well.

3. Garnish with cilantro and serve.

NUTRITIONAL FACTS (PER ½-CUP SERVING)

Calories: 60   Carbohydrates: 9.2 g   Cholesterol: 2 mg
Fat: 0.2 g   Fiber: 0 g   Protein: 5.6 g   Sodium: 186 mg

SUGGESTED ACCOMPANIMENTS

Royal Spiced Lamb with Rice (page 80) and Mixed Vegetable Curry (page 106).

HELPFUL HINT

- You can make this salad up to 8 hours in advance, but don't add the salt or cilantro until just ready to serve. The salt will cause the cucumber to release water, resulting in a thin, watery salad.

Cucumber Tomato Salad

Kakdi aur Tamatar ka Raita

This cool, colorful salad is generally eaten as a side dish but can also be enjoyed by itself.

Yield: *4 servings*

1½ cups plain nonfat yogurt

½ teaspoon sugar

1 pinch ground cumin (optional)

½ medium cucumber, peeled and finely chopped

1 small tomato, finely chopped

½ teaspoon salt (or to taste)

1 tablespoon finely chopped fresh cilantro

1. Whisk together the yogurt, sugar, and cumin (if using) in a medium-sized bowl.

2. Add the cucumber and tomato and mix well.

3. Refrigerate about 1 hour.

4. Stir in the salt, garnish with cilantro, and serve chilled.

NUTRITIONAL FACTS (PER ½-CUP SERVING)

Calories: 39   Carbohydrates: 5.9 g   Cholesterol: 1 mg
Fat: 0.2 g   Fiber: <1 g   Protein: 3.6 g   Sodium: 333 mg

SUGGESTED ACCOMPANIMENTS

Pumpkin Flatbread (page 90) and Stir-Fried Baby Corn (page 113).

Indian Potato Salad

Aloo ka Raita

Yield: *4 servings*

1 medium potato, boiled and cut into ½-inch cubes (about 1 cup)

1 cup plain nonfat yogurt

¼ teaspoon paprika

1 pinch ground cumin

1 teaspoon finely chopped fresh cilantro

1 teaspoon finely chopped fresh mint

Fresh herbs are used to flavor this dish, which is India's equivalent to American potato salad.

1. Place the potato cubes in a medium-sized salad bowl, and lightly mash with the back of a spoon.

2. Whisk together the yogurt, paprika, and cumin. Add to the potatoes and mix well.

3. Refrigerate 1 hour.

4. Garnish with cilantro and mint, and serve.

NUTRITIONAL FACTS (PER ½-CUP SERVING)

Calories: 61   Carbohydrates: 11.1 g   Cholesterol: 1 mg
Fat: 0.1 g   Fiber: <1 g   Protein: 3.8 g   Sodium: 45 mg

SUGGESTED ACCOMPANIMENTS

Green Pea Pilaf (page 70) and Sweet-and-Sour Eggplant with Potatoes (page 118).

 Pumpkin Yogurt Salad

Kaddoo ka Raita

This tasty yogurt-based salad is packed with valuable nutrients. Try it at your next Thanksgiving meal.

1. Place the pumpkin pieces in a single layer on a microwave safe dish. Cover with a paper towel and cook on High about 4 minutes or until tender. Transfer to a medium-sized bowl and mash with a fork. Cool thoroughly.

2. Combine the yogurt, mustard, sugar, and salt, and add to the pumpkin. Mix and set aside.

3. Place the oil in a small nonstick skillet over medium-high heat. When the oil is hot, add the cumin seeds. Fry a few seconds until the seeds begin to sizzle, then spoon the tempered oil over the pumpkin mixture and mix well.

4. Garnish with cilantro and serve.

Yield: *3 servings*

8 ounces fresh pumpkin, peeled and cut into ½-inch cubes (about 1½ cups)

¾ cup plain nonfat yogurt

¼ teaspoon Dijon-style mustard

1 teaspoon granulated white sugar

¼ teaspoon salt (or to taste)

½ teaspoon canola oil

¼ teaspoon cumin seeds

1 teaspoon finely chopped fresh cilantro

NUTRITIONAL FACTS: (PER ½-CUP SERVING)

Calories: 58   Carbohydrates: 9.3 g   Cholesterol: 1 mg
Fat: 0.9 g   Fiber: 0 g   Protein: 3.7 g   Sodium: 235 mg

SUGGESTED ACCOMPANIMENTS

Lentil and Spinach Curry (page 127) and Raised Indian Flatbread (page 92).

Radish Yogurt Salad

Mooli ka Raita

Yield: *4 servings*

1 cup plain nonfat yogurt

¼ teaspoon granulated white sugar

⅛ teaspoon mustard

6 small radishes, scrubbed and coarsely grated (about 1 cup)

¼ teaspoon salt (or to taste)

1 teaspoon finely chopped fresh cilantro

Grated raw radishes give this nutritious salad its pleasant crunch. The intense flavor of the radishes is muted by the yogurt. Serve as a side dish or as a relish.

1. Whisk together the yogurt, sugar, and mustard in a medium-sized bowl. Mix well.

2. Add the radishes to the yogurt mixture and mix well.

3. Refrigerate for 1 hour.

4. Stir in the salt, garnish with cilantro, and serve chilled.

NUTRITIONAL FACTS: (PER ½-CUP SERVING)

Calories: 37   Carbohydrates: 5 g   Cholesterol: 1 mg
Fat: 0.1 g   Fiber: 0 g   Protein: 3.3 g   Sodium: 189 mg

SUGGESTED ACCOMPANIMENTS

Minced Dry Lamb (page 159) and Potato Flatbread (page 89).

Smoked Eggplant Salad

Baingan ka Raita

The smoked eggplant and yogurt provide an unusual combination of flavors and textures in this salad. The perfect side dish to serve with legume dishes, it is also delicious as a dip for flatbreads or pitas.

1. Preheat the oven to 400°F. Line a 9-x-13-inch baking pan with foil. Lightly coat the foil with cooking spray.

2. Spread the eggplant cubes in a single layer in the pan, cover with foil, and bake for 30 minutes. Remove the foil and continue to bake another 15 minutes, stirring occasionally, until the eggplant is soft. Transfer to a medium-sized bowl and mash. Let cool.

3. Add the yogurt, onion, and salt to the eggplant and mix well.

4. Transfer to a serving dish and refrigerate for 1 hour.

5. Garnish with cilantro, and serve chilled.

Yield: *4 servings*

½ medium eggplant (about 8 ounces), peeled and cut into ½-inch cubes (about 2 cups)

1 cup plain nonfat yogurt

1 small yellow onion, finely chopped

¼ teaspoon salt (or to taste)

1 tablespoon coarsely chopped fresh cilantro

NUTRITIONAL FACTS (PER ½-CUP SERVING)

Calories: 49   Carbohydrates: 8.4 g   Cholesterol: 1 mg
Fat: 0.1 g   Fiber: <1 g   Protein: 3.9 g   Sodium: 189 mg

SUGGESTED ACCOMPANIMENTS

Sprouted Mixed Beans (page 139), Sweet-and-Sour Black-Eyed Peas (page 141), and Honey Wheat Flatbread (page 86).

Spinach Yogurt Salad

Palak ka Raita

Yield: *3 servings*

2½ cups thoroughly washed, chopped fresh spinach (leave wet)

1 cup plain nonfat yogurt

¼ medium yellow onion, finely minced

1 teaspoon white granulated sugar

⅛ teaspoon salt (or to taste)

This versatile and healthy spinach salad makes a great addition to any meal. It is also a great dip for crackers or pita bread.

1. Place the wet spinach in a medium-sized pan, cover, and place over medium heat. Without adding any water, steam the spinach about 5 to 8 minutes, or until tender. Transfer to a bowl and cool completely.

2. Add the yogurt, onion, sugar, and salt to the spinach and stir well.

3. Transfer to a bowl and serve.

NUTRITIONAL FACTS: (PER ½-CUP SERVING)

Calories: 62   Carbohydrates: 6.6 g   Cholesterol: 1.3 mg
Fat: 0.4 g   Fiber: 2 g   Protein: 5.8 g   Sodium: 190 mg

SUGGESTED ACCOMPANIMENTS

Cauliflower with Tomato (page 98) and Rice and Lentil Pilaf (page 75).

Crunchy Cabbage Salad

Pachadi

This crunchy salad is from southern India. Enjoy it as a side dish or all by itself.

Yield: *6 servings*

1. Place the cabbage in a medium-sized mixing bowl and set aside.

2. Place the oil in a small skillet over medium-high heat. When the oil is hot, add the mustard seeds. Cover the skillet with a splatter guard and allow the seeds to pop. When the seeds have finished popping (within 30 seconds), add the turmeric and remove from the heat. Add this tempered oil to the shredded cabbage and stir well.

3. Add sugar, salt, and peanuts (if using). Mix well.

4. Stir in the lemon juice just before serving.

3 cups finely shredded green cabbage

1 teaspoon canola oil

½ teaspoon black or yellow mustard seeds

½ teaspoon turmeric

½ teaspoon granulated white sugar

½ teaspoon salt (or to taste)

1 tablespoon coarsely ground unsalted peanuts (optional)

1 tablespoon lemon juice

NUTRITIONAL FACTS (PER ½-CUP SERVING)
Calories: 16   Carbohydrates: 2.2 g   Cholesterol: 0 mg
Fat: 0.8 g   Fiber: <1 g   Protein: 0.4 g   Sodium: 197 mg

SUGGESTED ACCOMPANIMENTS
Fish in Tomato Sauce (page 168) and Spicy Yellow Rice (page 79).

Shredded Cabbage with Split Mung Bean Salad

Bundh Gobi aur Mung Dal Kachumbar

Yield: *6 servings*

¼ cup dry split, skinned mung beans

2 cups finely shredded green cabbage

1 tablespoon lemon juice

½ green chile pepper, finely chopped

¼ teaspoon salt (or to taste)

2 tablespoons finely chopped fresh cilantro

The texture of the mung beans provides an interesting contrast with the crunchy cabbage in this delightful salad.

1. Pick through the dried beans for any grit or debris, then place them in a strainer and rinse thoroughly. Transfer the beans to a small bowl and add 1 cup of water. Soak for 2 to 3 hours until the beans are tender.

2. Place the cabbage in a medium-sized mixing bowl. Drain the beans and add them to the cabbage along with the lemon juice, chile, salt, and cilantro.

3. Toss well and serve.

NUTRITIONAL FACTS: (PER ½-CUP SERVING)

Calories: 28   Carbohydrates: 6.2 g   Cholesterol: 0 mg
Fat: 0.2 g   Fiber: 0 g   Protein: 1.8 g   Sodium: 102 mg

SUGGESTED ACCOMPANIMENTS

Shrimp Tomato Curry (page 171) and Quick Stir-Fried Rice with Vegetables (page 71).

Carrot Salad

Gajar ka Kachumbar

This colorful healthy salad uses very few ingredients and is easy to assemble.

Yield: *3 servings*

1. Put the grated carrots in a medium-sized serving bowl.

2. Add the remaining ingredients, mix well, and serve.

1¾ cups grated carrots (about 3 medium)

2 teaspoons finely chopped fresh cilantro

2 teaspoons lemon juice

¼ teaspoon salt (or to taste)

½ teaspoon white granulated sugar

NUTRITIONAL FACTS: (PER ½-CUP SERVING)

Calories: 14   Carbohydrates: 9.7 g   Cholesterol: 0 mg
Fat: 0 g   Fiber: 0 g   Protein: 0.3 g   Sodium: 93 mg

SUGGESTED ACCOMPANIMENTS

Raised Indian Flatbread (page 92) and Cauliflower, Peas, and Potato Curry (page 97).

Fenugreek with Split Mung Bean Salad

Methi ka Kachumbar

Yield: *4 servings*

½ cup dry split mung beans

1 cup thoroughly washed, finely chopped fresh fenugreek leaves

½ teaspoon canola oil

½ teaspoon black or yellow mustard seeds

⅛ teaspoon salt (or to taste)

½ tablespoon lemon juice

The slightly bitter taste of fresh fenugreek leaves is complimented perfectly by the mildness of the mung beans. Try to use small fenugreek leaves, which are not as bitter as the larger ones.

1. Pick through the dried beans for any grit or debris, then place them in a strainer and rinse thoroughly. Transfer the beans to a small bowl and add 1 cup of water. Soak for 2 to 3 hours until the beans are tender. Drain and place in a medium-sized bowl.

2. Add the fenugreek to the beans and mix well. Set aside.

3. Place the oil in a small skillet over medium-high heat. When the oil is hot, add the mustard seeds. Cover the skillet with a splatter guard and allow the seeds to pop. When the seeds have finished popping (within 30 seconds), add the tempered oil to the fenugreek-mung bean mixture and stir well.

4. Add the salt and lemon juice. Mix and serve.

NUTRITIONAL FACTS: (PER ½-CUP SERVING)

Calories: 80   Carbohydrates: 12.7 g   Cholesterol: 0 mg
Fat: 0.8 g   Fiber: <1 g   Protein: 5.4 g   Sodium: 87 mg

SUGGESTED ACCOMPANIMENTS

Cauliflower with Tomato (page 98) and Raised Indian Flatbread (page 92).

Green Bean Salad

Farasbee ka Kachumbar

This easy-to-prepare salad goes especially well with barbecued meat dishes.

1. Place the oil in a medium-sized nonstick skillet and place over medium heat. When the oil is hot, add the cumin seeds. Fry a few seconds until the seeds begin to sizzle, then add the beans and water. Cover the skillet and steam the beans for about 5 to 8 minutes, or until just tender. Stir the beans occasionally to prevent them from sticking to the skillet. Transfer the beans to a medium-sized bowl and cool completely.

2. Add the lemon juice, sugar, salt, and coconut (if using). Stir well.

3. Transfer to a serving bowl and enjoy.

Yield: *4 servings*

¼ teaspoon canola oil

⅛ teaspoon cumin seeds

2 cups julienne-cut fresh green beans, (or frozen French-cut variety)

1 teaspoon water

2 teaspoons lemon juice

1 teaspoon white granulated sugar

¼ teaspoon salt (or to taste)

1 teaspoon grated coconut (optional)

NUTRITIONAL FACTS: (PER ½-CUP SERVING)

Calories: 26   Carbohydrates: 5.9 g   Cholesterol: 0 mg
Fat: 0.6 g   Fiber: 2 g   Protein: 0.6 g   Sodium: 154 mg

SUGGESTED ACCOMPANIMENTS

Tandoori Chicken Kabobs (page 22) and Rice with Yogurt (page 76).

Quick Garbanzo Bean Salad

Chane ki Chat

Yield: *4 servings*

15.5-ounce can garbanzo
  beans, drained

1 small yellow onion, finely
  chopped

1 small tomato, finely chopped

¼ teaspoon salt (or to taste)

1 jalapeño pepper, finely
  chopped (optional)

¼ teaspoon chat masala
  (optional)

1 tablespoon lemon juice

1 tablespoon finely chopped
  cilantro

This salad is popular in northern India where its preparation varies from house to house. This is our favorite version.

1. Place the garbanzo beans, onion, tomato, salt, jalapeño pepper (if using), chat masala (if using), and lemon juice in a medium-sized bowl. Mix well.

2. Garnish with cilantro and serve at room temperature.

NUTRITIONAL FACTS: (PER ½-CUP SERVING)

Calories: 138   Carbohydrates: 28.4 g   Cholesterol: 0 mg
Fat: 1.2 g   Fiber: 4 g   Protein: 5.8 g   Sodium : 462 mg

SUGGESTED ACCOMPANIMENTS

Potato-Stuffed Green Peppers (page 117) and Fenugreek Flatbread (page 84).

5.

Quick Rice Dishes

Rice is a staple ingredient in Indian cuisine. Of the more than twenty rice varieties grown throughout India, the fragrant long-grain basmati is the most popular. Basmati rice swells to three times its original size when cooked, while retaining its shape. This makes it the perfect choice for pilafs.

Indians combine rice deliciously with vegetables, meats, and legumes. Dishes such as Stir-Fried Cabbage Rice and Green Pea Pilaf are just a sampling of the vegetable rice dishes presented in this chapter. Legumes and rice complement each other perfectly in dishes such as Peas and Tomato Pancakes and Rice with Split Mung Beans. Looking for the perfect dish to use up leftover plain boiled rice? Look no further than the recipe for Stir-Fried Yellow Rice or Rice with Yogurt. These and all of the dishes presented in this chapter need only a yogurt-based salad (raita) as an accompaniment.

Before preparing rice, always read the package directions first. Unless otherwise instructed, do not wash the rice, which leads to loss of valuable nutrients. When directions call for washing, do so using a minimal amount of water.

When cooking rice, be sure to use the exact amount of water specified in the instructions. Too much water will result in loose, mushy rice, while too little water will produce thick clumps of undercooked grains. Different sized grains require different water amounts. As a general rule, one cup of a long-grain rice like basmati requires two cups of water. Shorter grained rice requires less.

As the rice cooks, do not constantly uncover the pot to check on it. This will cause the steam to escape and prevent the rice from cooking properly. And unless instructed, don't stir the rice as it cooks. This will cause it to break apart. When making pilafs that call for stir-frying the rice, be sure to do so gently.

Enjoy making and serving the delicious rice dishes in this chapter. All are low in fat and all will complement the other side dishes in an Indian meal.

Green Pea Pilaf

Mattar Pulao

Yield: *8 servings*

1½ teaspoons canola oil

1 teaspoon cumin seeds

1 bay leaf

1½ cups basmati rice

1 cup frozen green peas

1 teaspoon ground cumin

1 teaspoon salt (or to taste)

3¼ cups water

Enjoy this simple rice pilaf as a tasty accompaniment to most curry dishes. Exotic-flavored basmati rice is best, but any long-grain rice will do.

1. Spray a large heavy-bottomed saucepan with vegetable cooking spray. Add the oil and place over medium-low heat.

2. When the oil is hot, add the cumin seeds and bay leaf, and stir-fry a few seconds. Stir in the rice, peas, ground cumin, and salt. Continue to stir-fry about 2 minutes until the rice is well-coated.

3. Slowly add the water, increase the heat to high, and bring to a rapid boil. Reduce the heat to low, cover the pan tightly, and simmer about 15 minutes, or until all of the water has been absorbed and the rice is tender.

4. Remove the pan from the heat and keep covered for 5 minutes.

5. Discard the bay leaf, fluff the rice with a fork, and transfer to a serving dish. Serve hot.

NUTRITIONAL FACTS (PER ¾-CUP SERVING)

Calories: 141   Carbohydrates: 29.1 g   Cholesterol: 0 mg
Fat: 0.9 g   Fiber: <1 g   Protein: 4.0 g   Sodium: 235 mg

SUGGESTED ACCOMPANIMENTS

Fish in Tomato Sauce (page 168) and Cucumber Tomato Salad (page 57).

Quick Stir-Fried Rice with Vegetables

Sabzi Pulao

This quick stir-fried rice is made with frozen vegetables. It's a great choice when you're pressed for time.

1. Spray a large heavy-bottomed saucepan with vegetable cooking spray. Add the oil and place over medium heat.

2. When the oil is hot, add the cumin seeds and bay leaf, and stir-fry for a few seconds. Stir in the vegetables, ground coriander, and ground cumin. Continue to stir-fry for one minute until the vegetables are well-coated.

3. Add the rice and salt, then slowly stir in the water. Increase the heat to high and bring the ingredients to a rapid boil. Reduce the heat to low, cover the pan tightly, and simmer for about 15 minutes, or until all of the water has been absorbed and the rice is tender.

4. Remove from heat and keep covered for 5 minutes.

5. Discard the bay leaf and fluff the rice with a fork. Transfer to a serving bowl, garnish with cilantro, and serve hot.

Yield: *8 servings*

1½ teaspoons canola oil

1 teaspoon cumin seeds

1 large bay leaf

1 cup frozen mixed vegetables (carrots, green peas and green beans), thawed

1 teaspoon ground coriander

1 teaspoon ground cumin

1½ cups basmati rice

1 teaspoon salt (or to taste)

3½ cups water

1 tablespoon finely chopped fresh cilantro

NUTRITIONAL FACTS (PER ¾-CUP SERVING)
Calories: 139   Carbohydrates: 28.7 g   Cholesterol: 0 mg
Fat: 0.9 g   Fiber: <1 g   Protein: 3.6 g   Sodium: 298 mg

SUGGESTED ACCOMPANIMENTS

Tandoori Chicken Kabobs (page 22) and Indian Potato Salad (page 58).

Peas and Tomato Pancakes

Mattar Tamatar Uttapam

Yield: *8 pancakes*

½ cup dry split, skinned black lentils

2 cups white rice

¾ teaspoon salt (or to taste)

4 teaspoons cumin seeds

1 medium tomato, finely chopped

½ cup frozen peas, thawed

The bean and grain combination in this satisfying vegetarian dish provides complete protein.

1. Pick through the lentils for any grit or debris, then place in a strainer and rinse thoroughly. Transfer the lentils to a small bowl and add 1 cup water. Place the rice in a medium-sized bowl and add 1½ cups water. Cover both bowls and soak 8 hours or overnight.

2. Drain the lentils and rice, reserving the soaking water. Grind each separately in a food processor or blender, adding a tablespoon of the reserved water at a time until both the lentils and rice are ground to a smooth batter. (You'll need about 1 cup water.)

3. Transfer both batters to a large bowl. Add the salt and mix well, adding more water as needed to achieve a pancake batter consistency. Cover the bowl and let the batter sit in a warm place for 12 hours or overnight, until it has doubled in volume. Stir the batter.

4. Coat a large nonstick griddle with vegetable cooking spray, and preheat over medium heat. Pour ¾ cup of batter on the heated griddle. Using the back of a large spoon, spread the batter to an 8-inch circle. Sprinkle evenly with ½ teaspoon cumin seeds, 1 tablespoon chopped tomato, and 1 teaspoon peas. Cook 3 minutes, until the bottom of the pancake is light brown. Flip the pancake over, then press it gently and continue to cook another 2 minutes. Transfer to a plate and cover to keep warm. Continue making pancakes with remaining batter.

5. Serve the pancakes hot (peas and tomato side up). Either pick them up with your hands and eat them like bread, or enjoy them as you would an omelet with a knife and fork.

HELPFUL HINT

We usually soak the dal and rice first thing in the morning. In the evening, we grind them into a batter and allow the mixture to rise overnight. The batter will be ready in the morning. Covered and refrigerated, it will keep for two days.

NUTRITIONAL FACTS (PER PANCAKE)

Calories: 198   Carbohydrates: 43 g   Cholesterol: 0 mg
Fat: 0.2 g   Fiber: <1 g   Protein: 6.1 g   Sodium: 230 mg

SUGGESTED ACCOMPANIMENTS

South Indian Dal (page 136), and Cilantro Chutney (page 181) mixed with an equal amount of plain nonfat yogurt.

Stir-Fried Yellow Rice

Pyaz wale Peele Chawal

This popular western Indian dish is great for using up leftover rice. It is commonly served at breakfast and tea time.

1. Spray a medium-sized nonstick skillet with vegetable cooking spray. Add the oil and place over medium heat.

2. When the oil is hot, add the mustard seeds. Cover the skillet with a splatter guard and allow the seeds to pop. When the seeds have finished popping (within 30 seconds), add the turmeric, chile (if using), and onion. Sauté while stirring, until the onion is golden brown.

3. Add the rice and mix well. Reduce the heat to low, cover the pan, and heat through. Remove the skillet from the heat. Add the salt, lemon juice, and cilantro. Stir well, transfer to a serving dish, and enjoy hot.

Yield: *4 servings*

1 teaspoon canola oil

½ teaspoon black or yellow mustard seeds

¼ teaspoon turmeric

½ green chile pepper, coarsely chopped (optional)

½ medium yellow onion, finely chopped

3 cups cooked rice, preferably a day old

¼ teaspoon salt (or to taste)

3 teaspoons lemon juice

½ tablespoon finely chopped fresh cilantro

NUTRITIONAL FACTS (PER ¾-CUP SERVING)

Calories: 257 Carbohydrates: 16 g Cholesterol: 0 mg
Fat: 1.3 g Fiber: 0 g Protein: 3.2 g Sodium: 144 mg

SUGGESTED ACCOMPANIMENTS

Stir-Fried Shrimp with Scallions (page 173) and Sweet-and-Sour Pumpkin Curry (page 120).

Shrimp Pilaf

Jingey ka Pulao

Yield: *6 servings*

8 ounces medium shrimp, peeled and deveined

1½ teaspoons canola oil

1 teaspoon cumin seeds

1 medium bay leaf

1 large black cardamom pod

1 medium yellow onion, finely chopped

1 medium tomato, finely chopped

1 teaspoon peeled, finely chopped ginger

2 cloves garlic, minced

1 cup basmati rice

½ teaspoon ground cumin

½ teaspoon ground coriander

½ teaspoon curry powder

½ teaspoon salt (or to taste)

2½ cups water

SEASONING RUB

¼ teaspoon turmeric

¼ teaspoon chili powder

¼ teaspoon salt

Served with a garnish of lemon wedges, this delicious one-dish meal is a great choice when you're having guests for dinner. If you are pressed for time, use cooked cleaned shrimp instead of raw.

1. Place the shrimp in a medium bowl, and rub them with the turmeric, chili powder, and salt. Cover with plastic wrap and refrigerate for 2 hours.

2. Spray a medium-sized pot with vegetable cooking spray. Add the oil and place over medium heat. When the oil is hot, add the cumin seeds, bay leaf, cardamom, and onion, and stir-fry for 2 minutes, until the onion turns light golden brown.

3. Add the shrimp and sauté for a few minutes until they turn pink. Add the tomato, ginger, and garlic, and continue to cook for another 2 minutes.

4. Stir in the rice, ground cumin, ground coriander, curry powder, and salt, continue to stir-fry another minute or two.

5. Slowly stir in the water and bring to a rapid boil. Reduce the heat to low, cover the pan tightly, and simmer about 15 minutes, or until all of the water has been absorbed and the rice and shrimp are cooked.

6. Discard the bay leaf, fluff the rice with a fork, and transfer to a serving dish.

NUTRITIONAL FACTS (PER ¾-CUP SERVING)

Calories: 171   Carbohydrates: 26.7 g   Cholesterol: 58 mg
Fat: 1.9 g   Fiber: < 1 g   Protein: 10.8 g   Sodium: 346 mg

SUGGESTED ACCOMPANIMENTS

Spinach Yogurt Salad (page 62) and Whole Black Lentils (page 128).

Rice and Lentil Pilaf

Masoor Pulao

This complete protein dish is one your whole family will enjoy. Serve with plain nonfat yogurt or any curry dish.

Yield: *6 servings*

1. Pick through the lentils for any grit or debris, then place in a strainer and rinse thoroughly. Transfer the lentils to a small bowl and add 2 cups of water. Soak for 2 hours. Drain the lentils and set aside.

2. Spray a large heavy-bottomed saucepan with vegetable cooking spray. Add the oil and place over medium-low heat. When the oil is hot, add the chile, cumin seeds, and onion. Stir-fry for 2 minutes, or until the onion turns light brown.

3. Add the drained lentils and cook for about 2 minutes while stirring occasionally. Add 1½ cups of the water and bring to a rapid boil. Reduce the heat to low, cover the pan tightly, and simmer for 10 minutes, or until the water has been absorbed.

4. Stir in the rice, along with the ground coriander, ground cumin, and salt. Add the remaining 3 cups of water and bring to a boil. Reduce the heat to low and simmer, loosely covered, for 20 minutes, or until all of the water has been absorbed and the rice and lentils are tender.

5. Transfer to a serving bowl, garnish with cilantro, and serve hot.

½ cup dry lentils

1 teaspoon canola oil

1 small green chile, finely chopped

1 teaspoon cumin seeds

1 medium yellow onion, coarsely chopped

1½ cups basmati rice

1 teaspoon ground coriander

1 teaspoon ground cumin

¾ teaspoon salt (or to taste)

4½ cups water

1 tablespoon finely chopped fresh cilantro

NUTRITIONAL FACTS (PER ¾-CUP SERVING)

Calories: 233   Carbohydrates: 46.8 g   Cholesterol: 0 mg
Fat: 0.9 g   Fiber: 1 g   Protein: 8.5 g   Sodium: 295 mg

SUGGESTED ACCOMPANIMENTS

Carrot Yogurt Salad (page 54) and Cauliflower with Tomato (page 98).

Rice with Yogurt
Dhahi Bhat

Yield: *6 servings*

3 cups water

1 cup basmati rice

1½ cups plain nonfat yogurt

½ teaspoon salt (or to taste)

1 teaspoon sweet butter

½ teaspoon cumin seeds

6 curry leaves (optional)

1 green chile pepper, halved

1 teaspoon finely chopped fresh
   cilantro

Perfect for using up leftover rice, this family favorite is great with hot mango pickles on the side.

1. Bring 2½ cups of the water to boil in a large heavy-bottomed saucepan. Add the rice, stir, and reduce the heat to low. Cover the pan tightly and simmer for 15 minutes, or until the water has been absorbed and the rice is tender.

2. Using the back of a spoon, mash the rice until it no longer retains its shape. Stir in the yogurt, salt, and ¼ cup of the remaining water. Set aside.

3. Heat the butter in a small wok or saucepan over medium-high heat. Add the cumin seeds, chile, and curry leaves (if using). Stir-fry for a minute, then add this mixture to the rice. Stir to combine.

4. Add 1 tablespoon of the remaining water at a time to the rice until the mixture is creamy but not runny. (You may need a little more or less water to achieve this consistency.)

5. Transfer to a serving bowl, garnish with cilantro, and serve.

NUTRITIONAL FACTS (PER ¾-CUP SERVING)
Calories: 144   Carbohydrates: 27.6 g   Cholesterol: 2 mg
Fat: 0.8 g   Fiber: 0 g   Protein: 5.9 g   Sodium: 235 mg

SUGGESTED ACCOMPANIMENTS
Sprouted Mixed Beans (page 139) and Spicy Mango Chutney (page 180).

Rice and Wheat Pancakes

Dhirdee

Serve these nutritious main-dish pancakes topped with a little chutney or accompanied with a side dish of meat or vegetable curry.

1. Place the cream of wheat, cream of rice, and salt in a large bowl. Add 2 cups of the water and mix well. Cover the bowl and let the batter sit on the countertop for 8 hours or overnight.

2. Stir in the remaining water and baking soda to the batter. Add the cumin seeds, bell pepper, tomato, cilantro, and chile. Mix well.

3. Spray a medium-sized nonstick griddle with vegetable cooking spray and place over medium heat. Heat the griddle until a few drops of water dance and sizzle on the surface. Pour ¼ cup of batter onto the hot griddle. Cook 1 to 2 minutes, until the edges are dry and tiny bubbles appear on the surface. Flip the pancake over and cook another minute until the bottom is light brown. Repeat with the remaining batter.

4. Stack the pancakes on an ovenproof plate and keep warm in a 200°F oven until all of the pancakes are made. Serve immediately.

Yield: 16 pancakes

1 cup cream of wheat

1 cup cream of rice

1 teaspoon salt (or to taste)

3 cups water

¾ teaspoon baking soda

½ teaspoon cumin seeds

¾ cup green bell pepper, finely chopped

1 tomato, finely chopped

2 tablespoons finely chopped fresh cilantro

1 small green chile pepper, finely chopped

NUTRITIONAL FACTS (PER PANCAKE)

Calories: 70   Carbohydrates: 18.5 g   Cholesterol: 0 mg
Fat: 0.2 g   Fiber: <1 g   Protein: 1.6 g   Sodium: 167 mg

SUGGESTED ACCOMPANIMENTS

South Indian Dal (page 136), Mint Chutney (page 182).

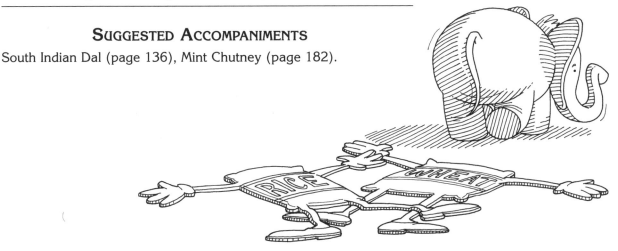

Rice with Split Mung Beans

Khichari

Yield: *6 servings*

¾ cups split dry mung beans

1 teaspoon canola oil

½ teaspoon black or yellow mustard seeds

½ teaspoon turmeric

6 curry leaves (optional)

3 very small yellow onions, peeled and quartered

1 ½ cups long-grain rice

1 teaspoon salt (or to taste)

½ teaspoon ground coriander

½ teaspoon ground cumin

½ teaspoon curry powder or sambar masala (page 132)

1 tablespoon shredded coconut(optional)

A healthy bean-grain combination, this dish is traditionally served (without onion) to toddlers because of its easy digestibility. Serve it hot with some pickles on the side.

1. Pick through the mung beans for any grit or debris, then place in a strainer and rinse thoroughly. Transfer the beans to a small bowl and add 2 cups water. Cover the bowl and let the beans soak 2 hours.

2. Spray a large pot with vegetable cooking spray. Add the oil and place over medium-low heat. When the oil is hot, add the mustard seeds. Cover the pot with a splatter guard and allow the seeds to pop. When the seeds have finished popping (within 30 seconds), add the turmeric and curry leaves (if using), and stir-fry for a few seconds. Add the onions and sauté about 2 minutes, until the onion begins to brown.

3. Drain the mung beans, reserving the soaking water. Stir in the beans, rice, salt, ground coriander, ground cumin, and curry powder, and stir-fry for 2 minutes. Add 5½ cups water (include the reserved soaking water), stir, and bring to a boil. Cover tightly, reduce the heat to medium-low, and cook for about 30 minutes, stirring occasionally, until all of the water has been absorbed and the rice and beans are tender.

4. Transfer to a serving dish, garnish with coconut (if using), and enjoy.

NUTRITIONAL FACTS (PER ¾-CUP SERVING)

Calories: 248   Carbohydrates: 50.9 g   Cholesterol: 0 mg
Fat: 1.1 g   Fiber: 0 g   Protein: 9.3 g   Sodium: 390 mg

SUGGESTED ACCOMPANIMENTS

Tomato Soup (page 47) and Spicy Mango Chutney (page 180).

Spicy Yellow Rice

Peele Chaval

For added flavor, simply add ⅛ teaspoon of your favorite sweet spice in Step 2. Cinnamon, saffron, and green cardamom are good choices.

Yield: *6 servings*

1. Coat a large heavy-bottomed pot with vegetable cooking spray. Add the oil and place over medium heat. When the oil is hot, add the cumin seeds, turmeric, and onion. Stir-fry about 2 minutes, or until the onion is just beginning to brown.

2. Add the cloves, cardamom, bay leaf, rice, and salt, and continue to stir-fry another minute.

3. Slowly stir in the water, increase the heat to high, and bring to a rapid boil. Reduce the heat to low, cover the pan tightly, and simmer about 15 minutes, or until all of the water has been absorbed and the rice is tender.

4. Remove from heat and keep covered for 5 minutes.

5. Discard the bay leaf, fluff the rice with a fork, and transfer to a serving dish.

1 teaspoon canola oil

1 teaspoon cumin seeds

½ teaspoon turmeric

1 small yellow onion, finely chopped

½ teaspoon ground cloves

2 black cardamom pods, crushed

1 medium bay leaf

1½ cups basmati rice

½ teaspoon salt (or to taste)

4½ cups water

NUTRITIONAL FACTS (PER ¾-CUP SERVING)

Calories: 171   Carbohydrates: 36 g   Cholesterol: 0 mg
Fat: 0.8 g   Fiber: 0 g   Protein: 4.1 g   Sodium: 192 mg

SUGGESTED ACCOMPANIMENTS

Shrimp Tomato Curry (page 171) and Radish Yogurt Salad (page 60).

Royal Spiced Lamb with Rice

Gosht Biryani

Yield: *7 servings*

¾ cups basmati rice

⅛ teaspoon saffron

¼ teaspoon canola oil

1-inch piece cinnamon stick

2 black cardamom pods

4 cloves

¼ teaspoon fennel seeds

3 cloves garlic, crushed

½ teaspoon peeled, grated
  ginger

1 small yellow onion, thinly
  sliced

12 ounces boneless lamb, cut
  into ½-inch cubes

½ teaspoon salt (or to taste)

½ teaspoon paprika

⅛ teaspoon chili powder
  (optional)

½ cup plain nonfat yogurt

¾ cups water

2 teaspoons slivered almonds
  (optional)

2 teaspoons raisins (optional)

This rich, one-dish meal needs only an accompaniment of plain yogurt to complement it perfectly.

1. Place the rice in a medium bowl, add 1 cup cold water, and soak for 15 to 30 minutes.

2. Place 2 teaspoons warm water in a small bowl. Pinching the saffron between your thumb and forefinger, add it to the water. Let steep about 10 to 15 minutes.

3. Spray a large nonstick skillet with vegetable cooking spray. Add the canola oil and place over medium heat. When the oil is hot, add the cinnamon, cardamom, cloves, and fennel. Reduce the heat to low, stir for 15 to 20 seconds, then add the garlic, ginger, and onion. Increase the heat to medium and continue to cook until the onion is pale and translucent. (Add a tablespoon or two of water as needed to prevent the onion from sticking to the skillet.) Stir in the salt and transfer the mixture to a dish. Set aside.

4. Increase the heat under the skillet to high and add the lamb. Sear and brown the lamb, reduce the heat to medium, and add the cooked onion mixture, salt, paprika, chili powder (if using), and yogurt. Stir well. Add ¾ cup water, cover, and simmer 50 to 60 minutes, until the lamb is tender. Uncover and continue to simmer until most of the pan juices are absorbed.

5. While the lamb is cooking, drain the rice, reserving the water. To this water add enough water to measure 3 cups. Place the water and soaked rice in a medium-sized pot and bring to a boil. Reduce the heat to low and simmer covered for 8 to 10 minutes, or until the rice is just tender. (As the rice simmers, do not uncover to test it.)

6. Spoon the rice onto one or two large platters, spreading it out evenly to cool completely. (This cooling period is necessary to prevent the rice from becoming mushy during the baking process.)

7. Preheat the oven to 350°F. Coat an 8-inch square casserole dish with vegetable cooking spray. Spread half the rice evenly on the bottom of the dish and top with the lamb mixture. Add the saffron water to the remaining rice, mix it well, and spoon it in an even layer on top of the lamb mixture.

8. Top the rice with the raisins and almonds (if using). Cover the dish with foil and bake about 10 minutes to heat through.

9. Spoon servings of the layered biryani into individual dishes and enjoy warm.

NUTRITIONAL FACTS (PER ¾-CUP SERVING)

Calories: 130   Carbohydrates: 17.9 g   Cholesterol: 22 mg
Fat: 1.9 g   Fiber: 0 g   Protein: 9.8 g   Sodium: 194 mg

SUGGESTED ACCOMPANIMENTS

Corn-Stuffed Tomatoes (page 99) and Cucumber Yogurt Salad (page 56).

HELPFUL HINT

- You can prepare this dish up to 24 hours before serving it. Tightly cover the prepared casserole with foil and refrigerate. Before serving, bake 35 to 45 minutes in a preheated 350°F oven, or until heated through.

Stir~fried Cabbage Rice

Masala Chawal

Yield: *8 servings*

2 teaspoons canola oil

½ teaspoon black or yellow mustard seeds

2 cloves garlic, crushed

1 medium yellow onion, halved and thinly sliced

2 cups finely shredded green cabbage

1 cup basmati rice, cooked according to package directions and cooled

½ teaspoon turmeric

¼ teaspoon paprika (optional)

¾ teaspoon salt (or to taste)

1 teaspoon ground cumin

1½ teaspoons lemon juice

1 tablespoon finely chopped fresh cilantro

This easy-to-prepare stir-fried rice dish is mildly spicy and quite nutritious.

1. Coat a large nonstick wok or skillet with vegetable cooking spray. Add the oil and place over medium heat. When the oil is hot, add the mustard seeds. Cover the wok with a splatter guard and allow the seeds to pop. When the seeds have finished popping (within 30 seconds), add the garlic and onion, reduce the heat to medium-low, and cook covered for 1 to 2 minutes until the onions are pale and translucent. (Add a tablespoon or two of water as needed to prevent the onion from sticking to the skillet.)

2. Add the cabbage, stir, and cover. Cook about 5 to 7 minutes until the cabbage is tender.

3. While the cabbage is cooking, sprinkle the rice with turmeric, paprika, and salt. Mix well.

4. Add the rice to the skillet and stir well. Cover for a minute to heat the rice, being careful not to let it stick to the bottom of the skillet. Mix in the ground cumin, lemon juice, and cilantro.

5. Transfer to a large serving bowl.

NUTRITIONAL FACTS (PER ¾-CUP SERVING)

Calories: 102   Carbohydrates: 21.3 g   Cholesterol: 0 mg
Fat: 1.2 g   Fiber: 0 g   Protein: 2.4 g   Sodium: 219 mg

SUGGESTED ACCOMPANIMENTS

Sesame Ginger Chicken (page 153) and Radish Yogurt Salad (page 60).

6.

Tasty Breads

Bread plays a very important role in Indian cuisine. Wheat, millet, and jowar—grains used to make delicious breads—are all grown in India, with whole wheat being the most widely used. Most breads, which are round, flat, and unleavened, are cooked on a flat iron griddle or skillet. Traditional leavened varieties are usually baked in a tandoor.

Popular Indian breads include:

Roti. Whole wheat unleavened flatbread that is dry-roasted on a skillet or in a tandoor.

Chapati. Whole wheat unleavened flatbread, similar to a roti, only thinner and more delicate in texture.

Kulcha. Yeast-leavened wheat flatbread, traditionally baked in a tandoor. To rewarm, kulchas are sometimes pan-fried in a lightly oiled skillet.

Naan. Yeast-leavened white-flour flatbread, traditionally baked in a tandoor.

Paratha. Whole wheat unleavened flatbread, similar to a roti, only cooked on an oiled skil-let. Can be plain or stuffed.

Thepla. Fenugreek leaves and whole wheat unleavened flatbread that is cooked on an oiled skillet.

Bread plays a central role in a traditional Indian meal. Served at the meal's onset, bread is torn into pieces, then dipped into the various curries, salads, and chutneys that comprise the meal. When the bread is eaten, it is generally replaced with rice—the meal's other central carbohydrate.

A fabulous variety of traditional Indian flatbreads are presented in this chapter. They range from such offerings as the hearty Potato Flatbread—a sumptuous addition to any meal—to the colorful and flavor-filled Green Pea Flatbread. Want to add a special touch to your Thanksgiving meal? Try the Pumpkin Flatbread for an exotic change.

No matter which breads you decide to try, we're sure you'll find them easy to make and absolutely delicious. You'll enjoy serving and eating them as well.

Fenugreek Flatbread

Methi Thepla

Yield: *12 theplas*

2 ½ cups thoroughly washed, coarsely chopped fenugreek leaves (about 5 ounces)

½ cup yellow split pea flour

1 cup whole wheat flour

1 cup unbleached flour

½ teaspoon salt (or to taste)

½ teaspoon turmeric

¾ cup water

Fresh fenugreek leaves, with their mildly bitter taste, are found in Indian grocery stores. Always choose fresh young leaves, which are usually milder and not as bitter as the more mature ones.

1. Place all of the ingredients, except the water, in a large bowl and combine well. Make a well in the center of the flour mixture, add the water, and mix with your hands. Knead to form a smooth, soft dough. Cover and let rest for about 10 minutes.

2. Place the dough on a clean work surface that has been dusted with flour. Roll the dough into a long, thick cylinder. Using a knife, cut the dough into 12 equal pieces. With floured hands, roll each piece into a ball.

3. Dust each ball with flour, then roll them out into 6-inch circles.

4. Place a medium-sized nonstick griddle or a frying pan over medium heat.

5. When the griddle is hot, add one piece of rolled-out dough and cook for 30 seconds, or until tiny bumps appear on the surface. Flip the flatbread over and cook another 30 seconds, or until it starts puffing up. Flip again and continue to cook for 30 to 60 seconds, or until both sides have light golden patches.

6. Place the bread in a tight-fitting container or wrap in aluminum foil to prevent it from drying out.

7. Continue cooking the remaining circles of dough.

8. Serve warm.

NUTRITIONAL FACTS: (PER THEPLA)

Calories: 87   Carbohydrates: 17.1 g   Cholesterol: 0 mg
Fat: 0.5 g   Fiber: 1 g   Protein: 3.7 g   Sodium: 100 mg

SUGGESTED ACCOMPANIMENTS

Mushrooms and Black-Eyed Peas (page 130) and Banana Yogurt Salad (page 52).

Green Pea Flatbread
Muttar ki Roti

This recipe is an adaptation of the classic paratha—stuffed fried bread of northern India. Cooked in an oilless skillet, this version is a healthy treat.

1. Bring the water to boil in a small saucepan. Add the peas and cook until tender. Drain the peas, reserving the cooking liquid in a measuring cup. To the cup add enough water to measure ½ cup. Place the peas in a food processor or blender and purée coarsely. Set aside.

2. Place the flours, cumin seeds, and salt in a large bowl and combine well. Add the puréed peas and rub it well into the flour. Slowly add the reserved water, mixing it with you hands. Knead to form a smooth, soft dough. Cover and let rest for 10 minutes.

3. Place the dough on a clean work surface that has been dusted with flour and roll it into a long, thick cylinder. Using a knife, cut the dough into 12 equal pieces. With floured hands, roll each piece into a ball. Dust each ball with flour, then roll them out into 5- or 6-inch circles.

4. Place a medium-sized nonstick griddle or a frying pan over medium heat. When the griddle is hot, add one piece of rolled-out dough and cook for 30 seconds, or until tiny bumps appear on the surface. Flip the flatbread over and cook another 30 seconds, or until it starts puffing up. Flip again and continue to cook for 30 to 60 seconds until both sides have light golden patches.

5. Place the bread in a tight-fitting container or wrap in aluminum foil to prevent it from drying out.

6. Continue cooking the remaining circles of dough. Serve warm.

Yield: *12 rotis*

1 cup water

1½ cups frozen green peas

1 cup unbleached flour

1 cup whole wheat flour

½ teaspoon cumin seeds

¼ teaspoon salt (or to taste)

NUTRITIONAL FACTS: (PER ROTI)
Calories: 82   Carbohydrates: 18 g   Cholesterol: 0 mg
Fat: 0.4 g   Fiber: 2 g   Protein: 3.4 g   Sodium: 66 mg

SUGGESTED ACCOMPANIMENTS
Mixed Legumes (page 129), Garlic-Flavored Fish Kabobs (page 175), and Creamy Plantain Curry (page 102).

Honey Wheat Flatbread

Khasti Roti

Servings: *12 rotis*

1 cup warm water

2 teaspoons active dry yeast

1 tablespoon honey

1 teaspoon salt (or to taste)

2 cups unbleached flour

1 cup whole wheat flour

Pushcart vendors throughout India sell this delicious flatbread much the same way that vendors in American cities sell hot pretzels. The flatbreads are sold along with a variety of tasty garnishes, such as boiled garbanzo beans, chopped onions and tomatoes, fresh cilantro, lemon juice, and a variety of dry spice combinations.

1. Place half the warm water in a large bowl. Stir in the yeast and honey and mix until dissolved. Set aside in a warm place for 5 minutes until foamy.

2. To the yeast mixture, add the salt and beat in the unbleached flour, 1 cup at a time, to form a smooth batter. Add the whole wheat flour and remaining water, and knead to form a smooth, soft dough. Cover the bowl with plastic wrap and a clean towel, and let the dough rise in a warm place for about 2 hours, or until doubled in size.

3. With a floured fist, punch down the dough, turn it onto a clean floured surface, and roll it into a long, thick cylinder. Using a knife, cut the dough into 12 equal pieces. With floured hands, roll each piece into a ball.

4. Dust each ball with flour, then roll them out into 5-inch circles. Cover the circles and let rest about 15 minutes.

5. Place a medium-sized nonstick griddle or a frying pan over medium heat.

6. When the griddle is hot, add one piece of rolled-out dough and cook for 30 seconds, or until tiny bumps appear on the surface. Flip the flatbread over and cook another 30 seconds, or until it starts puffing up. Flip again and continue to cook for 30 to 60 seconds until both sides have light golden patches.

7. Place the bread in a tight-fitting container or wrap in aluminum foil to prevent it from drying out.

8. Continue cooking the remaining circles of dough.

9. Serve warm.

Center Left: Shrimp Pilaf (page 74)
Bottom Left: Quick Spicy Garbanzos (page 131)
Bottom Right: Butterless Butter Chicken (page 148)

Top Left: Stir-Fried Yellow Rice (page 73) and
Spicy Buttermilk Drink (page 190)
Top Right: Cauliflower with Tomato (page 98)
Bottom: Ginger Chicken (page 147)

Top: Lamb with Poppy Seeds (page 160)
Center Left: Yellow Split Peas (page 142)
Center Right: Potato Flatbread (page 89)
Bottom Left: Sweet-and-Sour Pumpkin Curry (page 120)

NUTRITIONAL FACTS: (PER ROTI)
Calories: 105   Carbohydrates: 25.3 g   Cholesterol: 0 mg
Fat: 0.5 g   Fiber: 2 g   Protein: 3.4 g   Sodium: 193 mg

SUGGESTED ACCOMPANIMENTS

Butterless Butter Chicken (page 148) and Mixed Vegetable Curry
(page 106).

HELPFUL HINT

• You can prepare this dough up to 3 days before using it. After
  kneading the dough in Step 2, cover the bowl tightly and place it
  in the refrigerator, where it will rise slowly. When ready to use,
  remove the dough from the refrigerator, punch it down, then allow
  it to rise again. Continue as instructed.

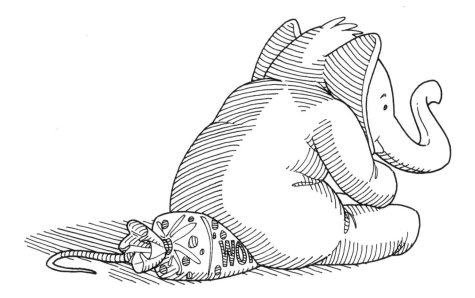

Herbed Onion Flatbread

Pyaz Wali Roti

Yield: *12 rotis*

1 cup warm water

¼-ounce package active dry
   yeast

1½ tablespoons honey

1 teaspoon salt (or to taste)

2½ cups unbleached flour

½ cup whole wheat flour

½ cup oat bran

1 teaspoon cumin seeds

1 small onion, very finely
   chopped

2 tablespoons finely chopped
   fresh cilantro

*This tasty version of the Honey Wheat Flatbread (page 86) is
flavored with onion and cilantro.*

1. Place half the warm water in a large bowl. Stir in the yeast and
honey and mix until dissolved. Set aside in a warm place for 5 minutes until foamy.

2. To the yeast mixture, add the salt and beat in the unbleached flour,
1 cup at a time, to form a smooth batter. Add the whole wheat flour,
oat bran, cumin seeds, onion, cilantro and remaining water, and
knead to form a smooth, soft dough. Cover the bowl with plastic wrap
and a clean towel, and let the dough rise in a warm place for about 2
hours, or until doubled in size.

3. With a floured fist, punch down the dough, turn it onto a clean
floured surface, and roll it into a long, thick cylinder. Using a knife,
cut the dough into 12 equal pieces, then roll each piece into a ball.

4. Dust each ball with flour, then roll them out into 5-inch circles.
Cover the circles and let rest about 15 minutes.

5. Place a medium-sized nonstick griddle or a frying pan over medium heat. When the griddle is hot, add one piece of rolled-out dough
and cook for 30 seconds, or until tiny bumps appear on the surface.
Flip the flatbread over and cook another 30 seconds, or until it starts
puffing up. Flip again and continue to cook for 30 to 60 seconds until
both sides have light golden patches.

6. Place the bread in a tight-fitting container or wrap in aluminum foil
to prevent it from drying out.

7. Continue cooking the remaining circles of dough. Serve warm.

NUTRITIONAL FACTS: (PER ROTI)

Calories: 116   Carbohydrates: 30.3 g   Cholesterol: 0 mg
Fat: 0.8 g   Fiber: 2 g   Protein: 4.0 g   Sodium: 193 mg

SUGGESTED ACCOMPANIMENTS

Corn with Potatoes (page 100) and Shrimp in Sweet, Sour, and
Spicy Curry (page 176).

Potato Flatbread

Aloo Roti

This is a simplified, fat-free version of Aloo Paratha, a traditional pan-fried potato bread.

1. Mix all of the ingredients together in a large bowl to form a smooth, soft dough. You may need a tablespoon more or less flour to achieve this consistency.

2. Place the dough on a clean work surface that has been dusted with flour, and roll it into a long, thick cylinder. Using a knife, cut the dough into 12 equal pieces. With floured hands, roll each piece into a ball.

3. Dust each ball with flour, then roll them out into 5-inch circles.

4. Place a medium-sized nonstick griddle or a frying pan over medium heat.

5. When the griddle is hot, add one piece of rolled-out dough and cook for 30 seconds, or until tiny bumps appear on the surface. Flip the flatbread over and cook another 30 seconds, or until it starts puffing up. Flip again and continue to cook for 30 to 60 seconds, or until both sides have light golden patches.

6. Place the bread in a tight-fitting container or wrap in aluminum foil to prevent it from drying out.

7. Continue cooking the remaining circles of dough.

8. Serve warm.

Yield: *12 rotis*

4 medium potatoes, boiled, peeled, and mashed

2 tablespoons finely chopped fresh cilantro

½ teaspoon cumin seeds

1 small green chile pepper, very finely chopped (optional)

½ teaspoon salt (or to taste)

1½ cups unbleached flour

NUTRITIONAL FACTS: (PER ROTI)

Calories: 79   Carbohydrates: 19.7 g   Cholesterol: 0 mg
Fat: 0.3 g   Fiber: 1 g   Protein: 2.3 g   Sodium: 99 mg

SUGGESTED ACCOMPANIMENTS

Lamb Curry (page 156) and Cabbage with Peas (page 96).

Pumpkin Flatbread

Kaddu ki Roti

Yield: *12 rotis*

¾ cup canned pumpkin

⅓ cup dark brown sugar, packed

½ teaspoon ground green cardamom

½ teaspoon ground cinnamon

¼ teaspoon ground cloves

1 cup whole wheat flour

½ cup unbleached flour

Try serving this sweet flatbread as an unusual and exotic addition to your Thanksgiving meal.

1. In a large bowl, combine the pumpkin and brown sugar. Mix well. Add the remaining ingredients and mix thoroughly. Knead to form a smooth, soft dough. Cover and let rest for about 10 minutes.

2. Place the dough on a clean work surface that has been dusted with flour and roll it into a long, thick cylinder. Using a knife, cut the dough into 12 equal pieces. With floured hands, roll each piece into a ball.

3. Dust each ball with flour, then roll them out into 6-inch circles.

4. Place a medium-sized nonstick griddle or frying pan over medium heat.

5. When the griddle is hot, add one piece of rolled-out dough and cook for 30 seconds, or until tiny bumps appear on the surface. Flip the flatbread over and cook another 30 seconds, or until it starts puffing up. Flip again and continue to cook for 30 to 60 seconds until both sides have light golden patches.

6. Place the bread in a tight-fitting container or wrap in aluminum foil to prevent it from drying out.

7. Continue cooking the remaining circles of dough.

8. Serve warm.

NUTRITIONAL FACTS: (PER ROTI)

Calories: 80   Carbohydrates: 19 g   Cholesterol: 0 mg
Fat: 0.3 g   Fiber: 2 g   Protein: 2.1 g   Sodium: 1 mg

SUGGESTED ACCOMPANIMENTS

Green Bean Salad (page 67) and Mixed Vegetable Curry (page 106).

Spinach Flatbread

Palak Wali Roti

Instead of fresh spinach, you can use frozen, thawed spinach for this recipe.

1. Place ¼ cup of the warm water in a small bowl. Stir in the yeast and sugar and mix until dissolved. Set aside in a warm place for 5 minutes until foamy.

2. In a large bowl, combine the flours, oat bran, spinach, garlic, and salt. Make a well in the center of the flour mixture. Add the yogurt, yeast mixture, and remaining water and mix with your hands. Knead to form a smooth, soft dough. Cover the bowl with plastic wrap and a clean towel, and let the dough rise in a warm place for about 2 hours, or until doubled in size.

3. With a floured fist, punch down the dough, and turn it onto a clean floured surface, and roll it into a long, thick cylinder. Cut the dough into 12 equal pieces, and roll each piece into a ball.

4. Dust each ball with flour, then roll them out into 6-inch circles. Cover the circles and let rest about 15 minutes.

5. Place a medium-sized nonstick griddle or a frying pan over medium heat. When the griddle is hot, add a circle of dough and cook for 30 seconds, or until tiny bumps appear on the surface. Flip the flatbread over and cook another 30 seconds, or until it starts puffing up. Flip again and continue to cook for 30 to 60 seconds until both sides have light golden patches.

6. Place the bread in a tight-fitting container or wrap in aluminum foil to prevent it from drying out.

7. Continue cooking the remaining circles of dough. Serve warm.

Yield: *12 rotis*

¾ cup warm water

¼-ounce package active dry yeast

1 teaspoon granulated white sugar

1 cup whole wheat flour

1 cup unbleached flour

⅓ cup oat bran

1½ cups finely chopped fresh spinach, packed

1 teaspoon salt (or to taste)

2 cloves garlic, peeled and minced

½ cup plain nonfat yogurt (room temperature)

NUTRITIONAL FACTS: (PER ROTI)

Calories: 82   Carbohydrates: 17.1 g   Cholesterol: 0 mg
Fat: 0.6 g   Fiber: 2 g   Protein: 3.7 g   Sodium: 250 mg

SUGGESTED ACCOMPANIMENTS

Corn-Stuffed Tomatoes (page 99), Cucumber Tomato Salad (page 57), and Mint Chutney (page 182)

Raised Indian Flatbread

Naan

Yield: *12 naans*

¾ cup warm water

¼-ounce package active dry yeast

1 teaspoon granulated white sugar

¾ cup plain nonfat yogurt

¼ cup skim milk

½ teaspoon baking powder

¼ teaspoon baking soda

3 cups unbleached flour

½ teaspoon salt (or to taste)

Cornmeal to sprinkle on oven bricks (optional)

Along with tandoori chicken, naan is probably the most popular Indian food eaten in the United States. Traditionally, naan is baked in a tandoor, however, we have provided instructions for baking this bread in a conventional oven on clean bricks or in a cast iron skillet.

1. Place ¼ cup of the warm water in a small bowl. Stir in the yeast and sugar and mix until dissolved. Set aside in a warm place for 5 minutes until foamy.

2. Mix the yogurt and milk together in a large microwave-safe bowl. Place in the microwave and heat for 20 to 30 seconds, or until the mixture is lukewarm.

3. Remove the bowl from the microwave and stir in the baking powder and baking soda (the mixture will foam). Set aside.

4. In another large bowl, combine the flour and salt. Make a well in the center of the flour mixture, add the yogurt mixture and the yeast mixture, and mix with your hands. Knead while slowly adding enough of the remaining water to form a smooth, soft dough. Cover the bowl with plastic wrap and a clean towel, and let the dough rise in a warm place for about 2 hours, or until doubled in size.

5. With a floured fist, punch down the dough, turn it onto a clean floured surface, and roll it into a long, thick cylinder. Using a knife, cut the dough into 12 equal pieces. With floured hands, roll each piece into a ball. Cover the balls and let them rest about 15 minutes until doubled.

6. Place the rack from a conventional oven in its lowest position, line it with clean clay bricks, then sprinkle the bricks with cornmeal. Preheat the oven to its hottest setting. Instead of bricks, you can bake the naan in a cast iron skillet that has been sprayed with vegetable cooking spray. If you are using a skillet, do not preheat it along with the oven.

7. Using your fingertips, gently press the balls of dough into 2½-inch circles. Then hold each circle with both hands and gently stretch it to a 5- to 6-inch circle that is about ⅛-inch thick. Do not use a rolling pin as this will flatten out the air bubbles. Lift up the circles of dough and place them on the oven bricks (or in the skillet). Bake 5 to 7 minutes, until they are flecked with golden spots.

8. Remove from the oven and let cool. Store the naan in a tight-fitting container or wrapped in aluminum foil.

9. Serve warm.

NUTRITIONAL FACTS: (PER NAAN)

Calories: 111   Carbohydrates: 28 g   Cholesterol: <1 mg
Fat: 0.6 g   Fiber: 1 g   Protein: 4.1 g   Sodium: 107 mg

SUGGESTED ACCOMPANIMENTS

Mushrooms and Black-Eyed Peas (page 130) and Stir-Fried Cabbage with Carrots (page 115).

7.

Good-for-You Veggies

Grown throughout India, vegetables are an integral part of that country's cuisine. Generally, vegetables—many of which are prepared in a number of ways—are enjoyed as side dishes in Indian meals.

Vegetables fall into three broad categories. These include leafy green varieties, such as spinach and fenugreek leaves; roots and tubers, like potatoes, carrots, onions, and sweet potatoes; and a final category that includes the fruits of various plants, such as eggplant, zucchini, cauliflower, and cabbage. Most Indian-style vegetables are either stir-fried, curried, or stuffed.

Stir-fried vegetables are usually shredded, sliced, cubed, or mashed, then cooked in oil and flavored with a wide assortment of herbs and spices. The stir-fried vegetables in this chapter are cooked in a skillet or wok that has been coated with vegetable cooking spray. Any additional oil used in the recipes has been kept to a minimum.

Curried vegetables are flavored with a wide variety of spices and cooked in a sauce.

Commonly, cream-based sauces or sauces with ginger-and-garlic or tomato-and-onion form the base for vegetable curries. Cream-based vegetable curries go best with kachumbar salads (those with fresh shredded vegetables). Stir-fried and stuffed vegetables go best with yogurt-based raitas.

Rice-Stuffed Green Peppers and Corn-Stuffed Tomatoes are examples of the stuffed vegetables in this chapter. Although stuffed vegetables are traditionally fried in generous amounts of oil, we find that baking them eliminates the fat while preserving the taste.

Remember to always choose fresh vegetables over canned, and be careful not to overcook them as heat can destroy their valuable vitamins and nutrients. When cooking or steaming vegetables, be sure to save any nutrient-rich cooking water to use in soups and other dishes.

So go ahead and enjoy these vegetable dishes with the flatbreads or rice dishes from this book.

Cabbage with Peas
Gobi Muttar

Yield: *4 servings*

1 teaspoon canola oil

½ teaspoon black or yellow
   mustard seeds

¼ teaspoon turmeric

1½ cups frozen green peas

3 cups finely shredded green
   cabbage

¼ teaspoon salt (or to taste)

½ teaspoon ground coriander

¼ teaspoon ground cumin

¼ teaspoon lemon juice

1 tablespoon finely chopped
   cilantro

*Healthy and economical, this stir-fried vegetable dish is commonly
served during winters in India, when fresh peas are abundant.*

1. Spray a medium-sized wok or skillet with vegetable cooking spray.
Add the oil and place over medium heat. When the oil is hot, add the
mustard seeds. Cover the skillet with a splatter guard and allow the
seeds to pop. When the seeds have finished popping (within 30 seconds), add the turmeric and peas. Stir-fry 30 seconds.

2. Add the cabbage. Cover and cook, while stirring occasionally, for
5 to 10 minutes, or until tender. (Add a tablespoon or two of water as
needed to prevent the cabbage from sticking to the wok.)

3. Stir in the salt, ground coriander, ground cumin, and lemon juice.
Mix well and continue to cook another minute or two.

4. Transfer to a bowl, garnish with cilantro, and serve warm.

NUTRITIONAL FACTS: (PER ⅔-CUP SERVING)

Calories: 70   Carbohydrates: 11.3 g   Cholesterol: 0 mg
Fat: 1.6 g   Fiber: 2.2 g   Protein: 3.8 g   Sodium : 155 mg

SUGGESTED ACCOMPANIMENTS

Indian Egg Curry (page 163) and Herbed Onion Flatbread (page
88).

Cauliflower, Peas, and Potato Curry

Rassa

We have Anita's husband, Girish, to thank for this delectable vegetable curry. He learned to make it during his college days in England. He claims that ketchup is the secret (not so secret anymore) ingredient that gives this dish a special touch.

1. Spray a medium-sized pot with vegetable cooking spray. Add the oil and place over medium heat. When the oil is hot, add the mustard seeds. Cover the pot with a splatter guard and allow the seeds to pop. When the seeds have finished popping (within 30 seconds), add the onion and turmeric, and stir-fry about 2 minutes, or until the onion just begins to turn brown.

2. Add the garlic, ginger, cauliflower, potato, and peas. Stir-fry about 2 minutes, then gradually add the water. Cover and cook, stirring occasionally, for 15 minutes, or until the vegetables are tender.

3. Add the ketchup and sprinkle with the ground cumin, ground coriander, and salt. Mix well and cook another 5 minutes.

4. Transfer to a serving bowl, garnish with cilantro, and serve hot.

NUTRITIONAL FACTS (PER ⅔-CUP SERVING)

Calories: 99   Carbohydrates: 18.6 g   Cholesterol: 0 mg
Fat: 1.8 g   Fiber: 2 g   Protein: 3.5 g   Sodium: 475 mg

SUGGESTED ACCOMPANIMENTS

Beet Yogurt Salad (page 53), Sweet-and-Sour Black-Eyed Peas (page 141), and Stir-Fried Yellow Rice (page 73).

Yield: *3 servings*

1 teaspoon canola oil

¼ teaspoon black or yellow mustard seeds

1 small yellow onion, finely chopped

¼ teaspoon turmeric

1 clove garlic, crushed

½ teaspoon peeled, grated ginger

1 cup cauliflower florets (1 inch)

1 medium potato, peeled and cut into 1-inch cubes

½ cup frozen green peas

1½ cups water

1 tablespoon low-sodium ketchup

½ teaspoon ground cumin

½ teaspoon ground coriander

½ teaspoon salt (or to taste)

1 tablespoon finely chopped fresh cilantro

Cauliflower with Tomato

Phool Gobi aur Tamatar

Yield: *4 servings*

½ teaspoon canola oil

½ teaspoon black or yellow mustard seeds

¼ teaspoon cumin seeds

¼ teaspoon turmeric

1 medium tomato, finely chopped

4 cups cauliflower florets (1 inch)

½ teaspoon salt

½ teaspoon ground cumin

½ teaspoon ground coriander

½ teaspoon paprika

2 tablespoons finely chopped fresh cilantro

The cauliflower florets are coated in a flavorful tomato-based sauce in this delectable side dish.

1. Spray a large nonstick wok or skillet with vegetable cooking spray. Add the oil and place over medium heat. When the oil is hot, add the mustard seeds. Cover with a splatter guard and allow the seeds to pop. When the seeds have finished popping (within 30 seconds), stir in the cumin seeds, turmeric, and tomato.

2. Increase the heat to high, and add the cauliflower and 1 tablespoon water. Cover quickly. Cook the cauliflower, stirring often, for 5 to 10 minutes, or until almost tender. (If the cauliflower starts to stick, reduce the heat to medium-low.)

3. Uncover and stir-fry for 5 minutes, or until all of the liquid has been absorbed.

4. Sprinkle with salt, ground cumin, ground coriander, and paprika. Mix well.

5. Transfer to a serving dish, sprinkle with cilantro, and serve.

NUTRITIONAL FACTS: (PER ⅔-CUP SERVING)

Calories: 40   Carbohydrates: 6.3 g   Cholesterol: 0 mg
Fat: 0.9 g   Fiber: 2.2 g   Protein: 2.2 g   Sodium: 304 mg

SUGGESTED ACCOMPANIMENTS

Cucumber Yogurt Salad (page 56) and Fenugreek Flatbread (page 84).

Corn~Stuffed Tomatoes

Makai Bhare Tamatar

This easy-to-prepare, eye-pleasing side dish is perfect to serve your guests. The fat-free filling is so delicious, we often make extra to enjoy as a salad. Be careful not to overcook the tomatoes.

Yield: *6 servings*

3 large, firm tomatoes

½ cup frozen corn, thawed

1 small onion, finely chopped

½ medium green bell pepper, finely chopped

1 tablespoon finely chopped fresh cilantro

½ teaspoon salt (or to taste)

1 teaspoon curry powder

¼ teaspoon chili powder (optional)

1. Preheat the oven to 375°F. Coat an 8-inch baking pan with vegetable cooking spray and set aside. Cut each tomato in half crosswise. Scoop out the pulp, leaving a thick shell so the tomato will hold its shape.

2. Coarsely chop the pulp and place it in a medium-sized bowl along with the remaining ingredients. Mix well.

3. Loosely fill each tomato shell with equal amounts of filling mixture, then arrange in the prepared pan. Bake uncovered about 25 minutes, or until the tomatoes are tender and the filling is heated through.

4. Transfer the stuffed tomatoes to a platter and serve warm.

NUTRITIONAL FACTS: (PER SERVING)

Calories: 43   Carbohydrates: 9.7 g   Cholesterol: 0 mg
Fat: 0.4 g   Fiber: 1 g   Protein: 1.8 g   Sodium: 205 mg

SUGGESTED ACCOMPANIMENTS

Sprouted Mung Bean Curry (page 140) and Spicy Yellow Rice (page 79).

HELPFUL HINT

• If the tomatoes halves do not sit well, cut a very thin slice from the bottom of each before filling and baking.

Corn with Potatoes

Aloo Makka Sabzi

Yield: *4 servings*

1 ½ teaspoons canola oil

1 teaspoon cumin seeds

½ teaspoon turmeric

6 curry leaves

1 small yellow onion, finely chopped

2 cups frozen corn, thawed

1 medium potato, boiled, skinned, and cut into ½-inch cubes

½ teaspoon ground cumin

½ teaspoon ground coriander

½ teaspoon salt (or to taste)

1 tablespoon finely chopped fresh cilantro

Here's a vegetable dish that your kids will love.

1. Spray a medium-sized nonstick skillet with cooking spray. Add the oil and place over medium heat. When the oil is hot, add the cumin seeds, turmeric, curry leaves (if using), and onion. Stir-fry about 2 minutes, or until the onion begins to brown.

2. Add the corn, reduce heat to low, and cook covered for 5 minutes. (Add a tablespoon or two of water as needed to prevent the vegetables from sticking to the skillet.)

3. Add the potato, ground cumin, ground coriander, and salt. Mix well. Cover and continue to cook another 5 minutes, stirring occasionally.

4. Transfer to a serving bowl, garnish with cilantro, and serve warm.

NUTRITIONAL FACTS: (PER ⅔-CUP SERVING)

Calories: 115   Carbohydrates: 23.1 g   Cholesterol: 0 mg
Fat: 2.6 g   Fiber: 1 g   Protein: 3.1 g   Sodium: 297 mg

SUGGESTED ACCOMPANIMENTS

Cucumber Tomato Salad (page 57), and
Spinach Flatbread (page 91).

Creamy Mixed Vegetables

Makhani Subzi

The original version of this recipe calls for fresh cream and butter, and is loaded with unwanted fat and calories. After many attempts, we developed this delicious low-fat variation.

1. Pour the milk into a medium-sized bowl. Add the ground cumin, ground coriander, paprika, turmeric, and sugar. Mix well and set aside.

2. Spray a medium-sized nonstick wok or skillet with vegetable cooking spray. Add the oil and place over medium heat. When the oil is hot, add the cumin seeds. Fry a few minutes until the seeds begin to sizzle, then add the onion. Stir-fry about 2 minutes. Add 1 tablespoon water, cover, and cook until the onion is pale and translucent.

3. Add the green pepper and stir-fry for 30 seconds. Add the mixed vegetables and stir-fry 2 minutes.

4. Add the milk mixture and salt, and bring to a rapid boil. Reduce the heat to low and simmer 2 to 3 minutes, or until the vegetables are cooked.

5. While the vegetables are cooking, dissolve the cornstarch in a tablespoon of water. Add this mixture to the wok, stirring constantly. Simmer about 30 seconds, or until the consistency of the sauce is like table cream.

6. Remove from the heat, cool a few minutes, then stir in the ketchup. Mix well and transfer to a serving dish. Sprinkle with cilantro and serve.

Yield: *4 servings*

2 cups 1% low-fat milk

1/4 teaspoon ground cumin

1/2 teaspoon ground coriander

1/2 teaspoon paprika

1/4 teaspoon turmeric

1/2 teaspoon granulated white sugar

1/4 teaspoon canola oil

1/4 teaspoon cumin seeds

1/4 medium yellow onion, finely chopped

1/2 cup coarsely chopped green pepper (1/2-inch pieces)

2 cups frozen mixed vegetables (any combination)

1/4 teaspoon salt (or to taste)

1 1/2 teaspoons cornstarch

2 tablespoons plus 1 teaspoon ketchup

1 teaspoon finely chopped fresh cilantro

NUTRITIONAL FACTS: (PER 2/3-CUP SERVING)

Calories: 117   Carbohydrates: 24 g   Cholesterol: 5 mg
Fat: 2 g   Fiber: 2.2 g   Protein: 6.5 g   Sodium: 342 mg

SUGGESTED ACCOMPANIMENTS

Mint-Flavored Shrimp Kabobs (page 177) and Honey Wheat Flatbread (page 86).

Creamy Plantain Curry

Kele ki Sabzi

Yield: *4 servings*

2 large ripe plantains

¼ teaspoon turmeric

¼ teaspoon cayenne pepper

1½ cups water

1½ teaspoon canola oil

½ teaspoon cumin seeds

6 curry leaves

¾ cup fat-free coconut milk
   (page 152)

1 medium yellow onion, finely
   chopped

1 tablespoon chopped fresh
   cilantro

We have replaced the high-fat coconut milk traditionally used in this Indian dish with our own fat-free version. Made by blending together nonfat ricotta cheese, skim milk, sugar, and coconut essence, this "coconut milk" saves on fat and calories, while providing great taste.

1. Peel the plantains and cut each in half crosswise. Then cut each half lengthwise into wedges. (There will be 4 wedges per plantain.) Chop each wedge into ½-inch pieces. Sprinkle the pieces with turmeric and cayenne pepper.

2. Place the plantains and water in a medium-sized saucepan over medium heat. Cook, partially covered, for 25 minutes, or until the plantains are tender and most of the water has evaporated.

3. Spray a medium-sized saucepan with vegetable cooking spray. Add the oil and place over medium heat. When the oil is hot, add the cumin seeds, curry leaves, and onions. Stir-fry until the onions are light golden brown.

4. Add the cooked plantains to the pan and toss gently. Stir in the coconut milk and bring to a gentle boil. Cook about 5 minutes, stirring occasionally.

5. Transfer to a serving bowl, garnish with cilantro, and serve hot.

NUTRITIONAL FACTS: (PER ⅔-CUP SERVING)

Calories: 115   Carbohydrates: 16.4 g   Cholesterol: 0 mg
Fat: 2 g   Fiber: <1 g   Protein: 5.6 g   Sodium: 106 mg

SUGGESTED ACCOMPANIMENTS

Green Bean Salad (page 67) and Quick Stir-Fried Rice with Vegetables (page 71).

Green Beans with Potatoes

Farazbee aur Aloo ki Sabzi

This simple vegetable dish is easy to prepare, especially if you have boiled potatoes on hand.

1. Spray a medium-sized nonstick skillet with vegetable cooking spray. Add the oil and place over medium heat. When the oil is hot, add the cumin seeds and turmeric. Fry a few seconds until the seeds begin to sizzle, then toss in the green beans. Cover and cook for 15 minutes, or until the beans are just tender. (Add a tablespoon or two of water as needed to prevent the beans from sticking to the skillet.)

2. Add the potato, ground cumin, ground coriander, paprika, and salt. Stir well and continue to cook another 2 minutes.

3. Remove from the heat, cover, and let stand a few minutes.

4. Transfer to a serving dish, garnish with cilantro, and serve.

Yield: *4 servings*

1 teaspoon canola oil

1 teaspoon cumin seeds

¼ teaspoon turmeric

3 cups green beans, trimmed and cut into 1-inch pieces*

1 medium potato, boiled, peeled, and cut into ½-inch cubes

½ teaspoon ground cumin

½ teaspoon ground coriander

¼ teaspoon paprika

¾ teaspoon salt (or to taste)

1 tablespoon finely chopped fresh cilantro

NUTRITIONAL FACTS: (PER ⅔-CUP SERVING)

Calories: 68   Carbohydrates: 12.7 g   Cholesterol: 0 mg
Fat: 1.1 g   Fiber: 2 g   Protein: 1.6 g   Sodium: 443 mg

SUGGESTED ACCOMPANIMENTS

Beet Yogurt Salad (page 53) and Raised Indian Flatbread (page 92).

*Can also use frozen, thawed green beans. If using frozen variety, cut the cooking time in Step 1 to 8 minutes.

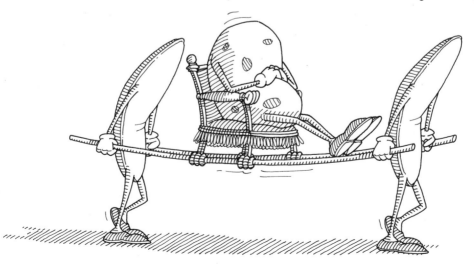

Green Pepper Curry

Mirchi Chi Bhaji

Yield: *4 servings*

1 teaspoon canola oil

¼ teaspoon black or yellow mustard seeds

½ teaspoon cumin seeds

¼ teaspoon turmeric

1 large potato, unpeeled and cut into ½-inch cubes (about 1 cup)

1 large carrot, cut into ¼-inch pieces

1 cup water

1 large green pepper, seeded and cut into 1-inch pieces

½ teaspoon ground cumin

½ teaspoon ground coriander

½ teaspoon salt (or to taste)

1 tablespoon finely chopped fresh cilantro

This delightful side dish with its flavorful sauce is wonderful served over a bed of hot, steaming rice.

1. Spray a medium-sized pot with vegetable cooking spray. Add the oil and place over medium heat. When the oil is hot, add the mustard seeds. Cover the skillet with a splatter guard and allow the seeds to pop. When the seeds have finished popping (within 30 seconds), add the cumin seeds and turmeric and fry a few seconds.

2. Add the potato and carrot, stir-fry for 1 minute, then add the water. Cover and cook 8 minutes, or until the carrots are nearly tender.

3. Add the green peppers. Cover and cook another 8 minutes, or until the peppers are tender.

4. Sprinkle with ground cumin, ground coriander, and salt. Mix well and cook another minute.

5. Transfer to a serving dish, garnish with cilantro, and serve hot.

NUTRITIONAL FACTS (PER ⅔-CUP SERVING)

Calories: 72   Carbohydrates: 11.3 g   Cholesterol: 0 mg
Fat: 1.4 g   Fiber: 1 g   Protein: 1.4 g   Sodium: 300 mg

SUGGESTED ACCOMPANIMENTS

Banana Yogurt Salad (page 52) and Stir-Fried Yellow Rice (page 73).

Potato Curry with Aniseed and Fenugreek Seeds

Sauf Methi ke Aloo

Traditionally, this curry is eaten with a deep-fried bread called puri.

Yield: *6 servings*

1. Spray a large nonstick wok or skillet with vegetable cooking spray. Add the oil and place over medium heat. When the oil is hot, add the cumin seeds, aniseed, and fenugreek seeds. Stir-fry for 1 or 2 minutes, until the spices emit a strong aroma.

2. Stir in the tomato and increase the heat to high. Cook while stirring constantly until most of the moisture from the tomatoes is reduced. (If the tomato starts to stick to the wok, reduce the heat a bit.)

3. Stir in the paprika, turmeric, and salt, then add the potatoes. Mix the ingredients together well.

4. Add the fenugreek leaves and water. Bring to a boil, then reduce the heat to medium-low and simmer uncovered about 8 minutes.

5. Transfer to a serving dish, sprinkle with cilantro, and serve.

1 teaspoon canola oil

½ teaspoon cumin seeds

½ teaspoon aniseed

¼ teaspoon fenugreek seeds

2 medium tomatoes, coarsely chopped

¾ teaspoon paprika

¼ teaspoon turmeric

½ teaspoon salt (or to taste)

3 medium potatoes, boiled, peeled, and cut into large 1½-inch pieces

1 teaspoon dried fenugreek leaves

1½ cups water

1 tablespoon finely chopped fresh cilantro

NUTRITIONAL FACTS: (PER ⅔-CUP SERVING)

Calories: 68   Carbohydrates: 12 g   Cholesterol: 0 mg
Fat: 1.6 g   Fiber: <1 g   Protein: 1.6 g   Sodium: 200 mg

SUGGESTED ACCOMPANIMENTS

Spinach Yogurt Salad (page 62), Ginger Chicken (page 147), and Spicy Yellow Rice (page 79).

Mixed Vegetable Curry

Palak aur Baingan ki Sabzi

Yield: *4 servings*

¼ cup dry yellow split peas

4 cups thoroughly washed coarsely chopped spinach (6 ounces)

1 small eggplant, stem removed and cut into chunks

½ small green pepper, cut into 1-inch pieces

½ cup ½-inch cauliflower florets

3 small red radishes, quartered

1 medium carrot, peeled and cut into ½-inch pieces

1 medium potato, peeled and coarsely chopped

1 small yellow onion, coarsely chopped

1 teaspoon peeled, grated ginger

1 small green chile pepper, coarsely chopped

1½ cups water

1 teaspoon ground coriander

½ teaspoon ground cumin

½ teaspoon black pepper

½ teaspoon salt (or to taste)

1 teaspoon canola oil

½ teaspoon black or yellow mustard seeds

¼ teaspoon turmeric

1 tablespoon lemon juice

1 tablespoon finely chopped fresh cilantro

A wonderful, nutritious, yet easy-to-prepare vegetable curry. Spinach and eggplant are the only required vegetables; the remaining choices are up to you. By simply adding 2 cups of water, you can serve this dish as a soup.

1. Pick through the dried peas for any grit or debris, then place them in a strainer and rinse thoroughly. Transfer the peas to a medium-sized pot along with 1½ cups water. Soak for 2 hours.

2. Place the pot with the peas and their soaking water over high heat and bring to a boil. Reduce the heat to medium, and cook loosely covered for 15 minutes, stirring occasionally.

3. Add the spinach, eggplant, green pepper, cauliflower, radishes, carrot, potato, onion, ginger, chile pepper, and water. Continue to cook another 30 minutes. As the vegetables cook, stir them occasionally, and mash them against the sides of the pot with the back of a spoon.

4. Sprinkle the ground coriander, ground cumin, black pepper, and salt on the vegetables. Stir well and continue cooking and mashing the vegetables.

5. Place the oil in a small skillet over medium heat. When the oil is hot, add the mustard seeds. Cover the skillet with a splatter guard and allow the seeds to pop. When the seeds have finished popping (within 30 seconds), add the turmeric. Add this tempered oil to the vegetable mixture, and continue cooking another 10 minutes.

6. Stir in the lemon juice, then transfer the mixture to a serving bowl. Garnish with cilantro and serve hot.

NUTRITIONAL FACTS: (PER ⅔-CUP SERVING)

Calories: 92   Carbohydrates: 16.3 g   Cholesterol: 0 mg
Fat: 1.9 g   Protein: 4.4 g   Fiber: 2 g   Sodium: 344 mg

SUGGESTED ACCOMPANIMENTS

Cucumber Tomato Salad (page 57) and plain boiled rice.

Sweet~and~Sour Okra Curry

Bhindi ki Sabzi

The tamarind pulp adds a wonderful tang to this dish. It also prevents the okra from becoming sticky as it cooks.

1. Spray a medium-sized saucepan with vegetable cooking spray. Add the oil and place over medium heat. When the oil is hot, add the mustard seeds. Cover the pan with a splatter guard and allow the mustard seeds to pop. When the seeds have finished popping (within 30 seconds), add the turmeric and chile, and fry a few seconds.

2. Add the onion and stir-fry about 2 minutes until light golden brown. Add the okra, tamarind pulp, and water. Cook uncovered, while stirring occasionally, for about 20 minutes, or until the okra is tender.

3. Stir in the ground coriander, ground cumin, and salt. Mix well and cook another 5 minutes.

4. Transfer to a serving dish, garnish with coconut, and serve warm.

NUTRITIONAL FACTS: (PER ⅔-CUP SERVING)

Calories: 51   Carbohydrates: 7 g   Cholesterol: 0 mg
Fat: 2.1 g   Fiber: 3 g   Protein: 1.2 g   Sodium: 311 mg

SUGGESTED ACCOMPANIMENTS

Sprouted Mung Bean Curry (page 140) and Honey Wheat Flatbread (page 86).

Yield: *4 servings*

1½ teaspoons canola oil

½ teaspoon black or yellow mustard seeds

¼ teaspoon turmeric

1 medium green chile, halved lengthwise

1 medium yellow onion, coarsely chopped

2 cups fresh or frozen okra, cut into ½-inch pieces

1 teaspoon tamarind pulp dissolved in 1 tablespoon warm water*

1 cup water

1 teaspoon ground coriander

½ teaspoon ground cumin

½ teaspoon salt (or to taste)

1 tablespoon grated coconut

*Can substitute 2 tablespoons lemon juice for the dissolved tamarind

Potatoes and Peas

Aloo Mattar

Yield: *6 servings*

1 teaspoon canola oil

½ teaspoon cumin seeds

½ teaspoon paprika

¼ teaspoon turmeric

2 cups frozen green peas

3 medium potatoes, boiled, peeled, and cut into 1-inch cubes

1 teaspoon ground cumin

2 teaspoons dried fenugreek leaves (optional)

1 teaspoon fresh mint, chopped (optional)

3 teaspoons lemon juice

¾ teaspoon salt (or to taste)

1 teaspoon finely chopped fresh cilantro

Our kids love this peas and potato combination, which is quick, easy, and economical to make.

1. Spray a medium-sized nonstick skillet with vegetable cooking spray. Add the oil and place over medium heat. When the oil is hot, add the cumin seeds. Fry a few seconds until the seeds begin to sizzle, then add the paprika, turmeric, and peas. Stir well, reduce the heat to low, and simmer covered for 1 minute to cook the peas.

2. Add the remaining ingredients, except the cilantro, and increase the heat to high. Stir well. Cook for 2 minutes until the ingredients are heated through.

3. Transfer to a serving dish, sprinkle with cilantro, and enjoy warm.

NUTRITIONAL FACTS: (PER ⅔-CUP SERVING)

Calories: 92   Carbohydrates: 17.5 g   Cholesterol: 0 mg
Fat: 1 g   Fiber: 2 g   Protein: 3.8 g   Sodium: 294 mg

SUGGESTED ACCOMPANIMENTS

Banana Yogurt Salad (page 52) and Spinach Flatbread (page 91).

Rice~Stuffed Green Peppers

Bhari Mirchi

This unusual combination of vegetables and rice has a tangy flavor. The original recipe calls for pan-frying the stuffed peppers, but we have found that baking eliminates unnecessary fat while preserving taste.

1. Slice the tops off the green peppers and set aside. Remove and discard the seeds from the peppers. Stand the hollowed peppers and their tops upright in a 4-quart saucepan. Add 1 inch of water and bring to a boil. Cover the pot, reduce the heat to medium, and cook for 5 minutes, or until the peppers are just tender. Remove and cool completely.

2. Bring the water to boil in a small saucepan. Add the peas, reduce the heat to medium, and cook uncovered for 30 to 60 seconds, or until the peas are just tender. Drain and set aside.

3. Preheat the oven to 350°F.

4. Place the rice in a large bowl along with the coriander, cumin, paprika, salt, tomato, cilantro, salsa (if using), and peas. Mix well.

5. Spoon the filling into the peppers. Top with mozzarella (if using), and cover with the pepper caps. Place the stuffed peppers in an 8-x-8-inch casserole dish, and lightly coat with cooking spray.

6. Bake uncovered for 10 to 15 minutes, until the peppers begin to brown and the filling is heated through.

7. Serve hot.

Yield: *4 servings*

4 medium green bell peppers

½ cup frozen green peas

½ cup water

⅔ cup cooked basmati rice

1 teaspoon ground coriander

½ teaspoon ground cumin

½ teaspoon paprika

¼ teaspoon salt (or to taste)

1 medium tomato, coarsely chopped

1 teaspoon finely chopped fresh cilantro

¼ cup Mexican salsa (optional)

¼ cup grated fat-free mozzarella cheese (optional)

NUTRITIONAL FACTS: (PER PEPPER)

Calories: 161   Carbohydrates: 15 g   Cholesterol: 0
Fat: 0.7 g   Fiber: 3 g   Protein: 5.3 g   Sodium: 153 mg

SUGGESTED ACCOMPANIMENTS

Lamb with Poppy Seeds (page 160) and Raised Indian Flatbread (page 92).

Sautéed Cauliflower with Green Peas

Flower ki Sabzi

Yield: *4 servings*

1 teaspoon canola oil

¼ teaspoon black or yellow mustard seeds

½ teaspoon cumin seeds

¼ teaspoon turmeric

2½ cups cauliflower florets (½-inch)

½ cup frozen peas

½ teaspoon ground coriander

½ teaspoon ground cumin

¼ teaspoon salt (or to taste)

1 tablespoon finely chopped fresh cilantro

We often double this recipe to ensure there will be enough left over to stuff into sandwiches the next day.

1. Spray a medium-sized nonstick wok or skillet with vegetable cooking spray. Add the oil and place over medium heat. When the oil is hot, add the mustard seeds. Cover the wok with a splatter guard and allow the seeds to pop.

2. When the seeds have finished popping, (within 30 seconds), add the cumin seeds and turmeric. Fry a few seconds until the seeds begin to sizzle, then toss in the cauliflower and stir-fry 2 to 3 minutes until the cauliflower begins to soften.

3. Stir in the peas and 2 tablespoons water, and reduce the heat to medium-low. Cook, covered, about 10 minutes, stirring occasionally. (Add a tablespoon or two of water as needed to prevent the cauliflower from sticking to the wok.)

4. Sprinkle with ground coriander, ground cumin, and salt. Mix well, cover, and cook another 5 minutes, or until the cauliflower is tender.

5. Transfer to a serving dish, sprinkle with cilantro, and serve hot.

NUTRITIONAL FACTS (PER ⅔-CUP SERVING)

Calories: 40   Carbohydrates: 5.9 g   Cholesterol: 0 mg
Fat: 1.3 g   Fiber: 2 g   Protein: 2.4 g   Sodium: 195 mg

SUGGESTED ACCOMPANIMENTS

Smoked Eggplant Salad (page 61) and Herbed Onion Flatbread (page 88).

Spinach with Cheese

Palak Paneer

This is one of the most popular dishes served in Indian restaurants. We have replaced the paneer—high-fat fried cheese—with tofu, which absorbs the flavor of the spinach and spices beautifully.

Yield: *3 servings*

10-ounce package frozen chopped spinach

1 teaspoon canola oil

½ teaspoon cumin seeds

6 ounces extra-firm lite tofu, cut into ½-inch pieces

¼ teaspoon salt (or to taste)

1. Cook spinach according to package directions. Cool and blend in a food processor.

2. Spray a medium-sized nonstick skillet with vegetable cooking spray. Add the oil and place over medium heat. When the oil is hot, add the cumin seeds. Fry a few seconds until the seeds begin to sizzle, then add the tofu, and stir-fry for 2 minutes.

3. Stir in the spinach and salt. Cook, stirring occasionally, for about 5 minutes.

4. Transfer to a serving dish and enjoy warm.

NUTRITIONAL FACTS (PER ⅔-CUP SERVING)

Calories: 61   Carbohydrates: 3 g   Cholesterol: 0 mg
Fat: 2.2 g   Fiber: 2 g   Protein: 6.3 g   Sodium: 379 mg

SUGGESTED ACCOMPANIMENTS

Carrot Yogurt Salad (page 54) and Raised Indian Flatbread (page 92).

Spinach with Potatoes

Aloo Palak

Yield: *5 servings*

1 teaspoon canola oil

½ teaspoon cumin seeds

½ teaspoon turmeric

2 small dried red chile peppers

1 medium yellow onion, finely chopped

2 medium potatoes, boiled, peeled, and cut into ½-inch cubes

10 cups thoroughly washed, chopped fresh spinach (about 20 ounces), packed

½ teaspoon ground cumin

½ teaspoon ground coriander

¼ teaspoon salt (or to taste)

This mild-tasting dish is a great way to prepare nutritious spinach. Our kids love it.

1. Spray a medium-sized nonstick wok or skillet with vegetable cooking spray. Add the oil and place over medium heat. When the oil is hot, add the cumin seeds. Fry a few seconds until the seeds begin to sizzle, then add the turmeric, chile peppers, onion, and 1 tablespoon water. Cover and cook, stirring occasionally, until the onion is pale and translucent. (Add a tablespoon or two of water as needed to prevent the onion from sticking to the skillet.)

2. Toss in the potatoes and mix well. Add the spinach and reduce the heat to medium-low. Cover and cook for 5 to 7 minutes, or until the spinach is tender.

3. Add the ground cumin, ground coriander, and salt. Mix well.

4. Transfer to a serving bowl and enjoy warm.

NUTRITIONAL FACTS: (PER ⅔-CUP SERVING)

Calories: 78   Carbohydrates: 16.9 g   Cholesterol: 0 mg
Fat: 1.4 g   Fiber: 4 g   Protein: 4.4 g   Sodium: 206 mg

SUGGESTED ACCOMPANIMENTS

Mixed Legumes (page 129), Easy Tandoori Fish (page 167), and Pumpkin Flatbread (page 90).

Stir~Fried Baby Corn

Makai ki Subzi

This aromatic stir-fried vegetable dish is quick and easy to prepare.

Yield: *4 servings*

1. Spray a large nonstick skillet with vegetable cooking spray. Add the oil and place over medium heat.

2. When the oil is hot, add the mustard seeds. Cover the skillet with a splatter guard and allow the seeds to pop. When the seeds have finished popping (within 30 seconds), add the turmeric, curry leaves, onion, and 1 tablespoon water. Cover and cook, stirring occasionally, until the onion is pale and translucent. (Add a tablespoon or two of water as needed to prevent the onion from sticking to the skillet.)

3. Stir in the ginger, then add the corn and tomato. Mix well.

4. Add the ground cumin, ground coriander, salt, and lemon juice. Mix well, cover, and steam for 30 seconds, or until the ingredients are heated through.

5. Transfer to a serving bowl, garnish with cilantro, and enjoy warm.

½ teaspoon canola oil

¼ teaspoon black or yellow mustard seeds

¼ teaspoon turmeric

3 curry leaves

1 medium yellow onion, thinly sliced

1 teaspoon peeled, julienned ginger

2 cans (14 ounces each) baby corn, drained and cut in half crosswise

1 medium tomato, finely chopped

½ teaspoon ground cumin

1 teaspoon ground coriander

½ teaspoon salt (or to taste)

1 teaspoon lemon juice

2 teaspoons finely chopped fresh cilantro

NUTRITIONAL FACTS: (PER ⅔-CUP SERVING)

Calories: 45   Carbohydrates: 11.5 g   Cholesterol: 0 mg
Fat: 0.7 g   Fiber: 2.2 g   Protein: 1.8 g   Sodium: 301 mg

SUGGESTED ACCOMPANIMENTS

Black Garbanzo Bean Curry (page 125) and Honey Wheat Flatbread (page 86).

Stir-Fried Broccoli

Broccoli Sabzi

Yield: *4 servings*

1 teaspoon canola oil

1 medium yellow onion, thinly sliced

6 cups broccoli florets (1 inch)

½ teaspoon salt (or to taste)

½ teaspoon ground cumin

1 teaspoon lemon juice

This quick and easy-to-prepare stir-fried vegetable dish tastes like a crunchy salad.

1. Spray a medium-sized nonstick pan with vegetable cooking spray. Add the oil and place over medium heat. When the oil is hot, stir in the onion. Add 1 tablespoon water, cover, and cook, stirring occasionally, until the onion is soft and pale. (Add a tablespoon or two of water as needed to prevent the onion from sticking to the skillet.)

2. Add the broccoli and 2 tablespoons of water. Cover the skillet and steam for 5 minutes, or until the broccoli is just tender. (Add water as needed to prevent sticking.)

3. Remove from the heat, and add the salt, cumin, and lemon juice. Stir thoroughly.

4. Transfer to a serving bowl. Enjoy warm.

NUTRITIONAL FACTS: (PER ⅔-CUP SERVING)

Calories: 60   Carbohydrates: 12.7 g   Cholesterol: 0 mg
Fat: 1.8 g   Fiber: 2 g   Protein: 4.4 g   Sodium: 224 mg

SUGGESTED ACCOMPANIMENTS

Red Kidney Bean Curry (page 134) and Herbed Onion Flatbread (page 88).

Stir~Fried Cabbage with Carrots

Gajar aur Gobi ki Sabzi

The light, crunchy texture of this vegetable dish is similar to that of a raw salad. Try it with your favorite flatbread.

1. Spray a medium-sized nonstick wok with vegetable cooking spray. Add the oil and place over medium heat.

2. When the oil is hot, add the mustard seeds. Cover the wok with a splatter guard and allow the seeds to pop. When the seeds have finished popping (within 30 seconds), stir in the turmeric, then add the chile pepper, cabbage, and carrot. Stir well, cover, and cook for 2 minutes, or until the vegetables are tender yet crisp.

3. Stir in the salt, cook another 2 minutes, and then remove from heat. Drizzle with lemon juice and stir.

4. Transfer to a serving bowl, garnish with cilantro, and serve.

Yield: *4 servings*

1 teaspoon canola oil

½ teaspoon black or yellow mustard seeds

½ teaspoon turmeric

1 green chile pepper, halved lengthwise

2 cups finely shredded green cabbage

1 cup finely grated carrot

¼ teaspoon salt (or to taste)

2 tablespoons fresh lemon juice

1 tablespoon finely chopped fresh cilantro

NUTRITIONAL FACTS: (PER ⅔-CUP SERVING)

Calories: 34   Carbohydrates: 5.5 g   Cholesterol: 0 g
Fat: 1.3 g   Fiber: 1 g   Protein: 0.8 g   Sodium: 168 g

SUGGESTED ACCOMPANIMENTS

Easy Tandoori Fish (page 167) and Raised Indian Flatbread (page 92).

Stir~Fried Tofu with Green Peppers

Paneer Bhurji

Yield: *4 servings*

2 teaspoons canola oil

½ teaspoon cumin seeds

1 medium yellow onion, finely chopped

½ medium green bell pepper, finely chopped

20 ounces extra-firm lite tofu, coarsely grated

2 medium tomatoes, finely chopped

2 tablespoons ketchup

1 teaspoon sugar

½ teaspoon salt (or to taste)

½ teaspoon ground cumin

2 teaspoons finely chopped fresh cilantro

Although this dish is traditionally made with a high-fat cheese called paneer, we use tofu with equally good results.

1. Spray a medium-sized nonstick skillet with vegetable cooking spray. Add the oil and place over medium heat. When the oil is hot, add the cumin seeds. Fry a few seconds until the seeds begin to sizzle, then add the onion and 1 tablespoon water. Cover and cook, stirring occasionally, until the onion is pale and soft. (Add a tablespoon or two of water as needed to prevent the onion from sticking to the skillet.)

2. Stir in the pepper, cover, and cook for 30 seconds until lightly steamed.

3. Add the tofu, tomatoes, and ketchup, and stir well. Stir in the sugar, salt, ground cumin, and cilantro. Mix gently and continue to cook about 30 seconds until the ingredients are heated through.

4. Transfer to a serving dish and enjoy warm.

NUTRITIONAL FACTS: (PER ⅔-CUP SERVING)

Calories: 124   Carbohydrates: 13.8 g   Cholesterol: 0 mg
Fat: 4.4 g   Fiber: 1 g   Protein: 13.2 g   Sodium: 506 mg

SUGGESTED ACCOMPANIMENTS

Quick Spicy Garbanzos (page 131) and Raised Indian Flatbread (page 92).

Potato~Stuffed Green Peppers

Aloo Bhari Simla Mirch

A quick baked dish that is great to serve when entertaining.

Yield: *8 servings*

1. Preheat the oven to 350°F. Line a 9-x-13-inch baking pan with foil. Lightly spray with vegetable cooking spray and set aside.

2. Remove and discard the stems from the green peppers. Halve the peppers lengthwise and remove the seeds.

3. In a saucepan large enough to hold the peppers, bring 4 cups of water to a boil. Gently and carefully add the peppers and boil for 5 minutes, or until just tender. Transfer the peppers to paper towels and let drain.

4. Spray a medium-sized nonstick frying pan with vegetable cooking spray. Add the oil and place over medium heat. When the oil is hot, add the cumin seeds. Fry a few seconds until the seeds begin to sizzle, then add the tumeric and onion, and stir-fry until light golden brown.

5. Add the paprika, salt, and mashed potatoes. Mix well and remove from the heat. Stir in the lemon juice and allow the filling to cool.

6. Spoon equal amounts of filling into each pepper half. Arrange in the baking pan, cover with foil, and bake for 30 minutes. Uncover and continue to bake another 10 minutes until the peppers are tender and the filling is hot.

7. Transfer the peppers to a platter and serve.

4 medium green peppers

1½ teaspoons canola oil

½ teaspoon cumin seeds

½ teaspoon turmeric

1 small yellow onion, finely chopped

½ teaspoon paprika

½ teaspoon salt (or to taste)

2 cups mashed potatoes

1 teaspoon lemon juice

2 tablespoons finely chopped fresh cilantro

NUTRITIONAL FACTS: (PER STUFFED PEPPER)

Calories: 52   Carbohydrates: 10.2 g   Cholesterol: 0 mg
Fat: 1.1 g   Fiber: <1 g   Protein: 1.1 g   Sodium: 148 mg

SUGGESTED ACCOMPANIMENTS

Mushrooms and Black-Eyed Peas (page 130) and Spicy Yellow Rice (page 79).

Sweet~and~Sour Eggplant with Potatoes

Ambat Goud Vangi Bhaji

Yield: *4 servings*

1 teaspoon canola oil

¼ teaspoon black or yellow mustard seeds

⅛ teaspoon turmeric

1 medium yellow onion, finely chopped

2 medium potatoes

½ medium eggplant

1 teaspoon paprika

½ teaspoon salt (or to taste)

¼ teaspoon ground cumin

½ teaspoon tamarind pulp dissolved in 1 tablespoon warm water*

1½ tablespoons brown sugar

¼ teaspoon homemade garam masala (page 133) or commercial variety, (optional)

1 teaspoon finely chopped fresh cilantro

*Can substitute 2–3 tablespoons lemon juice for the dissolved tamarind.

The sauce for this vegetable medley should be slightly sweet, a bit tangy, and quite thin.

1. Peel and cut the potatoes into ½-inch cubes and submerge in a bowl of cold water. Peel and cut the eggplant into ½-inch pieces and set aside on paper towels.

2. Spray a medium-sized pot with vegetable cooking spray. Add the oil and place over medium heat. When the oil is hot, add the mustard seeds. Cover the pan with a splatter guard and allow the seeds to pop. When the seeds have finished popping (within 30 seconds), add the turmeric and stir-fry a few seconds.

3. Add the onion and cover the pot. Cook, stirring occasionally, until the onion is soft and pale. (Add a tablespoon or two of water as needed to prevent the onion from sticking to the pot.)

4. Drain the potatoes and reserve 1½ cups of the soaking water. (You may need to add more water to achieve this measurement.) Set aside. Add the drained potatoes and 1 tablespoon of water to the pot. Reduce the heat to medium-low, cover the pot, and steam the potatoes for 8 to 10 minutes, or until tender.

5. Toss in the eggplant, paprika, salt, and cumin, and increase the heat to medium. Stir-fry for 30 seconds, then add the reserved potato water, and increase the heat to high. Bring to a boil, then reduce the heat to medium-low. Simmer covered for 3 to 4 minutes, or until the eggplant is tender. Add the tamarind and sugar. Mix well, simmer another minute or two, then remove from the heat.

6. Sprinkle with garam masala (if using) and cilantro. Mix well and transfer to serving dish. Enjoy warm.

NUTRITIONAL FACTS:(PER ⅔-CUP SERVING)

Calories: 94.5   Carbohydrates: 22.6 g   Cholesterol: 0 mg

Fat: 1.3 g   Fiber: 1.6 g   Protein: 2 g   Sodium: 292 mg

SUGGESTED ACCOMPANIMENTS

Carrot Salad (page 65) and Rice and Lentil Pilaf (page 75).

Zippy Corn

Makai ki Subzi

Enjoy this tasty side dish hot or cold. It's perfect to serve at your next barbecue.

1. Chop the scallions, keeping the green and white parts separate. Set aside.

2. Spray a medium-sized nonstick pan with vegetable cooking spray. Add the oil and place over medium heat. When the oil is hot, add the cumin seeds and tumeric. Fry a few seconds until the seeds begin to sizzle, then add the white part of the scallions. Stir-fry 30 seconds.

3. Add the corn, coriander, ground cumin, and water. Bring to a boil, then reduce the heat to low. Simmer uncovered for 8 to 10 minutes, or until most of the water has evaporated and the corn is cooked. Stir in the salt, sugar, and green part of the scallions. Remove from the heat.

4. Transfer to a serving dish, sprinkle with cilantro, and serve warm.

Yield: *6 servings*

6 scallions

2 teaspoons canola oil

1 teaspoon cumin seeds

½ teaspoon turmeric

6 cups frozen corn kernels

1 teaspoon ground coriander

½ teaspoon ground cumin

½ cup water

½ teaspoon salt (or to taste)

¼ teaspoon granulated white sugar

2 teaspoons finely chopped fresh cilantro

NUTRITIONAL FACTS: (PER ⅔-CUP SERVING)
Calories: 130   Carbohydrates: 34.5 g   Cholesterol: 0 mg
Fat: 1.4 g   Fiber: 2 g   Protein: 4.2 g   Sodium: 100 mg

SUGGESTED ACCOMPANIMENTS
Red Kidney Bean Curry (page 134) and Stir-Fried Cabbage Rice (page 82).

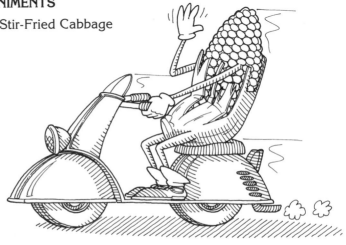

Sweet-and-Sour Pumpkin Curry

Kadoo ki Sabzi

Yield: *3 servings*

1 teaspoon canola oil

¼ teaspoon black or yellow mustard seeds

¼ teaspoon turmeric

½ teaspoon fenugreek seeds

1 pound pumpkin, unpeeled and cut into ½-inch cubes (about 2 cups)

⅓ cup water

1 teaspoon brown sugar

½ teaspoon salt (or to taste)

¼ teaspoon tamarind pulp dissolved in 1 tablespoon warm water

SPICE BLEND

1½ teaspoons sesame seeds

1½ teaspoons cumin seeds

1 tablespoon grated coconut (optional)

1 tablespoon poppy seeds

Here's an unusual way to serve pumpkin—as a zesty curry.

1. Place the spice blend ingredients in a small nonstick skillet. Place over medium heat and dry-roast while stirring frequently. Cool and place in a coffee or spice grinder. Finely grind into a dry masala. Set aside.

2. Spray a medium-sized nonstick saucepan with vegetable cooking spray. Add the oil and place over medium heat. When the oil is hot, add the mustard seeds. Cover the pan with a splatter guard and allow the seeds to pop. When the seeds have finished popping (within 30 seconds), add the turmeric, fenugreek seeds, and dry-roasted spice blend. Fry about 1 minute, or until the fenugreek seeds turn a light pink color.

3. Toss in the pumpkin and stir-fry about 2 minutes. Add the water, cover, and cook for 10 minutes, or until the pumpkin is almost cooked. Do not overcook.

4. Stir in the brown sugar, salt, and tamarind pulp. Continue cooking for another 5 minutes, or until the pumpkin is tender.

5. Transfer to a serving bowl and enjoy.

NUTRITIONAL FACTS: (PER ⅔-CUP SERVING)

Calories: 53   Carbohydrates 7.7 g   Cholesterol: 0 mg
Fat: 2.3 g   Fiber: 0 g   Protein: 0. 9 g   Sodium: 385 mg

SUGGESTED ACCOMPANIMENTS

Easy Mung Bean Curry (page 126) and Green Pea Flatbread (page 85).

Yellow Mashed Potatoes

Aloo Masala

Enjoy these unique mashed potatoes with a flatbread of your choice.

1. Peel the potatoes, cut into 1-inch cubes, and boil until just tender. Drain and set aside.

2. Spray a medium-sized nonstick wok or skillet with vegetable cooking spray. Add the oil and place over medium heat. When the oil is hot, add the mustard seeds. Cover the wok with a splatter guard and allow the seeds to pop.

3. When the seeds have finished popping (within 30 seconds), add the turmeric, chile pepper, onion, and 1 tablespoon water. Stir well, then cook covered until the onion is pale and soft. (Add a tablespoon or two of water as needed to prevent the onion from sticking to the wok.)

4. Add the peas and continue to cook another 30 seconds, while stirring.

5. Toss in the potatoes and paprika, and mix well. Add the water and bring to a boil. Cook until the all of the water has evaporated. As the potatoes cook, mash them against the sides of the wok with the back of a spoon.

6. Add the salt, cilantro, and lemon juice. Mix well.

7. Place in a serving bowl and enjoy hot.

Yield: *4 servings*

5 medium potatoes

1 teaspoon canola oil

½ teaspoon black or yellow mustard seeds

¼ teaspoon turmeric

1 dried red chile pepper

1 medium yellow onion, thinly sliced

½ cup frozen peas

¼ teaspoon paprika

1 cup water

½ teaspoon salt (or to taste)

1 teaspoon finely chopped fresh cilantro

½ teaspoon lemon juice

NUTRITIONAL FACTS: (PER ⅔-CUP SERVING)

Calories: 148   Carbohydrates: 33.7 g   Cholesterol: 0 mg
Fat: 1.3 g   Fiber: 2.2 g   Protein: 4.3 g   Sodium: 297 mg

SUGGESTED ACCOMPANIMENTS

Lentil and Spinach Curry (page 127) and Raised Indian Flatbread (page 92).

8.

Legumes for Health

Legumes are the dried peas and beans found within the hanging pods of leguminous plants. They are staples of Indian cuisine. One of the richest sources of vegetable protein, legumes can be eaten in their whole or split form. In their split form, legumes are referred to as dal. Although high in protein, legumes are lacking in one or more essential amino acids. In Indian cuisine, legumes are generally paired with a grain, such as rice or wheat, to form a complete protein dish.

Dry legumes must be cleaned and washed before they are cooked. To clean the legumes, pour them onto a large plate, then pick through them carefully, discarding any stones, empty shells, or bits of dirt. Place the legumes in a bowl or colander and rinse them under fresh running water, while rubbing them with your hand.

Once the legumes are washed, they are ready to be soaked. Place them in an appropriate sized bowl and cover them with approximately four times as much water. (The water should be at room temperature.)

Cover the bowl and allow the beans to soak on the countertop, not in the refrigerator. Soaking time will vary with each bean type. For your convenience, various soaking and cooking times for most pea and bean varieties are presented in Table 8.1 (page 124). Keep in mind that soaking cuts down on the cooking time.

Once legumes have been soaked, they are ready to be either cooked or sprouted (see Sprouting Legumes on page 138). Never discard the nutrient-rich soaking water, rather use it as part of the cooking water.

Just as soaking times vary with each legume variety, so do cooking times. Never add salt or acidic ingredients, such as tomatoes or tamarind pulp, to the water at the beginning of the cooking process. This will toughen the outer layer of the legumes, and they will not soften, no matter how long you cook them. Add such ingredients only after the legumes are thoroughly cooked and tender. As the beans cook, they will absorb most of the cooking water. If, however, an exces-

Table 8.1 Soaking and Cooking Times for Legumes

The following soaking and cooking information is based on ½-cup amounts of dried beans or peas. The figures presented below are approximate. Keep in mind that soaking and cooking times depend on how thick or thin you want the curry; other factors include pot size, heat used, and type of legume.

Legume (½ Cup)	Soaking Water	Soaking Time	Cooking Water	Cooking Time
Garbanzo beans	2 cups	12 hours or overnight	2 cups	45 minutes
Black garbanzo beans	2 cups	12 hours or overnight	1½ cups	1 hour
Red kidney beans	2 cups	12 hours or overnight	3 cups	1 hour
Whole moth beans	2 cups	12 hours or overnight	¾ cup	30 minutes
Whole mung beans	2 cups	12 hours or overnight	¾ cup	30 minutes
Whole black lentils	2 cups	12 hours or overnight	3 cups	1½ hours
Split mung beans	2 cups	2 hours	2 cups	30 minutes
Black-eyed peas	2 cups	12 hours or overnight	2 cups	40 minutes
Lentils	2 cups	2 hours	1½ cups	15 minutes
Split pigeon peas	2 cups	2 hours	1 cup	35 minutes
Yellow split peas	1½ cups	2 hours	1½ cups	30 minutes

sive amount of water remains, simply uncover the beans and cook them over medium-high heat for a few extra minutes.

Using a pressure cooker to cook certain legumes, such as split peas, pigeon peas, and lentils conveniently saves cooking time. Most Indian kitchens have at least two pressure cookers, which are regularly used for cooking dals and rice. In fact, using a pressure cooker cuts cooking time by two-thirds.

Enjoy making and serving the legume dishes presented in this chapter. All are wonderful alternatives to high-fat, high-cholesterol meat dishes. And all are delicious and satisfying enough to please everyone, even those with discriminating taste.

Black Garbanzo Bean Curry

Kala Chana

This exotic dish from northern India should be eaten warm with a flatbread of your choice.

1. Pick through the dried beans for any grit or debris, then place them in a strainer and rinse thoroughly. Transfer the beans to a medium-sized bowl along with 2 cups of water. Soak for 12 hours or overnight.

2. Drain the soaked beans, reserving the soaking water in a measuring cup. Add enough fresh water to measure 2 cups. Bring this water to boil in a medium-sized saucepan. Add the soaked beans, reduce the heat to low, and simmer loosely covered for 1 hour, or until the beans are tender. Drain the beans, reserving the stock (about 1¼ cups).

3. Spray a medium-sized nonstick wok with vegetable cooking spray. Add the oil and place over medium heat. When the oil is hot, add the garlic, ginger, and onion. Stir well, then cover and cook until the onion is translucent. (Add a tablespoon or two of stock as needed to prevent the onion from sticking to the wok.)

4. Add the tomato, increase the heat to high, and stir-fry until most of the liquid is absorbed. Reduce the heat to medium-low and add the paprika, turmeric, ground cumin, ground coriander, and salt. Stir well and add the yogurt. Continue to stir-fry until the ingredients are well-blended.

5. Add ¼ cup of the stock, 1 tablespoon at a time. Stir-fry until each tablespoon of stock is absorbed before adding the next.

6. Add the cooked beans along with the remaining stock, and bring to a boil. Reduce the heat to low and simmer 5 minutes. Transfer to a serving dish, sprinkle with cilantro, and serve.

Yield: *6 servings*

½ cup dried black garbanzo beans

1 teaspoon canola oil

2 cloves garlic, crushed

½ teaspoon peeled, grated ginger

1 small yellow onion, finely chopped

1 medium tomato, coarsely chopped

½ teaspoon paprika

¼ teaspoon turmeric

¼ teaspoon ground cumin

¼ teaspoon ground coriander

¼ teaspoon salt

1 tablespoon nonfat yogurt

1 teaspoon finely chopped fresh cilantro

NUTRITIONAL FACTS: (PER ⅔-CUP SERVING)

Calories: 158   Carbohydrates: 21 g   Cholesterol: 0 mg
Fat: 3.4 g   Fiber: 2 g   Protein: 7 g   Sodium: 216 mg

SUGGESTED ACCOMPANIMENTS:

Carrot Yogurt Salad (page 54) and Potato Flatbread (page 89).

Easy Mung Bean Curry

Mung Dal

Yield: *3 servings*

1 cup dry split, skinned mung beans

1 teaspoon canola oil

1 teaspoon cumin seeds

¼ teaspoon turmeric

2 cloves garlic, crushed

1 teaspoon ground cumin

¼ teaspoon cayenne pepper

1 teaspoon salt (or to taste)

1 tablespoon coarsely chopped fresh cilantro

Here is a great everyday curry that can be served with rice or whole wheat bread to form a complete protein dish. You can also dress it up with some chopped raw onion and tomatoes.

1. Pick through the dried beans for any grit or debris, then place them in a strainer and rinse thoroughly. Transfer the beans to a medium-sized bowl along with 4 cups of water. Soak for 2 hours.

2. Drain the soaked beans, reserving the soaking water in a measuring cup. Add enough fresh water to measure 4 cups. Set aside.

3. Spray a medium-sized saucepan with vegetable cooking spray. Add the oil and place over medium heat. When the oil is hot, add the cumin seeds, followed by the turmeric and garlic. Stir-fry a few seconds, add the soaked beans, and continue to stir-fry for 1 to 2 minutes.

4. Add the reserved soaking water and bring to a boil. Reduce the heat to medium-low, cover the pan loosely, and cook, stirring occasionally, for 30 minutes, or until the beans are tender.

5. Add the ground cumin, cayenne pepper, and salt. Mix well and continue to cook another 5 minutes.

6. Transfer to a serving dish, garnish with cilantro, and serve hot.

NUTRITIONAL FACTS: (PER ⅔-CUP SERVING)

Calories: 246   Carbohydrates: 39.9 g   Cholesterol: 0 mg
Fat: 2.3 g   Fiber: 3 g   Protein: 16.3 g   Sodium: 401 mg

SUGGESTED ACCOMPANIMENTS

Smoked Eggplant Salad (page 61) and Fenugreek Flatbread (page 84).

Lentil and Spinach Curry

Masoor aur Palak ka Saag

This simple yet tasty curry dish combines lentils with fresh spinach.

Yield: *3 servings*

1. Pick through the lentils for any grit or debris, then place them in a strainer and rinse thoroughly. Transfer the beans to a medium-sized pot along with 2 cups of water. Soak for 2 hours.

2. Place the pot with the lentils and their soaking water over medium heat. Cook loosely covered for 15 minutes, or until the lentils are tender (do not overcook).

3. Spray a large saucepan with vegetable cooking spray. Add the oil and place over medium heat. When the oil is hot, add the cumin seeds, followed by the chile and turmeric. Add the spinach, ginger, and 2 tablespoons of water. Cover the pan and cook about 10 minutes, or until the spinach is tender.

4. Add the cooked lentils and salt to the spinach and stir. Cook uncovered for 5 minutes. Using the back of a large spoon, lightly mash the lentils against the sides of the pan.

5. Stir the lemon juice into the mixture and transfer to a serving bowl. Enjoy hot.

½ cup lentils

1 teaspoon canola oil

½ teaspoon cumin seeds

1 small green chile, finely chopped

¼ teaspoon turmeric

8 ounces thoroughly washed fresh spinach, coarsely chopped

½ teaspoon peeled, grated ginger

½ teaspoon salt (or to taste)

1 tablespoon lemon juice

NUTRITIONAL FACTS: (PER ⅔-CUP SERVING)

Calories: 125   Carbohydrates: 19.3 g   Cholesterol: 0 mg
Fat: 1.6 g   Fiber: 2.4 g   Protein: 9.1 g   Sodium: 384 mg

SUGGESTED ACCOMPANIMENTS

Spicy Yellow Rice (page 79) and a Cucumber Tomato Salad (page 57).

Whole Black Lentils

Makhani Dal

Yield: *3 servings*

⅓ cup whole black lentils

2 cloves garlic, crushed

½ teaspoon peeled, grated ginger

1 medium yellow onion, finely chopped

1 medium tomato, coarsely chopped

1 cup water

2 tablespoons plain nonfat yogurt

1 teaspoon ground coriander

1 teaspoon ground cumin

¼ teaspoon homemade garam masala (page 133) or commercial variety

½ teaspoon canola oil

¼ teaspoon cumin seeds

½ teaspoon paprika

2 tablespoons finely chopped fresh cilantro

1 tablespoon half-and-half (optional)

This creamy legume dish, which is popular in northern India, is a bit heavy on the stomach. A small portion served with steamed rice is perfect. We find this dish to be even more flavorful the day after it is made.

1. Pick through the dried lentils for any grit or debris, then place them in a strainer and rinse thoroughly. Transfer to a medium-sized bowl along with 2 cups of water. Soak for 12 hours or overnight.

2. Drain the soaked lentils, reserving the soaking water in a measuring cup. Add enough fresh water to measure 2 cups. Bring this water to boil in a medium-sized saucepan. Add the soaked beans, garlic, ginger, and half of the onion. Reduce the heat to medium low, and simmer, loosely covered, for 1 to 1½ hours, or until the water is absorbed and the lentils are tender.

3. Add the tomato and 1 cup water. Continue to simmer over medium heat about 10 minutes, or until the legumes are creamy.

4. Increase the heat to medium-high and add the yogurt, ground coriander, ground cumin, and garam masala. Bring to a boil and remove from the heat. Set aside.

5. Spray a small nonstick skillet with vegetable cooking spray. Add the oil and place over medium heat. When the oil is hot, add the cumin seeds, paprika, and the remaining onion. Stir-fry until the onion is deep golden brown. Add this mixture to the cooked dal.

6. Transfer the legumes to a serving dish, sprinkle with cilantro, and drizzle with half-and-half (if using).

NUTRITIONAL FACTS: (PER ⅔-CUP SERVING)

Calories: 76   Carbohydrates: 21.4 g   Cholesterol: 0 mg
Fat: 1 g   Fiber: <1 g   Protein: 5 g   Sodium: 350 mg

SUGGESTED ACCOMPANIMENTS

Beet Yogurt Salad (page 53) and Fenugreek Flatbread (page 84).

Mixed Legumes

Dal

The following protein-packed recipe includes four different kinds of legumes.

1. Pick through all of the dried legumes for any grit or debris, then place them in a strainer and rinse thoroughly. Transfer the legumes to a medium-sized bowl along with 2 cups of water. Soak for 2 hours.

2. Drain the soaked beans, reserving the soaking water in a measuring cup. Add enough fresh water to measure 2 cups. Place the water in a medium-sized pot and bring to a boil. Add the beans, reduce the heat to low, and simmer loosely covered for 30 to 35 minutes, or until most of the water has been absorbed and the beans are tender.

3. Remove the pot from the heat, and coarsely mash the beans with the back of a spoon against the sides of the pan. Stir in 1 cup of water and set aside.

4. Spray a medium nonstick wok with vegetable cooking spray. Add the oil and place over medium heat. When the oil is hot, add the cumin seeds. Fry a few seconds until the seeds begin to sizzle, then add the jalapeño pepper (if using), turmeric, garlic, and onion. Reduce the heat to medium-low and cook covered until the onions are pale and translucent. (Add a tablespoon or two of water as needed to prevent the onion from sticking to the wok.)

5. Add the paprika and tomato. Increase the heat to high and stir-fry the tomato until well-cooked. If the tomato begins to stick to the wok, reduce the heat. Add the cooked beans, stir, and bring to a boil. Boil for 30 seconds, then remove from the heat. Stir in the salt, cilantro, and lemon juice.

6. Transfer to a serving bowl.

Yield: *5 servings*

¼ cup yellow split peas

1 tablespoon split pigeon peas

1 tablespoon split, skinned mung beans

1 tablespoon lentils

1 teaspoon canola oil

½ teaspoon cumin seeds

½ medium jalapeño pepper (optional)

¼ teaspoon turmeric

2 cloves garlic, crushed

½ small yellow onion, thinly sliced

¼ teaspoon paprika

1 medium tomato, chopped

¼ teaspoon salt (or to taste)

1 tablespoon finely chopped fresh cilantro

¼ teaspoon lemon juice

NUTRITIONAL FACTS: (PER ⅔-CUP SERVING)
Calories: 86   Carbohydrates: 10 g   Cholesterol: 0 mg
Fat: 1.6 g   Fiber: <1 g   Protein: 4.4 g   Sodium: 128 mg

SUGGESTED ACCOMPANIMENTS

Quick Stir-Fried Rice with Vegetables (page 71) and Spinach Yogurt Salad (page 62).

Mushrooms and Black-Eyed Peas

Kumbh aur Lobia ki Sabzi

Yield: *4 servings*

1 teaspoon canola oil

½ teaspoon cumin seeds

1 medium yellow onion, finely chopped

1 clove garlic, crushed

⅛ teaspoon turmeric

1 cup sliced button mushrooms

16-ounce can black-eyed peas, undrained

1 large tomato, coarsely chopped

½ teaspoon ground cinnamon

1 teaspoon curry powder

¼ teaspoon black pepper

¼ cup water

1 teaspoon lemon juice

Mushrooms and peas form a pleasing combination of flavors in this delicious side dish. It's perfect served over boiled rice and accompanied by a yogurt-based salad. As canned peas are used, this dish is quick to prepare.

1. Spray a medium-sized nonstick saucepan with vegetable cooking spray. Add the oil and place over medium heat. When the oil is hot, add the cumin seeds, onion, garlic, and turmeric. Stir-fry until the onions are golden brown. (Add a tablespoon or two of water as needed to prevent the onions from sticking to the pan.)

2. Add the mushrooms and peas. Stir well and cook covered for 5 minutes over medium heat.

3. Stir in the tomato, cinnamon, curry powder, black pepper, and water. Continue to cook about 10 minutes, or until the mushrooms are cooked.

4. Drizzle with lemon juice, stir well, and transfer to a serving bowl.

NUTRITIONAL FACTS: (PER ⅔-CUP SERVING)

Calories: 104   Carbohydrates: 18.5 g   Cholesterol: 0 mg
Fat: 1.3 g   Fiber: 3 g   Protein: 5.8 g   Sodium: 339 mg

SUGGESTED ACCOMPANIMENTS

Raised Indian Flatbread (page 92) Indian Potato Salad (page 58), and plain boiled rice.

Quick Spicy Garbanzos

Chole

This quick, colorful one-skillet dish is traditionally eaten with plain yogurt and deep-fried bread called bhatoora or puri.

1. Spray a medium-sized nonstick skillet with vegetable cooking spray. Add the oil and place over medium heat. When the oil is hot, add the garlic, then the onion. Cover and cook about 5 to 7 minutes, or until the onion is pale and translucent. (Add a tablespoon or two of water as needed to prevent the onion from sticking to the skillet.)

2. Add the ketchup and tomato, and stir-fry for 1 minute. Increase the heat to high and bring the mixture to a boil, stirring often. Cover the skillet, reduce the heat to medium, and cook, stirring frequently, until the tomato is well-cooked.

3. Uncover and continue to cook until most of the liquid has evaporated. Add the ground cumin, ground coriander, salt, turmeric, paprika, sugar, and chat masala (if using). Stir-fry for 30 seconds.

4. Add the beans and garam masala. Bring to a boil, then reduce the heat to low and simmer uncovered about 5 minutes, until the sauce starts to thicken.

5. Transfer to a serving bowl, garnish with cilantro, and enjoy warm.

Yield: *3 servings*

- 1 teaspoon canola oil
- 1 clove garlic, crushed
- ½ medium yellow onion, thinly sliced
- 1 tablespoon no-salt added ketchup
- 1 large tomato, finely chopped
- 1 teaspoon ground cumin
- 1 teaspoon ground coriander
- ¼ teaspoon salt (or to taste)
- ½ teaspoon turmeric
- ¼ teaspoon paprika
- ½ teaspoon granulated white sugar
- ½ teaspoon chat masala (optional)
- 15-ounce can garbanzo beans, undrained
- ¼ teaspoon homemade garam masala (page 133) or commercial variety
- 1 tablespoon finely chopped fresh cilantro

NUTRITIONAL FACTS: (PER ⅔-CUP SERVING)

Calories: 212   Carbohydrates: 32.6 g   Cholesterol: 0 mg
Fat: 3.4 g   Fiber: 6 g   Protein: 8 g   Sodium : 640 mg

SUGGESTED ACCOMPANIMENTS

Raised Indian Flatbread (page 92) and Cucumber Yogurt Salad (page 56).

Making Your Own Masala

Masalas—special wet or dry spice blends—add flavor and aroma to a number of traditional Indian foods. Generally, a masala is added to a dish during the actual cooking process, although some varieties, like garam masala, are added to a dish once the cooking is completed. You can find a number of different dry masala blends in Indian markets, gourmet shops, and most major grocery stores. You can also make your own. Recipes for the most common varieties are provided below. Stored in an airtight jar or container and kept in a cool, dry place, masalas will stay fresh up to six months.

Sambar Masala

Yield: ¾ cup

10 fresh curry leaves, dried*

3 tablespoons coriander seeds

1 tablespoon cumin seeds

½ teaspoon whole black peppercorns

½ teaspoon black or yellow mustard seeds

½ tablespoon fenugreek seeds

2 tablespoons dry yellow split peas

2 tablespoons dry split, skinned black lentils

2 tablespoons long-grain white rice

½ teaspoon turmeric

1 teaspoon cayenne pepper (or to taste)

* To dry the fresh curry leaves, first wash them, then pat dry. Line a medium-sized plate with paper towels. Place the curry leaves on the plate and allow them to air dry for a couple of days until they become dry and crisp.

A hot blend of spices, sambar masala is used mainly in southern Indian dishes, especially legume-based curries. You can use ground coriander and ground cumin instead of the whole seeds. Simply add them in Step 4.

1. Place a small nonstick frying pan over medium heat. Add the coriander seeds and dry-roast them until light pink. Transfer to a medium-sized bowl.

2. Continue to individually dry-roast the cumin seeds, black peppercorns, mustard seeds, fenugreek seeds, yellow split peas, black lentils, and rice, and add them to the bowl.

3. Allow the roasted ingredients to cool completely, then place them along with the curry leaves in a coffee or spice grinder, and grind into a fine powder. Transfer to a bowl, add the turmeric and cayenne pepper, and mix well.

4. Spoon the masala into a clean, airtight jar or container, and store in a cool, dry place.

5. Use within 6 months.

Garam Masala

A classic blend of hot and aromatic spices, garam masala is generally sprinkled on top of prepared dishes, especially those from northern India.

1. Place all of the ingredients in a bowl and mix well.

2. Spoon the masala into a clean, airtight jar or container, and store in a cool, dry place.

3. Use within 6 months.

Yield: 1/2 cup

2 tablespoons ground coriander

2 tablespoons ground cumin

2 teaspoons ground cinnamon

2 teaspoons ground cloves

2 teaspoons ground bay leaves

1/2 teaspoon ground nutmeg

1/2 teaspoon ground black pepper

1/2 teaspoon ground dry ginger

Tandoori Masala

Tandoori masala is generally blended with non-fat yogurt, crushed garlic, and grated ginger into a flavorful paste that is used to marinate meat, poultry, and seafood that is to be roasted in a tandoor.

1. Place all of the ingredients in a bowl and mix well.

2. Spoon the masala into a clean, airtight jar or container, and store in a cool, dry place.

3. Use within 6 months.

Yield: 1/2 cup

3 tablespoons ground coriander

3 tablespoons paprika

1 1/2 teaspoons ground cumin

1/2 teaspoon ground, dried fenugreek leaves

1 teaspoon salt

1/8 teaspoon nutmeg

1/8 teaspoon ground bay leaves

1/8 teaspoon dry ginger

1/8 teaspoon ground cloves

1/8 teaspoon garlic powder

1 pinch cinnamon

Red Kidney Bean Curry

Rajmah

Yield: *3 servings*

½ cup dry red kidney beans

½ teaspoon peeled, grated ginger

3 cloves garlic, crushed

1 teaspoon canola oil

1 small yellow onion, finely chopped

1 small tomato, finely chopped

½ teaspoon salt (or to taste)

½ teaspoon paprika

¼ teaspoon ground cumin

½ teaspoon ground coriander

¼ teaspoon homemade garam masala (page 133) or commercial variety

1 teaspoon lemon juice

1 tablespoon finely chopped fresh cilantro

This flavor-packed curry is from the northern part of India. We usually double the recipe and freeze half to enjoy at another time.

1. Pick through the dried beans for any grit or debris, then place them in a strainer and rinse thoroughly. Transfer the beans to a medium-sized saucepan along with 2 cups of water. Soak for 12 hours or overnight.

2. Bring the beans, soaking water, ginger, garlic, and another 2½ cups of water to a gentle boil over high heat. Reduce the heat to medium and cook loosely covered, stirring occasionally, for 1 hour. Remove from the heat, stir, and cover the pan tightly for 30 minutes.

3. Spray a medium-sized nonstick pan with vegetable cooking spray. Add the oil and place over medium heat. When the oil is hot, add the onion and stir-fry until golden brown.

4. Stir in the tomato, kidney beans, and ½ cup of water. Add the salt, paprika, cumin, coriander, and garam masala. Stir and bring to a boil. Reduce heat to low and simmer uncovered about 5 minutes. Stir in the lemon juice.

5. Transfer to a serving bowl, garnish with cilantro, and serve warm.

NUTRITIONAL FACTS: (PER ⅔-CUP SERVING)

Calories: 146   Carbohydrates: 23.9 g   Cholesterol: 0 mg
Fat: 2.1 g   Fiber: 2 g   Protein: 8.3 g   Sodium: 401 mg

SUGGESTED ACCOMPANIMENTS

Stir-Fried Cabbage with Carrots (page 115) and Fenugreek Flatbread (page 84).

*Center Left: Mushrooms and
Black-Eyed Peas (page 130)
Bottom Right: Easy Tandoori Fish
(page 167)
Bottom Left: Spinach with Cheese
(page 111)*

Top: Cilantro Chutney (page 181)
Top Right: Honey Wheat Flatbread
(page 86)
Left: Mixed Vegetable Curry
(page 106)
Bottom Right: Stir-Fried Shrimp
with Scallions (page 173)

Top: Spinach Yogurt Salad (page 62)
with pita bread
Right: Green Pea Pilaf (page 70)
Left: Shrimp Tomato Curry
(page 171) with Spicy Mango
Chutney (page 180)

Top: Indian Chicken Salad
(page 26)
Center: Red Kidney Bean Curry
(page 134)
Bottom: Cucumber Tomato Salad
(page 57)

Sour-and-Spicy Garbanzo Bean Curry

Khatta Channa

The tea and roasted ground spices give this dish its color and distinctive flavor.

1. Pick through the dried beans for any grit or debris, then place them in a strainer and rinse thoroughly. Transfer the beans to a medium-sized bowl along with 4 cups of water. Soak for 12 hours or overnight.

2. Drain the soaked beans, reserving the soaking water in a measuring cup. Add enough fresh water to measure 4 cups. Bring this water, the soaked beans, and the tea bag to boil in a medium-sized saucepan. Add the garlic and ginger, reduce the heat to medium-low, and simmer loosely covered for 45 minutes, or until the beans are tender.

3. While the beans are cooking, place the spice-blend ingredients in a small skillet. Place over medium heat and dry-roast while stirring constantly. Continue to roast about 5 to 7 minutes, or until the spices emit a strong aroma and become dark brown in color (a shade or two lighter than ground coffee). Be careful not to burn. Remove from the heat and allow the spices to cool. Transfer to a coffee or spice grinder and grind to a fine powder. Set aside.

4. When the beans are cooked, discard the tea bag, and add the paprika, turmeric, and salt. Stir well and continue to cook until the stock has been absorbed.

5. Add the roasted spice blend, along with the ginger (if using), chile pepper, garam masala, and ¾ cup water. Simmer over medium-low heat until most of the water has evaporated.

6. Stir in the lemon juice (if using) and cilantro, and transfer to a serving dish.

NUTRITIONAL FACTS: (PER ⅔-CUP SERVING)
Calories: 120   Carbohydrates: 15.4 g   Cholesterol: 0 mg
Fat: 1.9 g   Fiber: <1 g   Protein: 5.6 g   Sodium: 300 mg

SUGGESTED ACCOMPANIMENTS

Pumpkin Yogurt Salad (page 59) and Herbed Onion Flatbread (page 88).

Yield: *6 servings*

1 cup dry garbanzo beans

1 tea bag

4 cloves garlic, crushed

½ teaspoon peeled, grated ginger

1 teaspoon paprika

½ teaspoon turmeric

¾ teaspoon salt (or to taste)

½ teaspoon peeled, grated ginger (optional)

1 small green chile pepper, julienned

1 teaspoon homemade garam masala (page 133) or commercial variety

¾ cup water

1 teaspoon lemon juice (optional)

1 tablespoon finely chopped fresh cilantro

SPICE BLEND

3 teaspoons dry mango powder (aamchoor)*

6 black peppercorns

12 cloves

2 teaspoons coriander seeds

1 teaspoon cumin seeds

1 black cardamom pod

¼-inch piece cinnamon stick

* For true authentic taste, mango powder is best; however, you can use 2 tablespoons lemon juice in a pinch. If using lemon juice, do not include with the roasted spices, rather add it to the existing lemon juice ingredient.

South Indian Dal

Sambar

Yield: *4 servings*

¾ cup dry split pigeon peas

½ teaspoon tamarind pulp, dissolved in 1 tablespoon warm water*

½ teaspoon homemade sambar masala (page 132) or commercial variety

½ teaspoon granulated white sugar

1 teaspoon canola oil

½ teaspoon black or yellow mustard seeds

¼ teaspoon turmeric

1 medium yellow onion, cut into 8 chunks

½ teaspoon salt (or to taste)

1 small tomato, coarsely chopped

1 teaspoon finely chopped fresh cilantro

*Can substitute 2–3 teaspoons lemon juice for the dissolved tamarind.

The distinctive flavor of this dish comes from sambar masala and tamarind pulp. Both are readily available in Indian grocery stores.

1. Pick through the dried peas for any grit or debris, then place them in a strainer and rinse thoroughly. Transfer the peas to a medium-sized bowl along with 1½ cups water. Soak for 2 hours.

2. Drain the soaked peas, reserving the soaking water in a measuring cup. Add enough fresh water to measure 1½ cups. Bring this water to boil in a medium-sized saucepan. Add the soaked beans, reduce the heat to low, and simmer loosely covered about 35 minutes, or until most of the water has been absorbed and the beans are tender. Using the back of a spoon, mash the peas against the side of the pan. Add 1 cup water and set aside.

3. In a small bowl, combine the tamarind, sambar masala, and sugar. Set aside.

4. Spray a large nonstick wok with vegetable cooking spray. Add the oil and place over medium heat. When the oil is hot, add the mustard seeds. Cover the skillet with a splatter guard and allow the seeds to pop. When the seeds have finished popping, add the turmeric and onion. Stir-fry until the onion is golden, then add the sambar masala, salt, and tomato. Continue to stir-fry until the tomato is well-cooked. If the tomato starts sticking to the skillet, reduce the heat to low.

5. Add the cooked peas to the tomato mixture, increase the heat to high, and bring to a boil. Remove from the heat, add the cilantro, and serve.

NUTRITIONAL FACTS: (PER ⅔-CUP SERVING)

Calories: 138   Carbohydrates: 21.4 g   Cholesterol: 0 mg
Fat: 1.6 g   Fiber: <1 g   Protein: 8 g   Sodium: 140 mg

SUGGESTED ACCOMPANIMENTS

Peas and Tomato Pancakes (page 72), and Cilantro Chutney (page 181).

Spicy Baked Beans

We serve these spicy beans with fresh whole wheat bread for a very satisfying, filling meal.

1. Place the baked beans, onion, red and green bell peppers, tomato, and radishes in a medium-sized stockpot. Stir in the chile, garlic, ginger, and tamarind, and mix well.

2. Sprinkle the ground cumin, ground coriander, and paprika (if using) into the pot and stir to mix. Add the water and stir again.

3. Cook uncovered over medium heat for 10 minutes, stirring occasionally, until the vegetables are just beginning to soften (they should retain some of their crispness).

4. Transfer to a serving bowl, garnish with cilantro, and serve hot.

NUTRITIONAL FACTS (PER ⅔-CUP SERVING)

Calories: 136   Carbohydrates: 27.6 g   Cholesterol: 0 mg
Fat: 0.2 g   Fiber: 6 g   Protein: 6.9 g   Sodium: 418 mg

SUGGESTED ACCOMPANIMENTS

Potato-Stuffed Green Peppers (page 117) and Honey Wheat Flatbread (page 86).

Yield: *4 servings*

16-ounce can vegetarian baked beans in tomato sauce

1 small yellow onion, coarsely chopped

½ medium red bell pepper, coarsely chopped

½ medium green bell pepper, coarsely chopped

1 medium ripe tomato, finely chopped

6 small red radishes, grated

1 medium green chile, finely chopped

1 clove garlic, minced

1 teaspoon peeled, grated ginger

¼ teaspoon tamarind pulp dissolved in 1 tablespoon warm water*

½ teaspoon ground cumin

½ teaspoon ground coriander

¼ teaspoon paprika (optional)

¾ cups water

1 tablespoon finely chopped fresh cilantro

*Can substitute 1 teaspoon lemon juice for the dissolved tamarind

Sprouting Legumes

Peas, beans, and seeds are packed with vitamins, minerals, proteins, and carbohydrates. To sprout legumes, you can use either a special "sprouter," sold in most health food stores, or a cheesecloth and clean bowl. Simply follow the steps presented below.

Before cooking the sprouted beans, sort through them, discarding any that have not sprouted. Use the beans immediately or store them loosely covered in the refrigerator, where they will keep for about one day. Please note that sprouted beans require the same cooking time as unsprouted varieties.

1. Soak the legumes for 24 hours in four times the amount of water.

2. Drain the soaked legumes and place them in the center of a large piece of moistened cheesecloth.

3. Tie the cheesecloth into a knot and place it in a glass or plastic bowl. Cover and place in a dark cupboard away from direct sunlight.

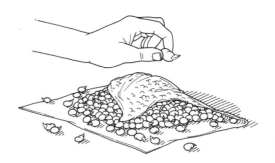

4. Sprouts will appear within 24 to 48 hours. When the sprouts are about ¼ inch long, the beans will be ready to cook.

Sprouted Mixed Beans

Mod Alay Lee Usal

This dish spotlights a flavorful combination of sprouted whole beans. Sambar masala adds distinctive flavor, but curry powder can be used instead. For sprouting instructions, see inset on page 138.

1. Spray a large nonstick pan with vegetable cooking spray. Add the oil and place over medium heat. When the oil is hot, add the mustard seeds. Cover the pan with a splatter guard and allow the seeds to pop. When the seeds have finished popping (within 30 seconds), add the turmeric, chile pepper, and onion. Fry until the onion turns golden brown.

2. Stir in the sprouted legumes and cook about 5 minutes. Add the water and cook, loosely covered, about 45 minutes, stirring occasionally until the legumes are tender.

3. Add the cumin, coriander, sambar masala, and salt. Stir well and continue cooking another 10 minutes, or until most of the water is absorbed and the beans are tender.

4. Transfer to a serving bowl, garnish with cilantro, and serve hot.

NUTRITIONAL FACTS: (PER ⅔-CUP SERVING)
Calories: 112   Carbohydrates: 17.1 g   Cholesterol: 0 mg
Fat: 2.1 g   Fiber: 1 g   Protein: 6.5 g   Sodium: 296 mg

SUGGESTED ACCOMPANIMENTS

Green Pea Pilaf (page 70) and Carrot Yogurt Salad (page 54).

HELPFUL HINT

- 2 heaping tablespoons of whole dried legumes yield approximately ½ cup sprouted.

Yield: *4 servings*

1½ teaspoons canola oil

½ teaspoon black or yellow mustard seeds

½ teaspoon turmeric

1 small green chile pepper, finely chopped

1 medium yellow onion, finely chopped

½ cup sprouted whole mung beans

½ cup sprouted moth beans

½ cup sprouted black-eyed peas

½ cup sprouted lentils

2 cups water

½ teaspoon ground cumin

½ teaspoon ground coriander

½ teaspoon homemade sambar masala (page 132) or commercial variety*

½ teaspoon salt (or to taste)

1 tablespoon coarsely chopped fresh cilantro

* Can substitute curry powder for the sambar masala.

Sprouted Mung Bean Curry

Moogachi Usal

Yield: *4 servings*

1 teaspoon canola oil

¼ teaspoon black or yellow mustard seeds

¼ teaspoon turmeric

1 small fresh green chile, finely chopped

1 small yellow onion, finely chopped

2 cups sprouted mung beans (*see* Sprouting Legumes on page 138)

2 cups water

½ teaspoon ground cumin

½ teaspoon ground coriander

½ teaspoon salt (or to taste)

1 tablespoon grated coconut (optional)

This mild bean curry can be eaten as a side dish or served as a salad. Instead of sprouted beans, you can use 2 cups unsprouted whole beans that have been soaked overnight.

1. Spray a medium-sized nonstick skillet with vegetable cooking spray. Add the oil and place over medium heat. When the oil is hot, add the mustard seeds. Cover the skillet with a splatter guard and allow the seeds to pop. When the seeds have finished popping (within 30 seconds), add the turmeric, chile, and onion. Fry until the onion is light golden brown.

2. Add the sprouted beans and stir-fry about 2 minutes. Stir in the water and cook loosely covered, about 40 minutes, or until most of the water has been absorbed and the beans are tender.

3. Add the ground cumin, ground coriander, salt, and coconut (if using). Stir and cook uncovered another 5 minutes. The curry will thicken as it cools.

4. Transfer to a serving dish and enjoy warm.

NUTRITIONAL FACTS: (PER ⅔-CUP SERVING)

Calories: 101   Carbohydrates: 15.6 g   Cholesterol: 0 mg
Fat: 1.5 g   Fiber: 1 g   Protein: 6.2 g   Sodium: 295 mg

SUGGESTED ACCOMPANIMENTS

Beet Yogurt Salad (page 53) and Spinach Flatbread (page 91).

Sweet~and~Sour Black~Eyed Peas

Khatti Meethi Lobia

This sweet-and-sour bean dish is typically served in the western part of India. For added zip, increase the amount of paprika.

Yield: *3 servings*

1. Pick through the dried peas for any grit or debris, then place them in a strainer and rinse thoroughly. Transfer the peas to a medium-sized bowl along with 3 cups of water. Soak for 12 hours or overnight.

2. Drain the soaked peas, reserving the soaking water in a measuring cup. Add enough fresh water to measure 3 cups. Bring this water to boil in a medium-sized saucepan. Add the soaked beans, reduce the heat to low, and simmer loosely covered for 40 minutes, or until the peas are tender. Drain the peas, reserving the stock.

3. Spray a large nonstick wok with vegetable cooking spray. Add the oil and place over medium heat. When the oil is hot, add the mustard seeds. Cover the wok with a splatter guard and allow the seeds to pop. When the seeds have finished popping (within 30 seconds), add the turmeric, paprika, garlic, and onion. Cover and cook, stirring often, for 5 minutes, or until the onion is pale and translucent. (Add a tablespoon or two of the reserved stock as needed to prevent the onion from sticking to the wok.)

4. Add the tamarind, brown sugar, salt, ground coriander, and ground cumin. Stir-fry a minute, then add the cooked beans, tomato, and ¾ cup of the reserved stock. Simmer for 5 minutes, then add the lemon juice (if using) and cilantro.

5. Transfer to a serving bowl and enjoy warm.

¾ cup black-eyed peas

1 teaspoon canola oil

½ teaspoon black or yellow mustard seeds

¼ teaspoon turmeric

¼ teaspoon paprika

1 clove garlic, crushed

1 medium yellow onion, finely chopped

½ teaspoon tamarind pulp dissolved in 1 tablespoon warm water*

1½ tablespoons brown sugar

½ teaspoon salt (or to taste)

½ teaspoon ground coriander

¼ teaspoon ground cumin

1 medium tomato, coarsely chopped

1 teaspoon finely chopped fresh cilantro

*Can substitute 2–3 teaspoons lemon juice for the dissolved tamarind.

NUTRITIONAL FACTS: (PER ⅔-CUP SERVING)

Calories: 194   Carbohydrates: 34.5 g   Cholesterol: 0 mg
Fat: 2g   Fiber: 2 g   Protein: 11.2 g   Sodium: 334 mg

SUGGESTED ACCOMPANIMENTS

Honey Wheat Flatbread (page 86), Cucumber Tomato Salad (page 57), and Spinach with Cheese (page 111).

Yellow Split Peas

Chana Dal

Yield: *4 servings*

¾ cup split yellow peas

1 medium yellow onion, finely chopped

2 cloves garlic, crushed

½ teaspoon peeled, grated ginger

½ teaspoon ground cumin

1 teaspoon ground coriander

½ teaspoon salt (or to taste)

¼ medium jalapeño pepper (do not chop)

1 large tomato, coarsely chopped

½ cup water

1 tablespoon finely chopped fresh cilantro

½ teaspoon lemon juice

½ teaspoon canola oil

¼ teaspoon cumin seeds

¼ teaspoon paprika

The original recipe for this northern Indian dish is made with butter. We believe our low-fat version is every bit as delicious.

1. Pick through the dried peas for any grit or debris, then place them in a strainer and rinse thoroughly. Transfer the peas to a medium-sized bowl along with 2 cups of water. Soak for 2 hours.

2. Drain the soaked peas, reserving the soaking water in a measuring cup. Add enough fresh water to measure 2 cups. Place this water, along with the soaked peas, half the onion, the garlic, ginger, ground cumin, ground coriander, salt, and jalapeño pepper in a medium-sized saucepan. Bring to a boil, then reduce the heat to medium-low. Simmer loosely covered for 20 minutes.

3. Add the tomato and continue to simmer another 10 minutes.

4. Uncover, increase the heat to high, and bring the ingredients to a vigorous boil. Boil about 5 minutes, while stirring, until most of the water has been absorbed and the peas are tender.

5. Remove from the heat and cool a bit. Remove and discard the jalapeño pepper. Using the back of a spoon, mash the peas against the side of the pan. Stir in ½ cup water, the cilantro, and the lemon juice. Transfer to a serving dish, cover, and set aside.

6. Spray a small nonstick skillet with vegetable cooking spray. Add the oil and place over medium heat. When the oil is hot, add the cumin seeds and the remaining onion. Stir-fry until the onion is golden brown. Add the paprika and mix well.

7. Pour the tempered oil over the cooked peas. Serve warm.

NUTRITIONAL FACTS: (PER ⅔-CUP SERVING)

Calories: 150   Carbohydrates: 22.6 g   Cholesterol: 0 mg
Fat: 2.6 g   Fiber: <1 g   Protein: 7.8 g   Sodium: 284 mg

SUGGESTED ACCOMPANIMENTS

Corn with Potatoes (page 100) and Honey Wheat Flatbread (page 86).

Yellow Split Pea Flour Pancakes

Besan Dhirdee

These pancakes can be made in no time with little preparation.

Yield: *5 Pancakes*

1. Place all of the ingredients except the water and 1½ teaspoons of the lemon juice in a medium-sized bowl and mix well. Slowly add the water while stirring the ingredients. Be sure the batter is smooth. Set aside.

2. Spray a medium-sized nonstick skillet with vegetable cooking spray and place over medium heat. Heat the skillet until a few drops of water dance and sizzle on the surface. When the skillet is ready, pour ¼ cup of the batter in the center. Using the back of a spoon, spread out the batter to a ¼-inch thickness.

3. Cook the pancake until tiny air bubbles appear on the surface and it is dry around the edges. Flip the pancake over to cook the other side. Transfer to a serving plate and cover to keep warm. Continue making pancakes with the remaining batter.

4. Drizzle with lemon juice and serve warm.

- ¾ cup split yellow pea flour
- 1 small green chile pepper, finely chopped
- 1 teaspoon finely chopped fresh cilantro
- ½ teaspoon salt (or to taste)
- ⅛ teaspoon ground black pepper
- ⅛ teaspoon turmeric
- ¼ teaspoon cumin seeds
- ⅛ teaspoon paprika
- 3½ teaspoons lemon juice
- ½ teaspoon baking soda
- ½ cup water

NUTRITIONAL FACTS: (PER PANCAKE)

Calories: 66   Carbohydrates: 10.2 g   Cholesterol: 0 mg
Fat: 0.6 g   Fiber: 1 g   Protein: 4.2 g   Sodium: 233 mg

SUGGESTED ACCOMPANIMENTS

South Indian Dal (page 136) and Mint Chutney (page 182).

9.

Chicken, Lamb, and Egg Dishes

Although the majority of Indians are vegetarian, the country includes a number of non-vegetarians as well. Chicken and goat meat are popular choices for those Indians who eat meat (Hindus do not eat beef and Moslems do not eat pork). While chicken is a popular dietary choice in the United States, goat is not. We have found lamb, which is readily available in American grocery stores, to be the perfect substitute for goat. Both chicken and lamb are rich sources of protein and vitamins, and each can be included in a healthy, low-fat diet, provided only lean cuts are used and they are eaten in moderate amounts. Be aware, however, that all chicken parts and cuts of lamb are not created equal.

If eaten without skin, chicken is lower in fat and calories than most meats, with the white meat portions substantially lower in fat than the dark. Even a white meat chicken breast, if eaten with the skin, can contain more fat than some cuts of beef. A 3.5-ounce serving of skinless white meat chicken contains 4.5 grams of fat (10.9 grams with the skin). The same size portion of skinless dark meat chicken contains 9.7 fat grams. That's almost twice the fat content! All of our chicken recipes call for skinless, boneless breasts.

One popular Indian cooking method for preparing chicken is to roast it in a tandoor. Tandoors are huge clay ovens that are partially set into the ground and heated with coal to intense temperatures of over 500°F. The marinated chicken is usually skewered and set inside the tandoor to roast. An outdoor barbecue, although not able to reach the same intense heat as a tandoor, can be used as a substitute. Stir-frying and/or simmering cubed pieces of marinated chicken in wet or dry curries are other popular cooking methods.

When buying lamb, always choose lean cuts that are trimmed of all visible fat. A 3-ounce loin lamb chop that has been trimmed of fat contains only 4.1 fat grams. Untrimmed, the same chop contains 23.4 grams. Lean, trimmed cuts from the shank are also fairly low in fat—a 3-ounce serving has 5 to 6 grams of fat.

American meals tend to include huge servings of meats and poultry. Authentic Indian dishes, on the other hand, use smaller amounts of meat in curries and are always served with rice or flatbreads.

The chicken and lamb recipes presented in this chapter are low-fat versions of traditional Indian dishes. Although they may be slightly higher in fat than the other recipes in this book, the fat content is still relatively low.

Egg dishes are also popular in India, and we have included a number of them in this chapter. While eggs may be very nutritious, their yolks are high in fat and cholesterol. It is for this reason that our recipes call for fat-free egg substitute or egg whites instead of whole eggs. The result? Authentic-tasting egg dishes that are both delicious as well as nutritious.

Whether you choose the Chicken Vindaloo, Lamb in Coconut Curry, or Indian Egg Curry, know that you can feel good about eating these or any of the other dishes found in this chapter. All are tasty, satisfying, and nutritionally sound.

Ginger Chicken

Adraki Murgi

Julienned strips of ginger and sliced onions add great flavor and crisp texture to this stir-fried chicken dish.

Yield: *4 servings*

1. Place the chicken cubes in a medium-sized mixing bowl. Sprinkle with garlic, paprika, turmeric, and salt. Mix to coat the chicken. Set aside.

2. Spray a large nonstick skillet with vegetable cooking spray. Add the oil and place over medium heat. When the oil is hot, add the cumin seeds and ginger. Stir-fry 15 to 20 seconds.

3. Stir in the onion, reduce the heat to medium-low, and cover. Cook the onion, stirring occasionally, until it is golden. (Add a tablespoon or two of water as needed to prevent the onion from sticking to the skillet.)

4. Increase the heat to medium-high, add the chicken, and stir-fry until cooked on the outside. If necessary, add a spoon or two of water to keep the chicken from sticking to the bottom of the skillet.

5. Add the coriander followed by the tomato sauce. Cook while stirring for 30 seconds, add 2 tablespoons water, and cover. Reduce the heat to low and simmer about 5 to 7 minutes, until the chicken is cooked through and no pink remains.

6. Uncover and let all of the liquid evaporate, stirring occasionally. Remove from the heat, add the lemon juice and cilantro, and mix well.

7. Transfer to a serving bowl and enjoy warm.

1 pound skinless, boneless chicken breasts, cut into ½-inch cubes

6 cloves garlic, crushed

2 teaspoons paprika

1 teaspoon turmeric

¾ teaspoon salt (or to taste)

1 teaspoon canola oil

½ teaspoon cumin seeds

2 teaspoons peeled and julienned ginger

1 medium yellow onion, finely sliced

2 teaspoons ground coriander

¼ cup tomato sauce

2 teaspoons lemon juice

2 teaspoons finely chopped fresh cilantro

NUTRITIONAL FACTS: (PER ⅔-CUP SERVING)

Calories: 226   Carbohydrates: 8 g   Cholesterol: 96 mg
Fat: 6.4 g   Fiber: 0 g   Protein: 25.8 g   Sodium: 524 mg

SUGGESTED ACCOMPANIMENTS

Pumpkin Yogurt Salad (page 59), Yellow Mashed Potatoes (page 121) and Fenugreek Flatbread (page 84).

Butterless Butter Chicken

Makhani Murg

Yield: *4 servings*

8 ounces skinless, boneless chicken breasts, cut into 1-inch chunks (about 16 pieces)

1 large tomato, cut into large pieces

7-ounce can peeled, diced tomatoes

1 teaspoon canola oil

2 cloves garlic, crushed

1 teaspoon paprika

1 tablespoon ketchup

¼ teaspoon salt (or to taste)

1 teaspoon dried fenugreek leaves

¼ cup nonfat sour cream

½ cup water

½ teaspoon granulated white sugar

⅛ teaspoon homemade garam masala (page 133) or commercial variety

¼ cup evaporated skim milk

1 teaspoon finely chopped fresh cilantro

CHICKEN MARINADE

2 cloves garlic, crushed

¼ teaspoon peeled, grated ginger

2½ teaspoons tandoori marinade paste

1 tablespoon nonfat yogurt

Butter chicken is a popular dish in Indian restaurants throughout the United States. Our low-fat version is as flavorful as the original. You can use leftover Tandoori Chicken Kabobs (page 22) to make this dish.

1. Combine the marinade ingredients in a medium bowl, add the chicken cubes, and toss to coat. Marinate in the refrigerator for 30 minutes.

2. Thread the marinated chicken on individual skewers and cook on a hot charcoal grill for 10 to 12 minutes, turning as it cooks. Or bake the chicken in a 450°F oven for 10 to 12 minutes. Remove the cooked chicken from the skewers and set aside.

3. Place the fresh and canned tomatoes in a blender. Blend until just puréed. Transfer to a bowl and set aside.

4. Spray a medium-sized nonstick wok with vegetable cooking spray. Place over medium-low heat, add the oil and garlic, and stir-fry for 30 seconds (do not let the garlic brown). Add the tomatoes, increase the heat to high, and bring to a boil. Stirring constantly, continue to cook about 5 minutes, or until the juice from the tomatoes begins to evaporate.

5. Reduce the heat to low, and add the paprika, ketchup, salt, and fenugreek. Stir to mix. Add the sour cream and water and mix well.

6. Add the chicken cubes, increase the heat to medium, and simmer for 1 minute. Stir in the sugar and garam masala, and mix well.

7. Remove from the heat and let cool a minute. Stir in the milk and cilantro.

8. Transfer to a serving dish and enjoy warm.

NUTRITIONAL FACTS: (PER ⅔-CUP SERVING)

Calories: 175   Carbohydrates: 8.7 g   Cholesterol: 48.8 mg
Fat: 4.2 g   Fiber: 0 g   Protein: 19.7 g   Sodium: 426 mg

SUGGESTED ACCOMPANIMENTS

Crunchy Cabbage Salad (page 63), Sweet-and-Sour Pumpkin Curry (page 120), and Raised Indian Flatbread (page 92).

Chicken Vindaloo

Murg Vindaloo

Serve this highly aromatic and tartly spiced chicken dish with a bowl of hot steaming rice. For a milder flavor, omit the red chile and black pepper.

1. To prepare the onion mixture, drop the chopped onion and chile pepper through the hole in the top of a running food processor. Add the vinegar and process to a fine paste. Transfer to a small bowl and add the cumin, coriander, turmeric, and black pepper. Set aside.

2. Spray a medium-sized nonstick 4-quart pot with vegetable cooking spray. Add the oil and place over medium heat. When the oil is hot, add the red chile pepper, cloves, cardamom, peppercorns, cinnamon stick, and bay leaves. Stir-fry about 2 to 3 minutes, until the spices emit a strong aroma.

3. Add the garlic, ginger, and onion. Reduce the heat to medium-low, cover, and cook until the onion is pale and translucent. (Add a tablespoon or two of water as needed to prevent the onion from sticking to the pot.) Increase the heat to medium, then toss in the chicken cubes and sear.

4. Reduce the heat to medium-low. Add the reserved onion mixture and stir-fry about 15 minutes, until the mixture begins to dry and clings to the chicken. (You may need to add a little more water.)

5. Add the salt, sugar, lemon juice, and water. Cover and simmer about 15 minutes, until the chicken is well-cooked.

6. Transfer to a serving dish, add the cilantro, and serve.

NUTRITIONAL FACTS (PER ⅔-CUP SERVING)

Calories: 210   Carbohydrates: 12.1 g   Cholesterol: 86 mg
Fat: 5.8 g   Fiber: 0 g   Protein: 32.2 g   Sodium: 334 mg

SUGGESTED ACCOMPANIMENTS

Quick Stir-Fried Rice with Vegetables (page 71) and Beet Yogurt Salad (page 53).

Yield: *4 servings*

1 teaspoon canola oil

1 dried red chile pepper

2 cloves

1 green cardamom pod

5 whole peppercorns

½-inch piece cinnamon stick

2 bay leaves

4 garlic cloves, crushed

1 teaspoon peeled, grated ginger

1 medium yellow onion, thinly sliced

1 pound skinless, boneless chicken breast, cut into 1-inch cubes

½ teaspoon salt (or to taste)

½ teaspoon granulated white sugar

2 teaspoons lemon juice

½ cup water

1 tablespoon finely chopped fresh cilantro

ONION MIXTURE

1 medium yellow onion, coarsely chopped

1 medium green chile pepper, seeded and coarsely chopped

¼ cup vinegar

1 teaspoon ground cumin

2 teaspoons ground coriander

½ teaspoon turmeric

¼ teaspoon ground black pepper

Chicken Xacutti

Murg Xacutti

Yield: *6 servings*

1 pound skinless, boneless chicken breasts, cut into ½-inch cubes

½ teaspoon turmeric

1 teaspoon canola oil

5 cloves garlic, crushed

1 teaspoon peeled, grated ginger

1 medium yellow onion, very finely sliced

½ teaspoon paprika

2 medium tomatoes, coarsely chopped

¾ teaspoon salt

1 cup fat-free coconut milk (page 152)

¼ cup water

2 tablespoons finely chopped fresh cilantro

½ small green chile pepper, finely chopped (optional)

SPICE BLEND

2 medium dried red chile peppers

10 cloves

10 black peppercorns

1 black cardamom pod

1 teaspoon poppy seeds

½-inch piece cinnamon stick

2 teaspoons coriander seeds

1 teaspoon cumin seeds

1 teaspoon aniseeds

This is a traditional dish from Goa, a coastal region in Western India. After much experimenting, we were finally satisfied with this outstanding low-fat version of the high-fat original.

1. Place the chicken cubes in a medium-sized bowl and sprinkle with turmeric. Rub the turmeric into the chicken and set aside.

2. Place the spice blend ingredients in a small nonstick skillet over medium heat. Dry-roast the spices, stirring constantly, until they emit a strong aroma. Cool completely, then transfer to a spice or coffee grinder and grind to a fine powder. Set aside.

3. Spray a large nonstick pan with vegetable cooking spray. Add the oil and place over medium heat. When the oil is hot, add the garlic, ginger, and onion. Stir, then cover and cook about 1 minute, until the onion is pale. (Add a tablespoon or two of water as needed to prevent the onion from sticking to the pot.)

4. Add the chicken and increase the heat to medium-high. Stir-fry the chicken for 1 minute, then add the paprika, tomatoes, and 1 tablespoon water. Continue stir-frying until the tomatoes release their juice. Reduce the heat to low, cover the pot, and simmer until the chicken is cooked, stirring occasionally. Cover and cook the chicken until no pink remains.

5. Add the dry-roasted spice blend to the chicken and mix well. Remove the pan from the heat and stir in the salt, coconut milk, and water.

6. Transfer to a serving bowl, sprinkle with cilantro and green chile (if using), and serve hot.

NUTRITIONAL FACTS: (PER ⅔-CUP SERVING)

Calories: 180   Carbohydrates: 12.9 g   Cholesterol: 64 mg
Fat: 3.8 g   Fiber: 0 g   Protein: 28.6 g   Sodium: 370 mg

SUGGESTED ACCOMPANIMENTS

Zippy Corn (page 119) Carrot Yogurt Salad (page 54), and plain boiled rice.

Goan Chicken in Coconut Sauce

Narial wali Murgi

Using fat-free coconut milk instead of the regular variety saves a lot of unwanted fat and cholesterol in this traditional Indian favorite. For added "heat," sprinkle with some finely chopped green chile pepper before serving.

1. Combine the spice paste ingredients and mix until smooth. Set aside.

2. Spray a medium-sized pan with vegetable cooking spray. Add the oil and place over medium heat. When the oil is hot, add the green chile, garlic, and onion. Stir-fry until golden. (Add a tablespoon or two of water as needed to prevent the onion from sticking to the pan.)

3. Add the chicken, increase the heat to high, and stir-fry about 30 seconds. (If the chicken starts sticking to the pan, add 1 or 2 tablespoons water.) Add the spice paste and continue to cook for 1 minute, stirring well.

4. Reduce the heat to low, add the coconut milk, and bring to a gentle simmer. Cover the pan and cook about 10 minutes, or until the chicken is cooked through.

5. Remove from the heat cool a few minutes, then gently stir in the tamarind.

6. Transfer to a serving dish, sprinkle with cilantro, and serve hot.

NUTRITIONAL FACTS (PER ⅔-CUP SERVING)

Calories: 258	Carbohydrates: 11.2 g	Cholesterol: 44 mg
Fat: 4.8 g	Fiber: 0 g Protein: 40 g	Sodium: 440 mg

SUGGESTED ACCOMPANIMENTS

Green Bean Salad (page 67) and Cauliflower with Tomato (page 98).

Yield: *4 servings*

1 teaspoon canola oil

½ small green chile pepper

4 cloves garlic, crushed

1 medium onion, finely minced

1 pound skinless, boneless chicken breasts, cut into 2-x-¼-inch pieces

1½ cups fat-free coconut milk (page 152)

1 teaspoon tamarind pulp dissolved in 1 tablespoon water*

2 tablespoons finely chopped fresh cilantro

SPICE PASTE

1 teaspoon ground cumin

¼ teaspoon ground black pepper

¼ teaspoon chili powder

2 teaspoons paprika

½ teaspoon salt

1 tablespoon water

*Can substitute 2 teaspoons lemon juice for the dissolved tamarind.

Making Fat-Free Coconut Milk

Coconut milk, which is used in a number of traditional Indian dishes, especially curries, contributes rich, creamy taste, but a substantial amount of unwanted saturated fat. One cup of coconut milk has a whopping 57.2 grams of fat, of which 50.7 grams are saturated! Not willing to sacrifice the flavor of coconut milk in the dishes we love so well, we were determined to create a fat-free alternative. After much experimenting, we came up with just the right blend of ingredients that result in an outstanding fat-free coconut milk. The easy recipe, which is presented below, yields 1½ cups of "coconut milk."

1 cup nonfat ricotta cheese

½ cup skim milk

1 teaspoon granulated white sugar

1 teaspoon pure coconut essence

1. Process the ricotta in a blender or food processor until fairly smooth.

2. Add the skim milk, sugar, and coconut essence. Continue to blend until smooth and well-combined.

3. Use immediately or place in a tightly sealed container and refrigerate up to 1 week.

NUTRITIONAL FACTS: (PER ½-CUP SERVING)
Calories: 86   Carbohydrates: 7.2 g   Cholesterol: 0 mg
Fat: 0 g   Fiber: 0 g   Protein: 10.7 g   Sodium: 248 mg

Sesame Ginger Chicken

Til Adraki Murg

An unusual blend of sweetness and spice gives this chicken dish its unique taste.

1. Place the chicken, grated ginger, garlic, salt, and brown sugar in a medium-sized bowl. Mix well and set aside for 15 minutes.

2. Place the spice-blend ingredients in a small nonstick skillet over medium heat. Dry-roast the spices, stirring constantly, until they emit a strong, pleasant aroma and the poppy seeds are pale brown in color. Cool completely, then transfer to a spice or coffee grinder and grind to a fine powder. Set aside.

3. Dry-roast the sesame seeds in the same skillet until they are a pale brown color. Set aside separately from the other dry-roasted spices.

4. Spray a medium-sized nonstick wok with vegetable cooking spray, add the oil, and place over medium heat. When the oil is hot, add the mustard seeds. Cover the wok with a splatter guard and allow the seeds to pop. When the seeds have finished popping (within 30 seconds), add the chile and marinated chicken. Stir-fry about 1 minute.

5. Add the paprika, turmeric, tomatoes, julienned ginger (if using), and the dry-roasted spice blend. Stir-fry another 2 minutes, then add the water. Cover and cook for 5 minutes, stirring occasionally, until the chicken is no longer pink. Uncover and continue to cook 3 to 5 minutes, or until the curry thickens.

6. Stir in the lemon juice and transfer the chicken to a serving bowl. Sprinkle with roasted sesame seeds and serve.

NUTRITIONAL FACTS: (PER ⅔-CUP SERVING)

Calories: 241   Carbohydrates: 7.6 g   Cholesterol: 97.8 mg
Fat: 6.5 g   Fiber: 0.6 g   Protein: 36.2 g   Sodium: 383 mg

SUGGESTED ACCOMPANIMENTS

Green Pepper Curry (page 104), Spinach Yogurt Salad (page 62), and plain boiled rice.

Yield: *4 servings*

1 pound boneless, skinless chicken breast, cut into ½-inch cubes

1 teaspoon peeled, grated ginger

6 cloves garlic, crushed

½ teaspoon salt

2 tablespoons brown sugar

½ teaspoon sesame seeds

1 teaspoon canola oil

½ teaspoon black or yellow mustard seeds

1 dried red chile pepper

2 teaspoons paprika

¼ teaspoon turmeric

2 medium tomatoes, coarsely chopped

2 teaspoons julienned fresh ginger (optional)

½ cup water

1 teaspoon lemon juice

SPICE BLEND

1 tablespoon white poppy seeds

3 black cardamom seeds

4 cloves

1 teaspoon aniseeds

¼-inch piece cinnamon stick

Chicken with Dried Fenugreek Leaves

Methi murg

Yield: *4 servings*

1 pound boneless, skinless chicken breasts, cut into ½-inch cubes

1 teaspoon oil

1 teaspoon cumin seeds

1 medium yellow onion, finely chopped

4 cloves garlic, crushed

½ teaspoon ground coriander

½ teaspoon turmeric

1 teaspoon paprika

1 medium tomato, finely chopped

½ teaspoon salt

1 teaspoon dried fenugreek leaves

2 teaspoons lemon juice

1 tablespoon finely chopped cilantro

MARINADE

2 tablespoons nonfat yogurt

2 cloves garlic, crushed

An exotic stir fried chicken dish.

1. Place the chicken and marinade ingredients in a medium-sized bowl. Mix well and set aside for 15 minutes.

2. Spray a medium-sized nonstick wok with vegetable cooking spray. Add the oil and place over medium heat.

3. When the oil is hot, add the cumin seeds. Fry a few seconds until the seeds begin to sizzle, then add the onion and garlic. Stir well, cover, and cook until the onion is soft and pale. (Add a tablespoon or two of water as needed to prevent the onion from sticking to the wok.)

4. Increase the heat to high, and add the chicken cubes and marinade. Stir-fry about 5 minutes, or until the liquid begins evaporating. Reduce the heat to medium.

5. Add the ground coriander, turmeric, paprika, tomato, and salt. Stir-fry until the chicken is cooked through and the tomato forms a dryish sauce. If the chicken starts sticking to the wok, add a tablespoon of water.

6. Stir in the fenugreek and lemon juice and mix well. Transfer to a serving dish, garnish with cilantro, and serve hot.

NUTRITIONAL FACTS: (PER ⅔-CUP SERVING)

Calories: 236   Carbohydrates: 4.8 g   Cholesterol: 97.8 mg
Fat: 7 g   Fiber: 0.6 g   Protein: 36.4 g   Sodium: 385 mg

SUGGESTED ACCOMPANIMENTS

Stir-Fried Baby Corn (page 113), Beet Yogurt Salad (page 53), Raised Indian Flatbread (page 92).

Chicken with Apricots

Murg Khobani

A tangy stir-fried chicken dish that is quick and easy to make.

Yield: *4 servings*

1. Place 2 teaspoons of water in a small microwave-safe bowl and heat it for 15 seconds, or until warm. Add the saffron to the water by crumbling it between your thumb and forefinger. Set it aside and let steep at least 10 minutes.

2. Combine the marinade ingredients in a medium-sized bowl. Add the chicken cubes and toss to coat. Marinate about 15 minutes.

3. Spray a medium-sized nonstick wok with vegetable cooking spray. Add the oil and place over medium heat. When the oil is hot, add the cumin seeds. Fry a few seconds until the seeds begin to sizzle, then add the cardamom, chile, and onion. Cover and cook about 3 minutes until the onion is pale and translucent. (Add a tablespoon or two of water as needed to prevent the onion from sticking to the wok.)

4. Increase the heat to high and add the chicken. Stir fry for 2 to 3 minutes, adding a little water if the chicken starts to stick. Add the ground cumin, ground coriander, chili powder, salt, and tomato. Stir well, add ¼ cup water, and reduce the heat to medium.

5. Cover the wok and cook another 5 minutes, stirring occasionally. Add the saffron and apricots and cook uncovered for 2 to 3 minutes or until the apricots are just tender and most of the juice has evaporated.

6. Transfer to a serving dish, sprinkle with garam masala (if using), and serve.

NUTRITIONAL INFORMATION: (PER ⅔-CUP SERVING)

Calories: 256   Carbohydrates: 10.3 g   Cholesterol: 97.8 mg
Fat: 6.6 g   Fiber: 0.6g   Protein: 37.1 g   Sodium: 386 mg

SUGGESTED ACCOMPANIMENTS

Corn-Stuffed Tomatoes (page 99), Spinach Yogurt Salad (page 62), and Herbed Onion Flatbread (page 88).

¼ teaspoon saffron threads

1 pound boneless, skinless chicken breasts, cut into ½-inch cubes

1 teaspoon oil

½ teaspoon cumin seeds

1 black cardamom pod

1 small green chile pepper, chopped

1 medium yellow onion, thinly sliced

½ teaspoon ground cumin

½ teaspoon ground coriander

¼ teaspoon chili powder

½ teaspoon salt

1 medium tomato, finely chopped

¼ cup coarsely chopped dried apricots

¼ teaspoon homemade garam masala (page 133) or commercial variety, optional

MARINADE

2 tablespoons plain nonfat yogurt

3 cloves garlic, crushed

½ teaspoon peeled, grated ginger

Lamb Curry

Masala Gosht

Yield: *5 servings*

12 ounces trimmed lamb from leg, cut into ½-inch pieces

2 medium potatoes

1 medium tomato, very finely chopped

½ teaspoon salt (or to taste)

¼ teaspoon homemade garam masala (page 133) or commercial variety

1 tablespoon finely chopped fresh cilantro

MARINADE

1 cup plain nonfat yogurt

1 medium yellow onion, very finely chopped

½ teaspoon peeled, grated ginger

4 cloves garlic, crushed

2 teaspoons paprika

This mildly spiced curry dish is a wonderful choice to serve family and guests alike.

1. Place the lamb in a medium-sized mixing bowl. Add the marinade ingredients and stir to coat. Cover and refrigerate 2 to 3 hours.

2. Peel the potatoes, cut into 1-inch cubes, and place in a medium-sized bowl. Add enough cold water to cover the potatoes and set aside.

3. Spray a large nonstick wok or skillet with vegetable cooking spray and place over medium-high heat. When hot, add the lamb and marinade, and stir well. When the mixture begins to bubble, reduce the heat to medium-low and cover. Cook, stirring often, about 45 minutes.

4. Drain the potatoes, reserving ¾ cup of the soaking water. Add the potatoes, soaking water, and tomato to the lamb. Cover and simmer 15 to 20 minutes, or until the lamb is fully cooked, the potatoes are tender, and the curry is slightly thickened.

5. Remove from the heat, and stir in the salt and garam masala.

6. Transfer to a serving dish, sprinkle with cilantro, and serve hot.

NUTRITIONAL FACTS: (PER ⅔-CUP SERVING)
Calories: 203   Carbohydrates: 17.2 g   Cholesterol: 60.8 mg
Fat: 5.1 g   Fiber: <1 g   Protein: 23.6 g   Sodium: 319 mg

SUGGESTED ACCOMPANIMENTS
Smoked Eggplant Salad (page 61) and Raised Indian Flatbread (page 92).

Lamb with Spices

Rogan Gosht

This curry is a popular dish in Indian restaurants. Serve it warm over a bed of boiled rice.

1. Peel the potatoes and cut into 1-inch cubes. Place in a bowl and cover with cold water. Set aside.

2. Spray a large nonstick pot with vegetable cooking spray. Add the oil and place over medium heat. When the oil is hot, add the cardamom, cloves, bay leaf, and peppercorns. Stir-fry about 10 to 15 seconds, or until the spices emit a strong aroma.

3. Add the ginger, garlic, and onion, and stir-fry for 1 minute. Reduce the heat to low, cover, and cook while stirring occasionally, until the onion is pale and translucent. (Add a tablespoon or two of water as needed to prevent the onion from sticking to the pot.)

4. Increase the heat to medium-high, toss in the lamb, and stir-fry about 2 minutes to sear.

5. Add the turmeric, ground cumin, ground coriander, salt, cinnamon, and paprika. Continue to stir-fry a minute, then add the yogurt, 1 tablespoon at a time. (Wait for each tablespoon to be absorbed before adding the next.)

6. Drain the potatoes, reserving ½ cup of the soaking water. Add the soaking water to the pot and bring the ingredients to a boil. Cover, reduce the heat to medium-low, and simmer for 30 minutes.

7. Add the potatoes and carrot, and continue to simmer 10 to 15 minutes, stirring often, until the curry thickens and the lamb, potatoes, and carrots are tender.

8. Transfer to a serving dish, sprinkle with garam masala and cilantro, and serve hot.

NUTRITIONAL FACTS: (PER ⅔-CUP SERVING)

Calories: 210   Carbohydrates: 19.4 g   Cholesterol: 60 mg
Fat: 5.8 g   Fiber: 0 g   Protein: 23 g   Sodium: 542 mg

SUGGESTED ACCOMPANIMENTS

Spinach Yogurt Salad (page 62), Tomato Soup (page 47), and Rice-Stuffed Green Peppers (page 109).

Yield: *5 servings*

2 medium potatoes

1 teaspoon canola oil

2 black cardamom pods

5 cloves

1 bay leaf

10 black peppercorns

1½ teaspoons peeled, grated ginger

6 cloves garlic, crushed

1 large yellow onion, very finely chopped

12 ounces trimmed lamb from leg, cut into 1-inch cubes

½ teaspoon turmeric

1 teaspoon ground cumin

1 teaspoon ground coriander

1 teaspoon salt

¼ teaspoon ground cinnamon

¼ teaspoon paprika

¾ cup plain nonfat yogurt

1 medium carrot, peeled and chopped into 1-inch pieces

¼ teaspoon homemade garam masala (page 133) or commercial variety

2 teaspoons finely chopped fresh cilantro

Lamb in Coconut Curry

Mutton Baffad

Yield: *5 servings*

1 teaspoon canola oil

1 medium yellow onion, thinly sliced

1 small green chile pepper, finely chopped

4 cloves garlic, crushed

1 teaspoon peeled, grated ginger

1 pound trimmed lamb from leg, cut into 1-inch cubes

1 teaspoon paprika

½ teaspoon turmeric

⅛ teaspoon fresh ground black pepper

1 teaspoon ground cumin

1 teaspoon ground coriander

1 pinch ground cinnamon

¼ teaspoon ground cloves

¾ cup fat-free coconut milk (page 152)

1 cup water

1 medium tomato, coarsely chopped

½ teaspoon salt (or to taste)

3 tablespoons vinegar

¼ teaspoon homemade garam masala (page 133) or commercial variety

1 teaspoon finely chopped fresh cilantro

This recipe, which hails from Goa, a coastal region of western India, is traditionally made with coconut milk.

1. Spray a large pot with vegetable cooking spray. Add the oil and place over medium heat. When the oil is hot, add the onion, chile, garlic, and ginger. Stir-fry until the onion is golden brown. (Add a tablespoon or two of water as needed to prevent the onion from sticking to the pot.)

2. Increase the heat to medium-high, toss in the lamb, and stir-fry about 2 minutes to sear. (If the lamb starts sticking to the pan, add 1 or 2 tablespoons water.) Add the paprika, turmeric, black pepper, cumin, coriander, cinnamon, and cloves. Continue stir-frying until the meat and spices are sizzling (but not burning).

3. Pour in the coconut milk and water. Bring to a boil, then reduce the heat to low. Cover and simmer about 45 to 60 minutes. Add the tomato and salt. Continue to cook another 15 minutes, or until the lamb is tender and the curry is thick.

4. Remove from the heat, cool a few minutes, then stir in the vinegar, garam masala, and cilantro. Mix well.

6. Transfer to a serving dish. Enjoy warm.

NUTRITIONAL FACTS: (PER ⅔-CUP SERVING)

Calories: 200   Carbohydrates: 7.9 g   Cholesterol: 74 mg
Fat: 6.8 g   Fiber: <1 g   Protein: 27.6 g   Sodium: 334 mg

SUGGESTED ACCOMPANIMENTS

Carrot Salad (page 65), Corn-Stuffed Tomatoes (page 99), and plain boiled rice.

Minced Dry Lamb

Keema

You may have to go to your local butcher for the ground lamb called for in this recipe, or you can grind lean chunks of lamb at home in a food processor. We have added a little ground turkey to reduce the dish's total fat content. In addition to serving this as a side dish, you can use it as a filling for Turkey-Lamb Samosas (page 32).

1. Spray a medium-sized nonstick skillet with vegetable cooking spray and place over medium heat. Add the ground lamb and turkey, and brown.

2. Add the onion and mix with the meat. Stir-fry until the onion is beginning to brown.

3. Remove from the heat and stir in the chile pepper, lemon juice, salt, and cilantro.

4. Transfer to a serving dish and enjoy warm.

Yield: *4 servings*

10 ounces lean ground leg of lamb

6 ounces ground turkey breast

1 medium yellow onion, finely chopped

1 small green chile pepper, finely chopped

2 tablespoons lemon juice

½ teaspoon salt (or to taste)

2 tablespoons finely chopped fresh cilantro

NUTRITIONAL FACTS: (PER ⅔-CUP SERVING)

Calories: 226   Carbohydrates: 5.8 g   Cholesterol: 92 mg
Fat: 6.4 g   Fiber: 0 g   Protein: 34 g   Sodium: 366 mg

SUGGESTED ACCOMPANIMENTS

Spinach with Cheese (page 111), Indian Potato Salad (page 58), and Raised Indian Flatbread (page 92).

Lamb with Poppy Seeds

Maratha Lamb Curry

Yield: *4 servings*

2 medium potatoes

12 ounces trimmed lamb from leg, cut into 1-inch cubes

1 teaspoon canola oil

1-inch piece cinnamon stick

4 medium dried red chiles

2 bay leaves

1 medium yellow onion, finely chopped

1½ teaspoons ground coriander

2 teaspoons paprika

¾ teaspoon salt (or to taste)

½ teaspoon homemade garam masala (page 133) or commercial variety

2 teaspoons finely chopped fresh cilantro

MARINADE

¼ cup plain nonfat yogurt

6 cloves garlic, crushed

1 teaspoon peeled, grated ginger

SPICE BLEND

6 cloves

6 black peppercorns

2 teaspoons poppy seeds

1 teaspoon aniseeds

This very hot, spicy dish was created by the warrior caste of Hindus from India's western region. The chile has been dramatically reduced in this version.

1. Peel the potatoes and cut into 1-inch cubes. Place in a bowl, cover with cold water, and set aside.

2. Combine the marinade ingredients in a medium-sized bowl. Add the lamb and mix well. Cover and refrigerate 2 hours.

3. Place the spice-blend ingredients in a medium-sized nonstick skillet over medium heat. Dry-roast the spices, stirring constantly, until the poppy seeds turn light pink and the spices emit a pleasant aroma. Cool completely, then transfer to a spice or coffee grinder and grind to a fine powder. Set aside.

4. Once the skillet cools, spray it with vegetable cooking spray. Add the oil and place over medium heat. When the oil is hot, add the cinnamon, chiles, and bay leaves. When the spices emit a strong aroma, add the onion, reduce the heat to medium-low, and stir-fry until the onion is light brown and slightly dry. Remove from the heat and cool completely.

5. Remove the lamb cubes from the marinade and place on a plate. Spoon the marinade into a food processor along with the onion mixture and dry-roasted spices. Grind to a fine paste, adding 1 or 2 tablespoons of water as needed. Set aside.

6. Drain the potatoes, reserving ¾ cup of the soaking water.

7. Spray a medium-sized pot with vegetable cooking spray and place over medium heat. Toss in the lamb, and stir-fry about 2 minutes to sear.

8. Reduce the heat to medium-low, then add the yogurt-onion spice paste, ground coriander, and ¾ cup of the potato soaking water. Stir well, bring to a boil, and add the paprika and salt. Reduce the heat to low, cover, and simmer 45 to 60 minutes.

9. Add the potatoes and continue to cook another 10 to 15 minutes, or until the potatoes and lamb are tender. Remove from the heat, add the garam masala and cilantro, and mix well. The sauce for this dish should be thin and spicy.

10. Transfer to a serving bowl and enjoy warm.

NUTRITIONAL FACTS: (PER ⅔-CUP SERVING)

Calories: 290   Carbohydrates: 16.9 g   Cholesterol: 66 mg
Fat: 6.4 g   Fiber: 0 g   Protein: 23.8 g   Sodium: 450 mg

SUGGESTED ACCOMPANIMENTS

Banana Yogurt Salad (page 52), Green Beans with Potatoes (page 103), and plain boiled rice.

Indian Coddled Eggs

Makhan wale Ande

Serve this simple egg dish warm for breakfast. The tomato, cilantro, and chile pepper make for an unusual garnish.

Yield: *4 servings*

1. Whisk together the egg substitute and milk in a small bowl. Spray a medium-sized nonstick skillet with vegetable cooking spray and place over low heat. Add the egg mixture and cook, stirring constantly, until just set.

2. Remove immediately from the heat and add the salt and pepper. Stir to combine.

3. Divide the eggs equally among four dishes and garnish with tomato, cilantro, and chile.

4. Serve warm.

2 cups fat-free egg substitute

½ cup skim milk

¼ teaspoon salt (or to taste)

⅛ teaspoon ground black pepper

1 medium tomato, finely chopped

2 tablespoons finely chopped fresh cilantro

1 green chile pepper, finely chopped

NUTRITIONAL FACTS: (½-CUP SERVING)

Calories: 68   Carbohydrates: 3.8 g   Cholesterol: 0 mg
Fat: 0 g   Fiber: 0 g   Protein: 12.4 g   Sodium: 336 mg

SUGGESTED ACCOMPANIMENTS

Raised Indian Flatbread (page 92) and Spicy Indian Tea (page 192).

Indian Egg Omelette

Ande ka Omlette

Yield: *6 servings*

1 teaspoon canola oil

½ teaspoon whole cumin seeds

1 small yellow onion, finely chopped

1 small tomato, finely chopped

Pinch paprika

1½ cups fat-free egg substitute

¼ teaspoon salt (or to taste)

This Indianized version of a hearty egg omelette flavored with whole cumin seeds can be served for brunch or a light lunch. Serve warm.

1. Spray a large nonstick skillet with vegetable cooking spray. Add the oil and place over medium heat.

2. Add the cumin seeds and onion, and stir-fry about 2 minutes, or until the onion is pale and beginning to soften.

3. Stir in the tomato and paprika, and continue to stir-fry another 5 minutes, or until the tomatoes are soft.

4. Form six holes in the tomato-onion mixture, and pour ¼ cup of the egg substitute into each hole. Cover the skillet and cook about 5 minutes, or until the egg is cooked through.

5. Divide the omelet into sixths and transfer to individual dishes. Serve immediately.

NUTRITIONAL FACTS: (PER SERVING)

Calories: 39   Carbohydrates: 2 g   Cholesterol: 0 mg
Fat: 0.8 g   Fiber: 0 g   Protein: 6.2 g   Sodium: 192 mg

SUGGESTED ACCOMPANIMENTS

Raised Indian Flatbread (page 92) and Spicy Mango Chutney (page 180).

Indian Egg Curry

Ande ka Saag

Don't be intimidated by the number of ingredients and steps in this recipe. It is actually quite easy to make. Serve warm as a side dish.

Yield: *6 servings*

1. Halve the eggs lengthwise, and remove and discard the yolks.

2. Spray a medium-sized nonstick skillet with vegetable cooking spray. Add the oil and place over medium-high heat. Add the chile and cumin seeds, and fry a few seconds until the seeds begin to sizzle.

3. Stir in the onions and fry 5 minutes, or until golden brown. (Add a tablespoon or two of water as needed to prevent the onion from sticking to the skillet.)

4. Add the bay leaf, turmeric, ginger, and garlic and continue to fry a few seconds. Stir in the tomato. Reduce the heat to low, cover the skillet, and cook about 5 minutes, stirring occasionally, until the tomato is soft.

5. Stir in the ground coriander, ground cumin, garam masala (if using), and salt. Cook another 2 minutes.

6. Add the water, then add the yogurt a spoonful at a time, and bring to a boil.

7. Carefully add the egg halves to the skillet and continue to cook another 5 minutes.

8. Transfer the eggs, cut side up, to a serving dish, and spoon the remaining curry over the eggs, making sure to fill the holes where the yolks used to be. Sprinkle with cilantro and serve hot.

6 large hard-boiled eggs

1 teaspoon canola oil

1 green chile pepper, halved lengthwise

1 teaspoon whole cumin seeds

1 large yellow onion, finely chopped

1 bay leaf

¼ teaspoon turmeric

1 teaspoon peeled, grated ginger

2 cloves garlic, crushed

1 medium tomato, finely chopped

½ teaspoon ground coriander

½ teaspoon ground cumin

½ teaspoon garam masala (optional)

½ teaspoon salt (or to taste)

½ cup water

½ cup plain nonfat yogurt

1 tablespoon finely chopped fresh cilantro

NUTRITIONAL FACTS: (PER SERVING)

Calories: 52   Carbohydrates: 5.9 g   Cholesterol: 0 mg
Fat: 0.9 g   Fiber: 0 g   Protein: 5.1 g   Sodium: 259 mg

SUGGESTED ACCOMPANIMENTS

Cucumber Tomato Salad (page 57), Stir-Fried Cabbage with Carrots (page 115), and Spicy Yellow Rice (page 79).

10.

Delicious Seafood Dishes

Indians, especially those living along the country's coastal region, enjoy a bountiful variety of fresh seafood dishes. With the exception of mackerel and halibut, the kinds of fish found in India are different from the types enjoyed in the United States. In this chapter, we present Indianized versions of fish commonly eaten in the States.

The good news is that many fish varieties—catfish, cod, flounder, haddock, perch, pollack, and rockfish—are very low in fat. Other fish, such as bluefish, salmon, tuna, and swordfish, although moderately high in fat, provide essential omega-3 fatty acids. These acids help reduce blood cholesterol, lower blood pressure, and prevent the formation of dangerous blood clots. Most fish and shellfish (with the exception of shrimp) are low in cholesterol. And all seafood, including shellfish, is very low in saturated fat. This means that all fish, even the higher fat types, are considered healthful.

Today, many commercial fish are "farm-raised" (as opposed to wild varieties that are caught in their natural habitat). Farm-raised fish are fed grains instead of a natural diet of plankton and smaller fish. And while farm-raised fish contain as much or more fat than wild fish, they also contain significantly lower levels of omega-3 fatty acids. So, always choose naturally raised fish varieties whenever possible.

Another great quality of fish is that it cooks quickly. Whether baked in an oven, steamed or browned in a pan, or barbecued on an outdoor grill, fish can be ready to eat in a matter of minutes. Cooking time is determined by the thickness of its flesh. When testing for doneness, simply insert a fork into the thickest part of the fish. If it is no longer translucent and flakes easily with a fork, the fish is done.

When shopping for fresh fish, be sure to choose the freshest available. Fish fillets should have firm flesh and a clean, fresh scent. A "fishy" odor signifies lack of freshness. Because it is highly perishable, fish should be refrigerated and cooked the same day or shortly after it is purchased. When buying fresh shrimp, choose those that are white or gray in color. Never buy shrimp that smell like ammonia, which signifies spoilage.

The delicious seafood offerings found in this chapter include dishes that range from the basic, mild-tasting Whole Fish Stuffed with Mint Chutney to more exotic delicacies like hot and spicy Shrimp Tomato Curry. All of the recipes are low in fat, easy to prepare, and delicious.

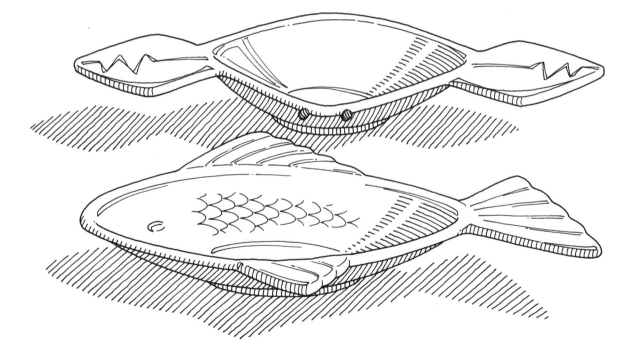

Easy Tandoori Fish
Tandoori Machchi

Ease of preparation and a minimum of ingredients characterize this flavorful fish dish that is traditionally cooked in a tandoor. We have provided instructions for baking the fish in a conventional oven, but feel free to use your outdoor barbecue.

1. Wash the perch fillets and pat dry with paper towels.

2. Combine the yogurt and tandoori masala in a large bowl. Add the fillets and turn to coat with the marinade. Cover and refrigerate 2 hours.

3. Preheat the oven to 450°F. Coat a large nonstick baking pan with cooking spray.

4. Arrange the fish skin side up in the baking pan. Bake for 10 minutes, then turn the fillets over and bake another 5 minutes, or until the fish is flaky and crumbles easily with a fork.

5. Transfer the fish to a serving platter and garnish with lemon wedges. Serve hot.

Yield: *4 servings*

1 pound ocean perch fillets

2 cups plain nonfat yogurt

2 tablespoons homemade tandoori masala (page 133) or commercial variety

1 lemon, cut into wedges

NUTRITIONAL FACTS (PER 4-OUNCE SERVING)
Calories: 166   Carbohydrates: 8.7 g   Cholesterol: 103 mg
Fat: 1.3 g   Fiber: 0 g   Protein: 28.5 g   Sodium: 156 mg

SUGGESTED ACCOMPANIMENTS
Spicy Onion with Vinegar Relish (page 184), Stir-Fried Cabbage with Carrots (page 115), and plain boiled rice.

Fish in Tomato Sauce

Tamatar Machchi

Yield: *4 servings*

1 pound haddock, pollock, or other firm-fleshed fish fillets (about 4 pieces)

1 cup finely chopped fresh cilantro

1 medium green chile pepper, coarsely chopped

1 teaspoon peeled, grated ginger

¼ teaspoon salt (or to taste)

¾ cup plain nonfat yogurt

¾ cup canned tomato sauce

1 teaspoon ground cumin

1 teaspoon homemade garam masala (page 133) or commercial variety

Served over a bed of plain steamed rice, this fairly mild, delicious curry dish is perfect for those who do not like overly spicy food.

1. Wash the fillets, cut into 3-inch pieces, and pat dry with paper towels (you should get about 12 pieces). Transfer the fish to a large bowl and set aside.

2. Place the cilantro, chile pepper, ginger, and salt in a mini food processor and grind to a fine paste. Coat the fish with this mixture, then cover and refrigerate 2 hours.

3. Combine the yogurt and tomato sauce in a medium bowl and set aside.

4. Spray a large nonstick skillet with vegetable cooking spray and place over medium heat. Arrange the fish in the skillet in a single layer, reserving any extra marinade. Cook the fish a few minutes on each side.

5. Add the extra marinade, yogurt-tomato sauce mixture, cumin, and garam masala to the skillet. Stirring gently, increase the heat to high and bring the ingredients to a gentle boil. Reduce the heat to medium and cook about 7 to 10 minutes, or until the fish is cooked and the curry has thickened.

6. Transfer the fish to a shallow serving bowl and serve warm.

NUTRITIONAL FACTS: (PER 4-OUNCE SERVING)

Calories: 138   Carbohydrates: 6.3 g   Cholesterol: 66 mg
Fat: 0.8 g   Fiber: 0 g   Protein: 24.7 g   Sodium: 449 mg

SUGGESTED ACCOMPANIMENTS

Crunchy Cabbage Salad (page 63), Potato-Stuffed Green Peppers (page 117), and Fenugreek Flatbread (page 84)

Goan Fish Curry

Goan Machchi

This is a popular dish from Goa, located in the western region of India. Be warned that this curry is fairly spicy, so adjust the red chile according to your taste.

1. Wash the fillets, cut them into 3-inch pieces, and pat dry with paper towels. Sprinkle with salt and turmeric, then rub it on both sides of the fish. Cover and refrigerate 2 hours.

2. Place the onion and chile in a mini food processor and grind to a fine paste. Set aside.

3. Generously spray a medium-sized nonstick skillet with vegetable cooking spray. Place over medium heat, add the onion-chile paste and ground coriander, and stir-fry until it turns light brown (Add a tablespoon or two of water as needed to prevent the onion from sticking to the skillet.) Add the coconut milk and bring to a gentle boil.

4. Add the fish to the skillet, reduce the heat to medium, and cook covered about 7 to 10 minutes. Remove from the heat and cool 5 minutes, then stir in the tamarind.

5. Transfer to a serving bowl, garnish with cilantro, and serve hot.

Yield: *4 servings*

1 pound haddock, pollock, or other firm-fleshed fish fillets

½ teaspoon salt (or to taste)

½ teaspoon turmeric

1 large yellow onion, quartered

2 medium green chile peppers, coarsely chopped

2 teaspoons ground coriander

1½ cups fat-free coconut milk (page 152)

1 teaspoon tamarind pulp dissolved in ¼ cup warm water*

2 tablespoons finely chopped fresh cilantro

*Can substitute 2 tablespoons lemon juice for the dissolved tamarind.

NUTRITIONAL FACTS (PER 4-OUNCE SERVING)
Calories: 183   Carbohydrates: 9.9 g   Cholesterol: 66 mg
Fat: 0.9 g   Fiber: 0 g   Protein: 30.2 g   Sodium: 552 mg

SUGGESTED ACCOMPANIMENTS

Fenugreek with Split Mung Bean Salad (page 66), Corn with Potatoes (page 100), and Green Pea Pilaf (page 70).

Pan-Fried Spicy Fish

Taali Hui Machchi

Yield: *4 servings*

12 ounces cod fillets

1½ teaspoons lemon juice

1 teaspoon turmeric

2 egg whites

2 cloves garlic, crushed

¼ teaspoon salt (or to taste)

¼ teaspoon peeled, grated
   ginger

3 tablespoons uncooked cream
   of wheat

½ teaspoon cumin seeds

½ teaspoon paprika

Dash ground black pepper

1 teaspoon canola oil

In the original version of this popular Indian dish, small pieces of fish are dipped in egg, coated with chick pea batter, then deep-fried. We have altered a few ingredients and pan-fry the coated fish in a minimal amount of oil. They're terrific.

1. Wash the fillets and dry thoroughly with paper towels. Sprinkle with lemon juice and half the turmeric, then rub it on both sides of the fish. Cover and refrigerate about 10 minutes.

2. In a small bowl, whisk the egg whites with a fork. Add the garlic, salt, and ginger, and mix well. Set aside.

3. In a small dish, combine the cream of wheat, cumin seeds, paprika, black pepper, and the remaining turmeric. Set aside.

4. Dip each piece of fish in the egg mixture, then coat in the seasoned cream of wheat. Place in a large nonstick skillet that has been sprayed with cooking spray and placed over medium heat. Drizzle the oil around the fish.

5. Cook the fish undisturbed for 3 minutes, then turn the pieces over. Add 1 tablespoon water to the skillet and quickly cover. Steam the fish another 2 to 3 minutes, depending on their thickness.

6. Transfer to a serving dish and enjoy warm with your favorite chutney or relish.

NUTRITIONAL FACTS (PER 4-OUNCE PIECE)
Calories: 141   Carbohydrates: 6.4 g   Cholesterol: 41 mg
Fat: 1.8 g   Fiber: <1 g   Protein: 23.2 g   Sodium: 249 mg

SUGGESTED ACCOMPANIMENTS

Quick Stir-Fried Rice with Vegetables (page 71) and Spicy Mango Chutney (page 180).

Shrimp Tomato Curry

Jhinga Tamatar Curry

A hot and delicious seafood delicacy, Shrimp Tomato Curry is great served over a bed of spicy yellow rice.

Yield: *4 servings*

1. Rinse the shrimp under cold water, pat dry with paper towels, and place in a medium-sized bowl. Sprinkle with salt, rub gently, and set aside.

2. Spray a large nonstick skillet with vegetable cooking spray. Add the oil and place over medium heat. Add the onion and stir-fry until golden brown.

3. Add the ginger, garlic, curry powder, coriander, and curry leaves. Stir-fry about 2 minutes, add the tomato, and continue to cook another 5 minutes.

4. Stir in the yogurt, a tablespoon at a time. Mix well.

5. Add the shrimp and water to the skillet, increase the heat to high, and bring to a boil. Reduce the heat to medium and cook uncovered about 10 minutes, until the shrimp turn pink.

6. Transfer to a serving bowl, garnish with cilantro, and serve hot.

1 pound medium-sized raw shrimp, peeled and deveined

½ teaspoon salt (or to taste)

1½ teaspoons canola oil

1 medium yellow onion, finely chopped

1 teaspoon peeled, grated ginger

4 cloves garlic, crushed

1 teaspoon curry powder

3 teaspoons ground coriander

10 curry leaves

1 large tomato, finely chopped

¾ cup plain nonfat yogurt

½ cup water

1 tablespoon finely chopped fresh cilantro

NUTRITIONAL FACTS (PER ⅔-CUP SERVING)

Calories: 162   Carbohydrates: 7.9 g   Cholesterol: 154 mg
Fat: 3.6 g   Fiber: <1 g   Protein: 23 g   Sodium: 434 mg

SUGGESTED ACCOMPANIMENTS

Smoked Eggplant Salad (page 61), Spicy Yellow Rice (page 79), and Mint Chutney (page 182).

Shrimp Vegetable Curry

Jhinga aur Sabzi ki Curry

Yield: *3 servings*

1 medium yellow onion, thinly sliced

½ teaspoon peeled and coarsely chopped ginger

2 cloves garlic, crushed

1 teaspoon canola oil

8 ounces medium-sized cooked shrimp

1 small red bell pepper, thinly sliced

1 cup frozen green peas

1 tablespoon tomato paste

½ cup plain nonfat yogurt

¾ cup water

¼ teaspoon salt (or to taste)

½ teaspoon ground cumin

½ teaspoon ground coriander

1 tablespoon finely chopped cilantro

The nonfat yogurt and tomato paste add a rich tang to this nutritious curry dish.

1. Place the onions, ginger, and garlic in a food processor and blend until smooth. Set aside.

2. Spray a medium-sized nonstick skillet with vegetable cooking spray. Add the oil and place over medium heat. When the oil is hot, add the onion mixture and stir-fry until it turns light golden brown. (Add a tablespoon or two of water as needed to prevent the onion from sticking to the skillet.)

3. Toss in the shrimp and stir to coat. Add the bell pepper, peas, tomato paste, yogurt, and water. Stir well, reduce the heat to low, and cook loosely covered about 15 minutes.

4. Stir in the salt, cumin, and coriander. Continue to cook another 5 minutes.

5. Transfer to a serving bowl, garnish with cilantro, and serve.

NUTRITIONAL FACTS (PER ⅔-CUP SERVING)

Calories: 154   Carbohydrates: 15.5 g   Cholesterol: 126 mg
Fat: 2.2 g   Fiber: 4 g   Protein: 18.6 g   Sodium: 343 mg

SUGGESTED ACCOMPANIMENTS

Beet Yogurt Salad (page 53), Rice and Lentil Pilaf (page 75), and Corn-Stuffed Tomatoes (page 99).

Stir-Fried Shrimp with Scallions

Taale Huae Jhinge

Here's a fantastic dish that takes just 10 minutes to prepare.

1. Generously spray a large nonstick skillet with vegetable cooking spray. Place over medium-high heat, then add the garlic, ginger, and scallions. Stir-fry about 2 minutes, until the scallions begin to brown.

2. Add the shrimp, turmeric, and salt. Stir-fry for 5 minutes until shrimp turn pink. Add the lemon juice, and continue to cook another minute.

3. Transfer to a serving bowl and garnish with lemon wedges. Serve hot.

Yield: *3 servings*

3 cloves garlic, crushed

½ teaspoon peeled, grated ginger

12 scallions, chopped

8 ounces medium-sized cooked shrimp

¼ teaspoon turmeric

¼ teaspoon salt (or to taste)

1 tablespoon fresh lemon juice

1 lemon, cut into wedges

NUTRITIONAL FACTS (PER ⅔-CUP SERVING)

Calories: 115   Carbohydrates: 3.9 g   Cholesterol: 142 mg
Fat: 1.9 g   Fiber: 0 g   Protein: 20.8 g   Sodium: 332

SUGGESTED ACCOMPANIMENTS

Rice with Yogurt (page 76), Cauliflower, Peas, and Potato Curry (page 97), and Cilantro Chutney (page 181).

Whole Fish Stuffed with Mint Chutney

Pudina Bhari Machchi

Yield: *6 servings*

2-pound whole red snapper or Pacific rockfish (with head), cleaned and scaled

¼ cup white distilled vinegar

6 tablespoons homemade Mint Chutney (page 182) or commercial variety

1 fresh lemon, cut into circles

Although this quick and easy-to-make fish dish is very low in fat, it is rich and delicious. In India, instead of foil, the fish is wrapped in fresh banana leaves then steamed.

1. Remove and discard the tail and fins from the fish. Rinse under cold water and pat dry with paper towels. Cut 4 diagonal slashes on each side.

2. Rub vinegar outside and inside the cleaned fish, and place in a medium-sized bowl. Cover and refrigerate 2 hours.

3. Preheat the oven to 400°F. Spray a large sheet of foil with cooking spray and set aside. (The foil should be large enough to wrap the whole fish. If using more than one fish, be sure to wrap them individually in foil before baking.)

4. Fill the slashes and rub the outside and inside of the fish with chutney. Wrap the fish in the foil, place on a baking sheet, and bake 30 minutes or until its flesh easily flakes with a fork.

5. Transfer the cooked fish to a serving platter, garnish with lemon, and serve immediately.

NUTRITIONAL FACTS: (PER 5-OUNCE SERVING)

Calories: 155   Carbohydrates: 0.7 g   Cholesterol: 55 mg
Fat: 1.9 g   Fiber: 0 g   Protein: 31.1 g   Sodium: 171 mg

SUGGESTED ACCOMPANIMENTS

Quick Stir-Fried Rice with Vegetables (page 71), Spinach with Potatoes (page 112), and plain nonfat yogurt.

Garlic~Flavored Fish Nabobs

Machchi ke Tikke

Generous amounts of garlic, ginger, cayenne pepper, and garam masala give this magnificent skewered fish its incomparable flavor.

1. Rinse the fish under cold water and pat dry with paper towels.

2. In a medium-sized bowl, combine all of the remaining ingredients, except the onion and 1 tablespoon lemon juice. Add the fish chunks and toss to coat. Cover and refrigerate 2 hours.

3. Skewer even amounts of marinated fish onto four skewers, then spray with vegetable cooking spray. Cook on a heated barbecue grill about 10 to 12 minutes, turning and basting with reserved marinade until the fish is cooked.

4. Arrange the kabobs on a serving platter, top with onion rings, and drizzle with lemon juice. Serve immediately.

NUTRITIONAL FACTS: (PER KABOB)

Calories: 131   Carbohydrates: 1.5 g   Cholesterol: 36 mg
Fat: 2.7 g   Fiber: 0 g   Protein: 23.8 g   Sodium: 205 mg

SUGGESTED ACCOMPANIMENTS

Spicy Vegetable Platter (page 28), Mint Chutney (page 182), and plain boiled rice.

Yield: *4 kabobs*

1 pound halibut, swordfish, or other firm-textured fish, skinned and cut into 1-x-1½-inch chunks (about 16 pieces)

1 teaspoon peeled, chopped ginger

4 cloves garlic, crushed

½ teaspoon cayenne pepper

1 teaspoon homemade garam masala (page 133) or commercial variety

2 tablespoons fresh lemon juice

¼ teaspoon salt (or to taste)

1 small red onion, cut into thin rings

1 tablespoon fresh lemon juice for garnish

Shrimp in Sweet, Sour, and Spicy Curry

Prawn Patia

Yield: *6 servings*

1 pound medium-sized raw shrimp, peeled and deveined

2 teaspoons canola oil

4 medium onions, very finely chopped

5 cloves garlic, crushed

2 green chiles, finely chopped

2 teaspoons ground cumin

4 teaspoons ground coriander

½ teaspoon turmeric

½ teaspoon cayenne pepper

1 teaspoon homemade garam masala (page 133) or commercial variety, (optional)

2 medium tomatoes, finely chopped

2 cups water

2 tablespoons white distilled vinegar

2 tablespoons fresh lemon juice

1 tablespoon dark brown sugar

½ teaspoon salt, or to taste

¼ cup finely chopped cilantro

This delicious seafood delicacy comes from the western part of India and is usually served on festive occasions. The heat from the chiles and cayenne pepper is offset by the sweet and sour taste of the lemon juice, tomatoes, vinegar, and brown sugar.

1. Rinse the shrimp under cold water, pat dry with paper towels, and set aside.

2. Spray a medium-sized nonstick skillet with cooking spray, add the oil, and place over medium heat. Add the onions and fry 15 to 20 minutes, until they are a light golden brown. (Add a tablespoon or two of water as needed to prevent the onion from sticking to the skillet.)

3. Add the garlic, chiles, ground cumin, ground coriander, turmeric, cayenne pepper, and garam masala (if using), and stir-fry for 1 minute. Stir in the tomatoes and reduce the heat to medium-low. Cover and cook about 5 minutes, stirring often until the tomatoes are soft.

4. Toss in the shrimp and stir-fry a minute. Add the water and bring the ingredients to a boil. Cook about 10 minutes until the shrimp are light pink and the curry is thick.

5. Add the vinegar, lemon juice, brown sugar, salt, and cilantro. Mix well and continue to cook about 2 minutes. Taste and adjust the sweet, sour, and hot flavors according to taste.

6. Transfer to a serving bowl and enjoy hot.

NUTRITIONAL FACTS: (PER ⅔-CUP SERVING)

Calories: 146   Carbohydrates: 12.7 g   Cholesterol: 115 mg
Fat: 3.2 g   Fiber: 1 g   Protein: 17 g   Sodium: 310 mg

SUGGESTED ACCOMPANIMENTS

Cucumber Yogurt Salad (page 56), Spicy Yellow Rice (page 79), and Easy Mung Bean Curry (page 126).

Mint~Flavored Shrimp Nabobs

Jhinge ke Tikke

Mint and tandoori masala combine to flavor succulent shrimps in this easy-to-make recipe. We like to serve the shrimp rolled up in flatbread.

1. Rinse the shrimp under cold water, pat dry with paper towels, and set aside.

2. In a medium-sized bowl, combine all of the remaining ingredients, except the lemon juice and mint sprigs. Add the shrimp and toss to coat. Cover and refrigerate 2 hours.

3. Reserving the marinade, thread even amounts of shrimp onto four "pairs" of skewers. Align the skewers so the shrimps lie flat. (You should get about 5 shrimp on each pair of skewers.)

4. Baste the shrimp with the reserved marinade, then lightly spray with vegetable cooking spray.

5. Cook on a heated barbecue grill for about 3 to 5 minutes, turning and basting with reserved marinade, until the shrimp is cooked.

6. Arrange the kabobs on a serving platter, drizzle with lemon juice, and garnish with mint sprigs. Serve immediately.

Yield: *4 kebabs*

1 pound jumbo raw shrimp (about 20), peeled and deveined

½ cup plain nonfat yogurt

1 teaspoon homemade tandoori masala (page 133) or commercial variety

1 tablespoon very finely chopped mint

2 cloves garlic, crushed

¼ teaspoon salt (or to taste)

1 tablespoon fresh lemon juice

Fresh mint sprigs for garnish

NUTRITIONAL FACTS: (PER KEBAB)

Calories: 136   Carbohydrates: 3.2 g   Cholesterol: 174 mg
Fat: 2 g   Fiber: 0 g   Protein: 24.6 g   Sodium: 333 mg

SUGGESTED ACCOMPANIMENTS

Crunchy Cabbage Salad (page 63) and Honey Wheat Flatbread (page 86).

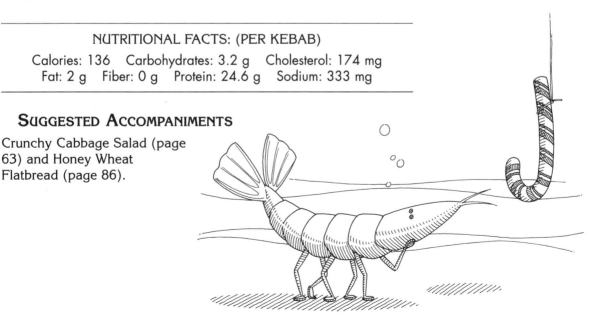

11.

Chutneys and Relishes

Indians would not be able to live without their chutneys and relishes. A combination of flavorful fruits, spices, and herbs, these condiments provide contrast in taste, flavor, and texture to a wide variety of dishes. The main difference between them lies in their texture—chutneys are finely ground, while relishes are slightly chunkier. Both are an important part of an Indian meal.

Certain relishes, like Spicy Onion with Vinegar, are generally used as garnishes for various tandoori-grilled meats, poultry, and seafood. Others, such as Yellow Split Pea with Mango Relish, offset the taste of mild or spicy curry dishes. In addition to adding a spark of flavor, relishes provide a textural contrast to the other items in an Indian meal.

Chutneys serve as both dipping sauces and flavoring agents. Tamarind Chutney, for instance, when added to plain nonfat yogurt, transforms it into a unique-flavored treat, while a little Cilantro or Mint Chutney makes a tasty sandwich spread. Most savory Indian-style snacks are served with a teaspoon or two of chutney on the side.

The chutneys and relishes offered in this chapter are perfect accompaniments to a number of dishes in this book. Table 11.1 lists these condiments and the foods with which they go especially well. Use them as we have suggested or feel free to enjoy them as you prefer. One thing is sure, no matter which foods you try them with, you will be sure to relish their taste.

Table 11.1 Recommendations for Chutneys and Relishes

The following table provides a listing of popular chutneys and relishes and the foods with which they are recommended.

Chutney or Relish	Taste	Goes Especially Well With:
Cilantro Chutney	Hot and garlicky	Lentils, vegetables, rice, bread, yogurt.
Mint Chutney	Hot and minty	Lamb dishes, seafood, lentils, vegetables, rice, bread.
Tamarind Chutney	Tart and sweet	Lentils, vegetables, rice, bread, yogurt.
Spicy Mango Chutney	Tart and spicy	Grilled meats, poultry, and seafood.
Spicy Onion with Vinegar Relish	Tart and pungent	Grilled meats, poultry, and seafood.
Yellow Split Pea with Mango Relish	Tart and sour	Curries (mild and spicy) and flatbreads.

Spicy Mango Chutney

Aam ki Chutney

Yield: *1 cup*

1 medium, slightly raw mango, peeled and cut into ¼-inch pieces

½ green chile pepper, finely chopped

2 teaspoons finely chopped fresh cilantro

½ teaspoon ground cumin

½ teaspoon chat masala, optional

This chutney, with its uniquely Indian flavor, is a great accompaniment to grilled meats, fish, and poultry. To achieve its characteristic tart, spicy flavor, use mangoes that are a bit on the raw side.

1. Place all of the ingredients in a medium-sized serving bowl and mix well.

2. Transfer to a serving bowl and serve immediately, or cover and refrigerate for later use.

NUTRITIONAL FACTS (PER TABLESPOON)

Calories: 9   Carbohydrates: 2.2 g   Cholesterol: 0 mg
Fat: < 1 g   Fiber: 0 g   Protein: < 1 g   Sodium: 39 mg

Cilantro Chutney

Dhania Chutney

This chutney gets its flavor from fresh cilantro and pungent garlic. Indians commonly use it as a dip that accompanies lentil and vegetable dishes, rice pilafs, bread, and yogurt. For an exotic treat, spread some of this chutney on two slices of bread, add a few sliced cucumbers and tomatoes, and enjoy a vegetarian sandwich.

1. Place the cilantro in a food processor, and process for 30 seconds. With the motor running, add the remaining ingredients through the access hole in the lid. Process to a fine paste, while scraping the sides of the bowl. (If necessary, add 1 or 2 tablespoons of water to achieve the desired consistency.)

2. Serve immediately, or cover tightly and store in the refrigerator for up to 5 days. You can also freeze this chutney up to 6 months.

Yield: 1 cup

4 cups coarsely chopped cilantro, packed

2 green chile peppers, coarsely chopped

4 cloves garlic

½ teaspoon salt (or to taste)

1 tablespoon lemon juice

NUTRITIONAL FACTS (PER TABLESPOON)

Calories: 2   Carbohydrates: 0.3 g   Cholesterol: 0 mg
Fat: 0 g   Fiber: 0 g   Protein: 0.2 g   Sodium: 76 mg

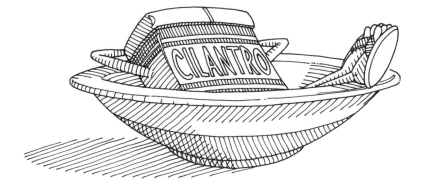

Mint Chutney

Podina Chutney

Yield: *1 cup*

1½ cups coarsely chopped
fresh cilantro leaves, tightly
packed

2½ cups coarsely chopped
fresh mint leaves

3 small green chile peppers,
coarsely chopped

1 tablespoon lemon juice

½ teaspoon salt

This hot, refreshing mint-flavored chutney goes especially well with lamb dishes. In addition, Indians enjoy it as an accent to other foods, such as lentils, vegetables, and rice.

1. Place the cilantro and mint in a food processor, and process for 30 seconds. With the motor running, add the remaining ingredients through the access hole in the lid. Process to a fine paste, while scraping the sides of the bowl. (If necessary, add 1 or 2 tablespoons of water to achieve the desired consistency.)

2. Serve immediately, or cover tightly and store in the refrigerator for up to 5 days. You can also freeze this chutney up to 6 months.

NUTRITIONAL FACTS (PER TABLESPOON)
Calories: 2   Carbohydrates: 0.2 g   Cholesterol: 0 mg
Fat: 0 g   Fiber: 0 g   Protein: 0.2 g   Sodium: 75 mg

Top Left: Spinach Flatbread (page 91)
Top Center: Fresh Lemonade (page 189)
Top Right: Potato-Stuffed Green Peppers (page 117)
Center Left: Beet Yogurt Salad (page 53)
Bottom Right: Stir-Fried Broccoli (page 114)

Top Left: Indian Ice Cream with Mango (page 199)
Top Right: Spicy Indian Tea (page 192)
Center: Indian Fresh Fruit Salad (page 196)
Bottom Right: Carrot Pudding (page 204)

Tamarind Chutney

Imli ki Chutney

This chutney has a taste that's both sweet and tart. It adds flavor to such dishes as Indian-Style Crisped Rice (page 35), and when a teaspoon or two is added to a cup of yogurt, the result is an unusual, yet flavorful yogurt.

Yield: *1 cup*

3 tablespoons tamarind pulp, dissolved in ½ cup warm water

⅓ cup light brown sugar

1 teaspoon ground cumin

½ teaspoon salt

½ teaspoon paprika

1. Place the tamarind in a medium-sized pan and place over medium-high heat. While stirring often, bring to a boil.

2. Add the sugar and reduce the heat to medium-low. Simmer, while stirring, until the sugar dissolves.

3. Add the remaining ingredients and mix thoroughly. Simmer another 2 minutes, then remove from the heat and cool completely.

4. Serve immediately, or cover tightly and store in the refrigerator for up to 2 weeks. You can also freeze this chutney up to 6 months. As it does not freeze solid, you can easily spoon out the amount you need.

NUTRITIONAL FACTS (PER TABLESPOON)

Calories: 24   Carbohydrates: 6.1 g   Cholesterol: 0 mg
Fat: 0.1g   Fiber: 0.3 g   Protein: 0.1 g   Sodium: 74 mg

Spicy Onion with Vinegar Relish

Sirka Wala Piyaas

Yield: ½ cup

1 medium yellow onion, very thinly sliced

½ teaspoon salt (or to taste)

Pinch turmeric

½ teaspoon paprika

2 tablespoons lemon juice

This pungent and delicious onion relish goes very well with tandoori dishes. Before preparing the relish, we soak the freshly sliced onion in cold water to help reduce its pungency.

1. Place the onion slices in a bowl of cold water and let sit for 15 minutes. Drain and cover with more fresh water and let sit another 10 minutes. Drain well.

2. Just before serving, add the salt, turmeric, paprika, and lemon juice, and toss well. Serve immediately at room temperature.

NUTRITIONAL FACTS (PER TABLESPOON)

Calories: 7   Carbohydrates: 2.8 g   Cholesterol: 0 mg
Fat: 0 g   Fiber: 0 g   Protein: 0 g   Sodium: 140 mg

Yellow Split Pea with Mango Relish

Vatli Dal

Yield: *2 cups*

In this relish, which also makes a great side dish, the tang of raw mango complements the flavor of the yellow split peas. If mango is unavailable, use lemon juice.

1. Pick through the dried peas for any grit or debris, then place them in a strainer and rinse thoroughly. Transfer the peas to a bowl along with 2 cups of water. Soak for 5 hours.

2. Drain the soaked peas, reserving the soaking water for another use, and place them in a food processor. Add the chile pepper and coarsely grind. Transfer the mixture to a bowl and set aside.

3. Heat the oil in a small nonstick skillet over medium heat. When the oil is hot, add the mustard seeds. Cover the skillet with a splatter guard and allow the seeds to pop. When the seeds have finished popping (within 30 seconds), add the turmeric and fry for a few seconds, then spoon this tempered oil onto the ground peas. Stir well to combine.

4. Add the mango and salt to the peas and mix well.

5. Serve immediately as a side dish or an accompaniment, or cover tightly and store in the refrigerator for up to 2 days. Garnish with cilantro before serving.

¾ cup dry yellow split peas

1 small green chile, finely chopped

1 teaspoon canola oil

¼ teaspoon black or yellow mustard seeds

¼ teaspoon turmeric

½ cup raw green mango, finely chopped, or 2 tablespoons lemon juice

½ teaspoon salt (or to taste)

1 tablespoon finely chopped fresh cilantro

NUTRITIONAL FACTS (PER TABLESPOON)

Calories: 20　Carbohydrates: 3 g　Cholesterol: 0 mg
Fat: 0.4 g　Fiber: <1 g　Protein: 1 g　Sodium: 40 mg

12.

Exotic Beverages

A wide variety of Indian beverages range from the very simple to the uniquely exotic. Traditional favorites include the buttermilk- or yogurt-based lassi and the mint- or cumin-flavored zeera pani. Cooling fruit juice-based beverages such as lemonade, and hot, soothing comfort drinks like tea and coffee are also among India's popular beverages.

The lassi—India's most popular dairy-based beverage—comes in sweet and savory varieties. A sweet lassi is made with sugar, rose water, and crushed ice, while the savory variety includes a ground spice such as cumin or ginger, and a sprinkling of salt. During hot summer months, lassi is commonly enjoyed as an after-lunchtime treat. In addition to being smooth and delicious, lassi and zeera pani help aid digestion. Fresh milk-based fruit shakes are also popular Indian snack drinks for children.

Summers in India are extremely hot. It is during these summer months that street vendors sell refreshing lemonade called nimbu pani and fresh sugar cane juice called ganne

ka russ. As crowds of busy people rush through the streets of India, most will stop to enjoy a cool glass of these thirst-quenching drinks.

Those living in India's northern region are predominantly tea drinkers. Certain regions like Darjeeling, located in the foothills of the Himalayan Mountains, are famous worldwide for the tea that is grown there. Indians prefer strong tea to which sweet spices, such as cardamom, cinnamon, and cloves, are often added, especially on special occasions. Many households prepare their own unique tea blends. Having visitors for tea is a common and welcomed practice in India.

Coffee is the beverage of choice for Indians living in the southern part of India. Fresh coffee beans are ground daily and brewed through a special percolation method. The ground beans are placed in the top half of a special stainless steel container that is filled with tiny holes at its base. Hot water is poured over the coffee, then left to drip and collect in the bottom half of the container—a process that takes 2 to 3 hours.

The dense, thick coffee concentrate is ready to be mixed with milk and water and brought to a boil. Sugar is added and the coffee is ready. On special occasions, nutmeg can be added for extra flavor.

Be sure to try the following low-fat drinks. They are perfect to enjoy with meals, snacks, or by themselves.

Fresh Lemonade

Nimbu Pani

In India, street vendors sell fresh lemonade from clay containers that keep it frosty cold all day without ice.

1. Place the lemon juice, water, sugar, salt, and cardamom in a mixing bowl, and stir well to dissolve the sugar.

2. Pour into ice-filled glasses and serve immediately.

Yield: *4 servings*

6 tablespoons freshly squeezed lemon juice

4 cups cold water

¼ cup white granulated sugar

⅛ teaspoon salt

½ teaspoon ground cardamom

Ice cubes

NUTRITIONAL FACTS: (PER 8-OUNCE SERVING)
Calories: 48   Carbohydrates: 12.4 g   Cholesterol: 0 mg
Fat: 0 g   Fiber: 0 g   Protein: 0 g   Sodium: 72 mg

Mango Lassi

Aam ki Lassi

The sweetness of mango adds a pleasant contrast to the slight tang of buttermilk in this nonfat drink. When ordering Mango Lassi in an Indian restaurant, be sure that it is made with either low-fat or nonfat buttermilk.

1. Place the mango, buttermilk, and sugar in a mixing bowl, and stir well to dissolve the sugar.

2. Pour into ice-filled glasses and serve immediately.

Yield: *3 servings*

1 cup sweetened, canned mango

2 cups nonfat buttermilk, chilled

1 tablespoon granulated white sugar

Ice cubes

NUTRITIONAL FACTS: (PER 8-OUNCE SERVING)
Calories: 118   Carbohydrates: 23.5 g   Cholesterol: 3 mg
Fat: 0.1g   Fiber: 2 g   Protein: 5.6 g   Sodium: 86 mg

Mango Milkshake

Aam ka Milkshake

Yield: *4 servings*

2 cups sweetened canned mango

2 tablespoons granulated white sugar

2 cups 1% reduced-fat milk

As kids, we enjoyed this thick, creamy mango drink every afternoon during the summer.

1. Place the purée and sugar in a blender, and blend about 30 seconds, until the sugar has dissolved.

2. Slowly add the milk, and blend another 30 seconds.

3. Pour into individual glasses and serve immediately.

NUTRITIONAL FACTS: (PER 8-OUNCE SERVING)

Calories: 165   Carbohydrates: 77.1 g   Cholesterol: 5 mg
Fat: 1.7 g   Fiber: 1 g   Protein: 4.7 g   Sodium: 64 mg

Sweet Buttermilk Drink

Meethi Lassi

Yield: *4 servings*

4 cups nonfat buttermilk, chilled

¼ cup sugar

2 tablespoons rose water

Crushed ice

This refreshing buttermilk drink gets its delicate flavor from rose water. Covered and refrigerated, it will keep up to 12 hours.

1. Place the buttermilk, sugar, and rose water in a mixing bowl, and stir well to dissolve the sugar.

2. Pour into ice-filled glasses and serve immediately.

NUTRITIONAL FACTS: (PER 8-OUNCE SERVING)

Calories: 128   Carbohydrates: 24.4 g   Cholesterol: 4 mg
Fat: 0 g   Fiber: 0 g   Protein: 8 g   Sodium: 125 mg

Spicy Mint Drink

Jal Jeera

Try serving this refreshing exotic minty drink at your next outdoor barbecue. You can purchase packaged jal jeera powder at Indian grocery stores.

1. Place the jal jeera powder in a medium-sized mixing bowl.

2. Slowly add the chilled water to the powder, while stirring. Continue to mix until the powder is dissolved.

3. Add the cilantro and mint, and stir well.

4. Pour into ice-filled glasses and serve immediately.

Yield: *4 servings*

2 tablespoons plus 2 teaspoons jal jeera powder

4 cups chilled water

1½ teaspoons very finely chopped fresh cilantro

1 tablespoon very finely chopped fresh mint

Crushed ice

NUTRITIONAL FACTS: (PER 8-OUNCE SERVING)

Calories: 0   Carbohydrates: 0 g   Cholesterol: 0 mg
Fat: 0 g   Fiber: 0 g   Protein: 0 g   Sodium: 287 mg

Spicy Indian Tea

Masala Chai

Yield: *2 cups*

1¾ cups water

1-inch piece cinnamon stick or ½ teaspoon ground

4 green cardamom pods

4 whole cloves or ½ teaspoon ground

2 teaspoons granulated white sugar (or to taste)

½ cup evaporated skim milk

2 tea bags, regular or decaffeinated

Pinch ground cinnamon for garnish

The following recipe is for a sweet and spicy tea that is one of our all-time favorites. For a ginger version, add a ¼-inch piece of fresh grated ginger in Step 1.

1. Bring the water, cinnamon, cardamom, and cloves to boil in a medium-sized saucepan over high heat. Reduce the heat to medium, and simmer partially covered for 7 to 10 minutes.

2. Add the sugar, milk, and tea bags, and bring to a boil.

3. Remove from the heat, and immediately strain into individual tea cups.

4. Sprinkle with ground cinnamon, and serve immediately.

NUTRITIONAL FACTS: (PER CUP)

Calories: 65   Carbohydrates: 11.2 g   Cholesterol: 2 mg
Fat: 0.2 g   Fiber: 0 g   Protein: 4.8 g   Sodium: 74 mg

Spicy Buttermilk Drink

Masale Wali Lassi

Filled with plenty of crushed ice, this frosty drink is a refreshing favorite during India's hot summer months. Also a digestive aid, Spicy Buttermilk Drink is often served with a heavy meal. Covered and refrigerated, this drink will keep up to 12 hours. Be sure to add the cilantro just before serving.

1. Place the buttermilk and water in a blender, and blend for 20 seconds.

2. Add the ginger, chile salt, black pepper, and cumin, and blend another 10 seconds.

3. Pour into ice-filled glasses, garnish with cilantro, and serve immediately.

Yield: *2 servings*

1 cup nonfat buttermilk, chilled

1 cup water

1/8 teaspoon peeled, grated ginger

1/4 small green chile pepper, finely chopped

1/4 teaspoon salt

Dash ground black pepper

1/8 teaspoon ground cumin

1 teaspoon finely chopped fresh cilantro

Crushed ice

NUTRITIONAL FACTS: (PER 8-OUNCE SERVING)

Calories: 49   Carbohydrates: 6 g   Cholesterol: 4 mg
Fat: 0 g   Fiber: 0 g   Protein: 4.1 g   Sodium: 402 mg

13.

Delightfully Light Desserts

Characteristically, Indian desserts are loaded with fat and packed with sugar. With a few minor adjustments and some ingredient substitutions, we have transformed a number of popular high-fat Indian desserts into reduced-fat delights. All are filled with flavor and include less than 3 grams of fat per serving, with many containing even less fat.

On hot summer days, be sure to try a sweet, refreshing fruit dessert like the Indian Fruit Salad or Indian Ice Cream with Mango. If it's a rich, creamy dessert that you crave, there are a number of luscious puddings from which to choose, including Exotic Rice Pudding, Vermicelli Pudding, and Carrot Pudding. And they are nutritious as well as delicious! Looking for a decadent dessert that takes only minutes to prepare? The exotic-tasting Milk Delight is sure to fit the bill. And if you love yogurt but are tired of the same old flavors, give the Creamy Saffron Yogurt a try.

So go ahead, feel free to indulge your cravings for dessert. We guarantee that your sweet tooth will be satisfied while keeping you within your fat budget.

Indian Fresh Fruit Salad

Phal ka Salad

Yield: *6 servings*

¾ cup skim milk

2 tablespoons fat-free
  sweetened condensed milk

½ cup fresh ripe mango, cut
  into ½-inch pieces

½ cup fresh green seedless
  grapes, cut lengthwise in half

¼ cup fresh tangerine or
  orange segments

½ cup sliced red apples (about
  ¼ inch thick)

½ cup fresh peaches, cut into
  ¼-inch cubes

¼ teaspoon ground green
  cardamom

¼ teaspoon ground nutmeg

1 medium banana

This is a wonderful dessert to enjoy in the summer, when fresh fruit is abundant.

1. Combine the skim milk and condensed milk in a medium-sized mixing bowl. Add the mango, grapes, tangerines, apples, and peaches. Sprinkle with cardamom and nutmeg, and mix well.

2. Transfer to a serving bowl, cover, and refrigerate at least 2 hours.

3. Just before serving, cut the banana into thin slices and add them to the bowl. Mix and serve.

NUTRITIONAL FACTS: (PER ½-CUP SERVING)

Calories: 75   Carbohydrates: 17.1 g   Cholesterol: 0 mg
Fat: 0.3 g   Fiber: <1 g   Protein: 2 g   Sodium: 26 mg

Milk Cake

Burfi

This popular dessert is found in almost every neighborhood confectionary store in India.

Yield: *4 squares*

1. Place 2 teaspoons of water in a small microwave-safe bowl and heat it for 15 seconds, or until warm. Add the saffron to the water by crumbling it between your thumb and forefinger. Set it aside and let steep at least 10 minutes.

2. Place the part-skim and nonfat ricotta cheese in a large microwave-safe bowl. Cover with a paper towel and microwave on high power for 9 minutes, stirring well every 2 to 3 minutes to prevent scorching.

3. Stir in the sugar and microwave another 5 minutes, stirring halfway through. Add the steeped saffron and mix well.

4. Spray a medium-sized plate with vegetable cooking spray and place the cheese mixture on top. Spray a spatula with a little cooking spray and pat the mixture into a 2-x-2-inch square. Sprinkle with slivered almonds (if using), and press them gently into the mixture. Cool completely and cut into 4 squares.

5. Serve at room temperature.

1 pinch saffron threads (about $1/16$ teaspoon)

$1/2$ cup part-skim ricotta cheese

$1/2$ cup nonfat ricotta cheese

$1/4$ cup granulated white sugar

1 teaspoon slivered almonds (optional)

NUTRITIONAL FACTS: (PER SQUARE)

Calories: 115   Carbohydrates: 15.1 g   Cholesterol: 11.2 mg
Fat: 2.5 g   Fiber: 0 g   Protein: 5.4 g   Sodium: 79 mg

Milk Delight

Rabdi

Yield: *4 servings*

1½ cups evaporated skim milk

⅛ teaspoon saffron threads

1½ cups fat-free sweetened condensed milk

¼ cup crumbled white bread without crust

2 tablespoons slivered almonds (optional)

The bread crumbs give this unique dessert its texture. You can make Milk Delight up to two days in advance. In fact, this gives the saffron a chance to release all of its flavor and color.

1. Place 2 teaspoons of the skim milk in a small microwave-safe bowl and heat it for 15 seconds, or until warm. Add the saffron to the milk by crumbling it between your thumb and forefinger. Set it aside and let steep at least 10 minutes.

2. Combine the remaining evaporated skim milk and the condensed milk in a medium-sized bowl. Add the bread, almonds (if using), and steeped saffron mixture. Mix thoroughly, cover, and refrigerate at least 2 hours.

3. Spoon into individual bowls and serve.

NUTRITIONAL FACTS: (PER ¾-CUP SERVING)

Calories: 432   Carbohydrates: 27.7 g   Cholesterol: 18 mg
Fat: 0.6 g   Fiber: 0 g   Protein: 17.4 g   Sodium: 282 mg

Indian Ice Cream with Mango

Aam ki Kulfi

This exotic Indian ice cream called kulfi is rich, creamy, and delicious. When they are in season, mangoes are the most popular addition to kulfi. Special kulfi molds are sold in Indian markets; however, you can use popsicle molds or even ice cube trays to form this special ice cream.

Yield: *6 servings*

1½ cups skim milk

1½ cups evaporated skim milk

2 tablespoons granulated white sugar

½ cup sweetened mango pulp, or puréed fresh mango

1. Bring the skim milk and evaporated milk to boil in a medium-sized saucepan. Reduce the heat to medium, and cook the milk, stirring every minute or so for 20 to 30 minutes, or until the milk is about two-thirds reduced and has the consistency of heavy cream. (If "skin" forms on top, simply stir it in.)

2. Remove the pan from the heat and add the sugar, stirring until dissolved. Cover the pan tightly and cool completely.

3. Stir in the mango pulp, transfer the mixture to a plastic container, and place in the freezer.

4. Stir the mixture every 15 minutes for about an hour, or until it has the consistency of soft ice cream.

5. Stir the mixture thoroughly and spoon into individual kulfi or popsicle molds. Return to the freezer to set

6. Remove from the molds, slice, and serve.

NUTRITIONAL FACTS: (PER ½-CUP SERVING)

Calories: 198   Carbohydrates: 34 g   Cholesterol: 6 mg
Fat: 0.7 g   Fiber: 2 g   Protein: 13.9 g   Sodium: 212 mg

Mung Bean Dessert

Mung Dal ka Halwa

Yield: *4 servings*

½ cup dry skinned mung beans

1½ teaspoons sweet unsalted butter

¾ cup evaporated skim milk

¼ cup skim milk

⅓ cup granulated white sugar

½ teaspoon ground green cardamom

1 tablespoon golden seedless raisins

Here is an unusual dessert made from nutritious mung beans. Enjoy!

1. Pick through the dried beans for any grit or debris, then place them in a strainer and rinse thoroughly. Transfer the beans to a small bowl along with 1 cup of warm water. Soak for 2 hours.

2. Drain the soaked beans thoroughly, place them in a food processor, and coarsely chop. Do not overprocess.

3. Thoroughly coat a medium-sized nonstick pot with vegetable cooking spray. Add the butter and place over medium heat. As soon as the butter melts, add the mung beans and stir-fry about 15 minutes, or until they are browned slightly. You must stir constantly to prevent the beans from sticking to the pot.

4. Add the evaporated milk and skim milk to the beans and stir well. Continue cooking about 10 minutes, stirring occasionally, until most of the milk has evaporated and a thick pulp remains.

5. Stir in the sugar and continue cooking another 10 minutes. Remove from the heat, add the cardamom, and stir well.

6. Spray a medium-sized plate with vegetable cooking spray and pour the bean mixture on top. Spray a spatula with a little cooking spray and pat the mixture into a 2-x-2-inch square. Sprinkle with raisins, and press them gently into the mixture. Cool completely and cut into 4 squares.

7. Serve at room temperature.

NUTRITIONAL FACTS: (PER SQUARE)

Calories: 209   Carbohydrates: 39.6 g   Cholesterol: 6 mg
Fat: 2 g   Fiber: 0 g   Protein: 9.2 g   Sodium: 70 mg

Creamy Saffron Yogurt

Shrikhand

Shrikhand—commonly served at Indian weddings—has a smooth, creamy texture, rich flavor, and enticing aroma. Usually eaten with puris, shrikhand is also served topped with slices of mango and toasted slivered almonds. For best results, use yogurt with active cultures.

Yield: *4 servings*

4 cups plain nonfat yogurt

¼ cup nonfat sour cream

1 cup granulated white sugar

½ teaspoon ground green cardamom

4 teaspoons skim milk

⅛ teaspoon saffron threads

1. Line a strainer with cheesecloth and spoon the yogurt in the middle. Gather up the four corners and tie into a knot. Hang this bundle on the water faucet over a bowl and allow the whey to drain from the yogurt undisturbed for 12 hours, preferably overnight.

2. Squeeze the cheesecloth gently to drain any excess whey. Untie the bundle and, using a spatula, transfer the yogurt "cheese" to a medium-sized mixing bowl. Add the sour cream, sugar, and cardamom, and beat with a wire whisk until light and fluffy. (You can use a food processor, if you prefer.)

3. Place the skim milk in a small microwave-safe bowl and heat it for 15 seconds, or until warm. Add the saffron to the milk by crumbling it between your thumb and forefinger. Set it aside and let steep at least 10 minutes.

4. Add the steeped saffron to the yogurt mixture and stir well. Cover the bowl and refrigerate at least 2 hours.

5. Spoon into individual bowls and serve.

NUTRITIONAL FACTS: (PER ½-CUP SERVING)

Calories: 232   Carbohydrates: 93.5 g   Cholesterol: 0 mg
Fat: 0 g   Fiber: 0 g   Protein: 7.2 g   Sodium: 122 mg

Saffron

Orange-colored saffron threads are actually the dried stigmas from the Crocus sativas, a plant of the iris family. Although it is quite expensive, a little saffron goes a long way in adding unique flavor and deep yellow color to a number of dishes, especially rice.

Generally, the delicate saffron threads are crushed between one's thumb and forefinger into a spoonful or two of warm liquid and left to steep a few minutes before being added to the other ingredients. To achieve maximum flavor and color from the saffron, the threads should be very dry before crumbling. To dry out the threads, place them on a large steel spoon and heat over a flame about 30 seconds (see below). Once cool, the threads will be dry and easy to crush.

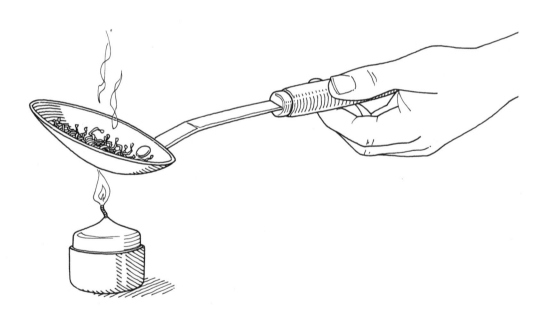

Heating Saffron Threads

Sweet Saffron Rice

Sakhar Bhat

Basmati rice and sweet spices complement each other in this exotic rice dessert that is surprisingly easy to prepare. Serve at room temperature.

Yield: *6 servings*

1 pinch saffron threads (about $1/16$ teaspoon)

$1\frac{1}{2}$ teaspoons sweet unsalted butter

2 whole cloves

1 cup basmati rice

2 cups boiling water to cook rice

1 tablespoon fresh lemon juice

$\frac{1}{4}$ cup water

$\frac{1}{2}$ cup granulated white sugar

$\frac{1}{2}$ teaspoon ground green cardamom

$\frac{1}{3}$ cups seedless golden raisins

1 tablespoon blanched slivered almonds (optional)

1. Place 2 teaspoons water in a small microwave-safe bowl and heat for 15 seconds, or until warm. Add the saffron to the water by crumbling it between your thumb and forefinger. Let steep at least 10 minutes.

2. Heat the butter in a medium-sized heavy-bottomed saucepan over medium-high heat. As soon as the butter melts, add the cloves and rice and stir-fry a few minutes until the rice is well-coated. Carefully stir in the boiling water, reduce the heat to low, and simmer partially covered until the water is absorbed.

3. Stir in the lemon juice, then transfer the mixture to a large flat dish. Fluff the rice with a fork and allow it to cool.

5. Dissolve the sugar in $\frac{1}{4}$ cup water in a medium-sized pot over medium heat. Cook, while stirring, about 4 minutes, until the sugar begins to caramelize.

6. Add the steeped saffron and cooked rice to the sugar water. Stir well, reduce the heat to low, and cook covered about 5 minutes, or until all of the water has been absorbed. Add the cardamom and raisins and mix well.

7. Remove from the heat, cover, and cool to room temperature.

8. Transfer the rice to a serving bowl, garnish with almonds (if using), and serve.

NUTRITIONAL FACTS: (PER $\frac{1}{2}$-CUP SERVING)

Calories: 207   Carbohydrates: 46.5 g   Cholesterol: 3 mg
Fat: 1 g   Fiber: 0 g   Protein: 3 g   Sodium: 1 mg

Carrot Pudding

Gajar ka Halwa

Yield: *4 servings*

6 medium carrots, shredded
(about 3 cups)

1½ cups evaporated skim milk

1½ cups skim milk

⅓ cup granulated white sugar

1½ teaspoons sweet unsalted
butter

1 teaspoon ground green
cardamom

¼ cups golden seedless raisins

1 tablespoon slivered almonds
(optional)

Halwa means "to-stir." To make this pudding properly, the ingredients must be stirred until the liquid thickens to a unique pudding of interesting flavors and textures.

1. Combine the carrots, evaporated milk, and skim milk in a medium-sized heavy-bottomed pan and bring to a boil. Reduce heat to medium-high and cook, stirring occasionally, for about 25 minutes.

2. Add the sugar and cook for another 5 to 10 minutes, or until the most of the liquid is evaporated and the mixture is beginning to thicken. Set aside.

3. Heat the butter in a medium-sized nonstick frying pan over medium-low heat. Add the carrot mixture and stir well. Cook about 5 minutes, or until the mixture turns a rich reddish color and begins to pull away from the sides of the pan. Remove from heat.

4. When cool, stir in the cardamom and raisins.

5. Transfer to a serving bowl and garnish with almonds (if using). Serve chilled or at room temperature.

NUTRITIONAL FACTS: (PER ½-CUP SERVING)

Calories: 260   Carbohydrates: 50.3 g   Cholesterol: 8 mg
Fat: 2.1 g   Fiber: 2 g   Protein: 11.7 g   Sodium: 197 mg

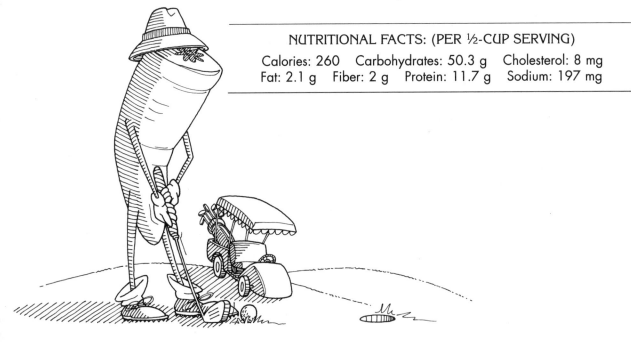

Cream of Wheat Pudding

Sheera

Both of our husband's claim this pudding is one of their favorite Indian desserts. We like it best served warm.

1. Place 2 teaspoons of water in a small microwave-safe bowl and heat it for 15 seconds, or until warm. Add the saffron to the water by crumbling it between your thumb and forefinger. Set it aside and let steep at least 10 minutes.

2. Melt the butter in a medium-sized wok over medium-low heat, then stir in the cream of wheat. Roast the cream of wheat about 30 minutes, stirring often, until it turns pale gold in color.

3. Stir in the water and quickly cover the wok for 30 seconds to steam the cream of wheat. Uncover and continue to cook 5 to 7 minutes, until most of the water has been absorbed. Add the sugar and mix well.

4. Cover and cook on low heat for 2 to 3 minutes, or until the remaining liquid has been absorbed and the mixture is thick. Add the saffron water and almonds (if using). Stir well and remove from the heat.

5. Transfer to a serving bowl or spoon into individual dishes. Serve warm.

Yield: *5 servings*

1 pinch saffron threads (about $\frac{1}{16}$ teaspoon)

1½ teaspoons sweet unsalted butter

½ cup dry cream of wheat cereal

1 cup water

¼ cup plus 2 tablespoons granulated white sugar

1 tablespoon slivered almonds (optional)

NUTRITIONAL FACTS: (PER ½-CUP SERVING)

Calories: 168   Carbohydrates: 46 g   Cholesterol: 6mg
Fat: 2.4 g   Fiber: <1 g   Protein: 2.8 g   Sodium: 60 mg

Exotic Rice Pudding

Chaval ki Kheer

Yield: *4 servings*

3 cups plus 1 tablespoon skim milk

3 cups evaporated skim milk

½ cup basmati rice

⅛ teaspoon saffron threads

2 tablespoons granulated white sugar

2 tablespoons golden seedless raisins

Instead of saffron, you can flavor this pudding with almond essence. Serve chilled or at room temperature

1. Combine 3 cups of the skim milk, the evaporated skim milk, and the rice in a medium-sized nonstick saucepan and bring to a boil. Reduce the heat to medium and cook, stirring frequently, for 25 minutes or until the rice is tender and half of the liquid has evaporated.

2. Place 1 tablespoon of skim milk in a small microwave-safe bowl and heat it for 15 seconds, or until warm. Add the saffron to the milk by crumbling it between your thumb and forefinger. Let steep at least 10 minutes.

3. To the rice-milk mixture, stir in the sugar and cook for another 5 minutes. Add the steeped saffron, stir, and remove from the heat. Cover the pan and allow the pudding to cool and thicken.

4. Stir and transfer to a serving bowl. Garnish with raisins and chill for at least 2 hours before serving.

NUTRITIONAL FACTS: (PER ½-CUP SERVING)

Calories: 317   Carbohydrates: 53.9 g   Cholesterol: 9 g
Fat: 0.9 g   Fiber: 0 g   Protein: 22.7 g   Sodium: 316 mg

Indian Bread Pudding

Shahi Tukde

This quick and easy dessert requires bread that is at least one or two days old. If you have only fresh bread on hand, lightly toast it before using.

1. Place 2 teaspoons of the milk in a small microwave-safe bowl and heat it for 15 seconds, or until warm. Add the saffron to the milk by crumbling it between your thumb and forefinger. Set it aside and let steep at least 10 minutes.

2. Place the remaining milk, egg white, and sugar in a pie plate or shallow dish. Stir well until the sugar dissolves. Add the steeped saffron and mix well. Set aside.

3. Spray a small nonstick skillet with vegetable cooking spray and place over medium heat. While the pan is heating up, coat both sides of one slice of bread in the milk mixture (don't soak more than 5 seconds per side).

4. Place the slice in the heated skillet. Gently press 6 or 7 raisins (if using) into the surface of the bread. Cook about 30 seconds, or until the bottom is golden brown. Using a spatula, gently flip the bread over to cook the other side.

5. Transfer the cooked bread to a warm plate and continue cooking the remaining bread.

6. Serve warm.

Yield: *4 servings*

½ cup evaporated skim milk

1 pinch saffron threads (about ¹⁄₁₆ teaspoon)

1 egg white, beaten

1½ tablespoon granulated white sugar

4 slices day-old white bread

1 tablespoon golden raisins (optional)

NUTRITIONAL INFORMATION: (PER SLICE)

Calories: 110   Carbohydrates: 21.2 g   Cholesterol: 1 mg
Fat: 1.0 g   Protein: 5.2 g   Fiber: <1 g   Sodium: 172 mg

Vermicelli Pudding

Sewain ki Kheer

Yield: *4 servings*

½ cup vermicelli, angel hair, or other very thin spaghetti, broken into 1-inch pieces

1½ cups plus 2 teaspoons skim milk

1 pinch saffron threads (about ¹⁄₁₆ teaspoon)

1 cup evaporated skim milk

3 tablespoons granulated white sugar

½ teaspoon ground green cardamom

3 tablespoons golden seedless raisins

2 tablespoons blanched, slivered almonds (optional)

Here's an old family favorite that came about as a creative way to use up leftover milk.

1. Place the vermicelli in a medium-sized nonstick frying pan over low heat. Dry roast while stirring gently until golden brown. Remove from the heat and set aside.

2. Place 2 teaspoons of the skim milk in a small microwave-safe bowl and heat for 15 seconds, or until warm. Add the saffron to the milk by crumbling it between your thumb and forefinger. Let steep at least 10 minutes.

3. Place the evaporated milk and 1½ cups of the skim milk in a medium-sized pot over medium-high heat. Bring to a gentle boil, add the vermicelli, and stir. Reduce the heat to medium-low and cook 12 to 15 minutes, stirring occasionally, until slightly thickened.

4. Add the sugar and cook another 2 minutes, stirring to dissolve. Remove from heat, add the steeped saffron and cardamom, and stir. Cover the pot and cool to room temperature.

5. Add the raisins and almonds (if using) to the cooled mixture, and stir.

6. Spoon into a serving bowl, cover, and refrigerate about 2 hours before serving.

NUTRITIONAL FACTS: (PER ½-CUP SERVING)

Calories: 153   Carbohydrates: 29.4 g   Cholesterol: 3 mg
Fat: 0.4 g   Fiber: 0 g   Protein 8.6 g   Sodium: 122 mg

Index

Metric Conversion Tables

Common Liquid Conversions

Measurement	=	Milliliters
$1/4$ teaspoon	=	1.25 milliliters
$1/2$ teaspoon	=	2.50 milliliters
$3/4$ teaspoon	=	3.75 milliliters
1 teaspoon	=	5.00 milliliters
$1\,1/4$ teaspoons	=	6.25 milliliters
$1\,1/2$ teaspoons	=	7.50 milliliters
$1\,3/4$ teaspoons	=	8.75 milliliters
2 teaspoons	=	10.0 milliliters
1 tablespoon	=	15.0 milliliters
2 tablespoons	=	30.0 milliliters

Measurement	=	Liters
$1/4$ cup	=	0.06 liters
$1/2$ cup	=	0.12 liters
$3/4$ cup	=	0.18 liters
1 cup	=	0.24 liters
$1\,1/4$ cups	=	0.30 liters
$1\,1/2$ cups	=	0.36 liters
2 cups	=	0.48 liters
$2\,1/2$ cups	=	0.60 liters
3 cups	=	0.72 liters
$3\,1/2$ cups	=	0.84 liters
4 cups	=	0.96 liters
$4\,1/2$ cups	=	1.08 liters
5 cups	=	1.20 liters
$5\,1/2$ cups	=	1.32 liters

Converting Fahrenheit to Celsius

Fahrenheit	=	Celsius
200—205	=	95
220—225	=	105
245—250	=	120
275	=	135
300—305	=	150
325—330	=	165
345—350	=	175
370—375	=	190
400—405	=	205
425—430	=	220
445—450	=	230
470—475	=	245
500	=	260

Conversion Formulas

LIQUID When You Know	Multiply By	To Determine
teaspoons	5.0	milliliters
tablespoons	15.0	milliliters
fluid ounces	30.0	milliliters
cups	0.24	liters
pints	0.47	liters
quarts	0.95	liters

WEIGHT When You Know	Multiply By	To Determine
ounces	28.0	grams
pounds	0.45	kilograms